REBEKAH

REBEKAH

WOMEN OF GENESIS

ORSON SCOTT CARD

SHADOW MOUNTAIN

CAr

Library of Congress Cataloging-in-Publication Data

Card, Orson Scott.
  Rebekah / Orson Scott Card.
    p. cm. — (Women of Genesis)
  ISBN 1-57008-995-7 (hardbound : alk. paper)
  1. Rebekah (Biblical matriarch)—Fiction.   2. Bible. O.T. Genesis—History of Biblical events—Fiction.   3. Women in the Bible—Fiction.   I. Title.
  PS3553.A655 R427   2001
  813'.54—dc21   2001005523

Printed in the United States of America   72082-6701
Publishers Press, Salt Lake City, Utah

10   9   8   7   6   5   4   3   2   1

To Zina

alight with all the graces

you are the joy of this old man's life

CONTENTS

PREFACE

I used all the sources that previously helped me in writing *Sarah*, the companion volume to this book, and in addition, Norman L. Heap's *Abraham, Isaac, and Jacob: Servants and Prophets of God* (Family History Publications, Greensboro NC, 1986, 1999). While Dr. Heap places more reliance on non-biblical sources than I do, he performed the valuable service of bringing together all the scattered verses about each figure in the stories of the patriarchs. In particular, his book called my attention to Deborah, the nurse of Rebekah, who had figured in none of my preliminary outlines because I had carelessly overlooked her. And figuring out why Rebekah, alone of all these women, was so close to her nurse throughout her life led me to the whole elaborate invention of the first half of this book.

The task in this novel was to show how good people can sometimes do bad things to those they love most. The story of Rebekah could easily be taken as a case study in how not to run a family. But if there's anything I've learned in my fifty years of life, it's that people doing the best they can often get it wrong, and all you can do afterward is try to ameliorate the damage and avoid the same mistakes in the future. Good people aren't good because they never cause harm to others. They're good because they treat others the best way they know how, with the understanding that they have. Too often in our public life we condemn people for well-meant errors, and then insist that everyone should forgive people whose errors were intentional and who attempted, not to make amends, but to avoid consequences. Good and bad have been stood on their head by people who should have known better. How do we live in such a world? Isaac was headed for a disastrously wrong decision; Rebekah chose an equally wrong method of stopping him. The question of which wrong was worse is not even interesting to me. They both meant well; they both acted badly; but in the end, the result was a good one because good people made the best of it despite all the mistakes.

Much of what goes on in this novel is speculation. I know that some people have a specific set of theological "meanings" assigned to Abraham's near-sacrifice of Isaac, and there is no room in their picture of these men for Isaac to have had anything other than perfect agreement with all that his father did. While that is not impossible, I find it highly unlikely. Prophets are human beings, too, and the feelings of human beings are not always responsive to our intellectual understanding. Isaac might well have agreed that his father made the right choice. But to me it seems inevitable that Isaac would come away from that scene on a mountain in Moriah with a great deal of pain at the knowledge that when his father was commanded to kill him, the old man did *not* love his son so much that he could not do it.

Believers in biblical inerrancy will be annoyed by some of my choices. For instance, I don't take literally all three accounts in Genesis of a husband passing off his wife as his sister in order to avoid getting killed by a king. It happens once with Sarah, Abraham, and Pharaoh; once with Sarah, Abraham, and Abimelech of Gerar; and a third time with Rebekah, Isaac, and Abimelech of Gerar. My conclusion that the two Abimelech versions of the story are really variant accounts of the same story is reinforced by the fact that both end with a newly-dug well being named "Beersheba." I chose to leave the digging and naming of Beersheba with Isaac, and the incident of deceiving a dangerous king with Abraham, Sarah, and Pharaoh. I'd rather think that the Bible has included three variants of the same story than to think that these people were so dumb that they would dig the same well and give it the same name twice. Not to mention what a slow learner Abimelech apparently was—even if, as some have speculated, the Abimelech who flirted with Rebekah was the son of the Abimelech who had the hots for Sarah.

In preparing this novel I am indebted, as always, to a small corps of friends and family who read the chapters as they spew forth from the LaserJet. Kristine, my wife, is always there to read and keep me from the most egregious errors. She was joined on this novel by my daughter Emily, who reads like the perceptive actor that she is, with a keen eye for what characters would and would not do, and by our friends Erin and Phillip Absher, who were with us for much of the summer when I wrote the book. Erin, in particular, alerted me to an imbalance in my portrayal of one of the characters;

unfortunately, she did so when I was right up against a deadline and had no time to make the substantial corrections that would be required. But once aware of the problem, I could never have allowed the book to be published as it was. So the deadline was pushed back one more day as I made the changes. It's a better book for her having had the courage to tell me such unwelcome news. Another whose prereading and comments were much appreciated is Kathryn H. Kidd, who was far too generous with her time during a month when she had precious little of it to spare. And Kay McVey's encouragement and enthusiasm for the book reassured me that maybe, despite all the difficulties, this story was going to work.

Passages of this book were written in such farflung places as Laie, Hawaii; the home of my beloved cousins Mark and Margaret Park in Los Angeles; in a rented beach house in Corolla, North Carolina; and on a grassy shore near Cape Canaveral, where I wrote a chapter and a half while waiting for our friend Dan Berry to take off on a mission in the space shuttle.

Cory Maxwell is the perspicacious publisher who first caught the vision of these books and made it possible for the project to go forward. Sheri Dew inherited the project when Deseret Book bought out Bookcraft; she became my mother confessor during some bleak days, and gave me a bucket to bail with more than once. My editors, Emily Watts and Richard Peterson, showed unbelievable patience when this book was shamefully late, and if it comes out on time, it's only because of the extraordinary lengths they and others at Deseret Book went to to compensate for my tardiness. Kathie Terry, Andrew Willis, and Tom Haraldsen did an excellent job of promoting this series outside the normal territory of the publishing company. And Tom Doherty astonished me by picking up the paperback rights to books that are definitely *not* science fiction or fantasy. You're too good to me, Tom! But don't stop.

During a very hard year in our lives, my family has stood by me—or, rather, we've all stood by each other. My wife, Kristine, and my children, Geoffrey, Emily, and Zina, have borne me up through all sorrows and given purpose to my work. Zina, especially, has dealt with more death than a child her age should see, and yet remains the light of my old age. And the two children who are not with us now were nevertheless very much in my heart as I wrote. I have written elsewhere of my love and gratitude for those who were good to Charlie Ben during his life and who reached out to us since his passing, as well as those who helped comfort us after the brief life of our youngest child, Erin Louisa. Given the story I have told in this book, it seems appropriate for me to use these pages to thank God for letting me have the joy of all these children in my life. No one brings you more woe, more worry, or more rejoicing than your children. Blessed is he who has a quiver full.

PART I

DEAF MAN'S DAUGHTER

CHAPTER 1

R ebekah's mother died a few days after she was born, but she never thought of this as something that happened in her childhood. Since she had never known her mother, she had never felt the loss, or at least had not felt it as a change in her life. It was simply the way things were. Other children had mothers to take care of them and scold them and dress them and whack them and tell them stories; Rebekah had her nurse, her cousin Deborah, fifteen years older than her.

Deborah never yelled at Rebekah or spanked her, but that was because of Deborah's native cheerfulness, not because Rebekah never needed scolding. By the time Rebekah was five, she came to understand that Deborah was simple. She did not understand many of the things that happened around her, could not grasp many of Rebekah's questions and explanations. Rebekah did not love her any the less; indeed, she appreciated all the more how hard Deborah worked to learn all the tasks she did for her. For answers and understanding, she would talk to her father, or to her older brother Laban. For comfort and kindness she could always count on Deborah.

Rebekah no longer played pranks or hid or teased Deborah, because she could not bear seeing her nurse's confusion when a prank was discovered. Rebekah soon made her brother Laban stop teasing Deborah. "It's not fair to fool her," said Rebekah, which made little impression on Laban. What convinced him was when Rebekah said, "It's what a coward does, to mock someone who can't fight back." As usual, when she finally found the right words to say, Rebekah was able to prevail over her older brother.

The real change in her life, the one that transformed Rebekah's childhood, was when her father, Bethuel, went deaf. He had not been a young man when she was born, but he was strong enough to carry her everywhere on his shoulders when she was little, letting her listen in on conversations with the men and women of his household, shepherds and farmers and craftsmen, cooks and spinners and weavers. Riding on his shoulders as she did, his voice became far more than words to her. It was a vibration through her whole body; she felt sometimes as though she could hear his voice in her knees and elbows, and when he shouted she felt as if it were her own voice, coming from her own chest, deep, manly tones pouring out of her own throat. Sometimes she resented the fact that in order to say her own words, she had only her small high voice, which sounded silly and inconsequential even to her.

But when she spoke, Father heard her, and since he was the most important man in the whole world, however weak her voice might be, it was strong enough. Even after she grew too big to ride his shoulders, she was at his side as much as possible, listening to everything, understanding or trying to understand every aspect of the life of the camp, the work and workings of the household. He, in turn, called her his conscience. The little voice always at his side, never intruding, but asking him wise questions whenever they were alone together.

And then, trying to keep a cart from sliding down a muddy bank into the cold water of a brook in spring flood, Father slipped himself and fell into the water, the cart tumbling after him. The men swore later that it was a gift of God that Bethuel was not killed, for the cart was held up by the spokes of its own broken wheel just enough that he was able to keep his mouth above water and breathe while the men hurriedly unloaded the cart enough that they could lift it off him. He seemed at first to be no worse the wear for the hour he spent in the cold water, but that night he awoke shivering and fevered, and for two weeks he came back and forth between fever and chills as if the icy water still had a place in him.

When he rose at last from his pallet, the world had gone silent for him. He shouted everything he said, and heard no one's answer, and when Rebekah ran to him and covered her ears and cried, "Father, why are you angry with me?" he bent down to her and shouted for her to speak up, speak up, he couldn't hear her. Louder and louder she spoke until she was red-faced with screaming and Father gathered her into his arms and wept. "Of all the sounds that I shall never hear again," he murmured into her hair, "the voice of my sweet girl is the one I will miss most of all."

Father remained master of his household, but there was no more ranging out in the hills to oversee the herds. There was too much danger to a man who could not hear a shouted warning, or the roar of a lion, or the cries of marauders. Instead, Father had no choice but to trust his servants to oversee his flocks and herds. It embarrassed him to have to ask people to repeat everything, to talk slowly, to pronounce their words carefully so he could try to read their lips. He did not have to tell Rebekah that she could not stay with him all the time that he was in camp, as she had used to. She could see that he did not want her there, partly because he was ashamed to show his weakness in front of her, and partly because, when she spoke to him, she saw how much it hurt him that he could not hear her anymore.

"Why don't you go with your father?" Deborah asked her. "He likes you beside him. He used to carry you when you were little. You're too big now."

Rebekah had to explain it to her several times. "Father is deaf now. That means he can't hear. So I can't talk to him anymore. He doesn't hear me."

And after a little while, Deborah understood and remembered. Indeed, she took to informing Rebekah. "You mustn't go to your father today. He's deaf, you know. He can't hear you when you talk to him." Rebekah didn't have the heart to rebuke Deborah for the frequent reminders. Instead, she would ask Deborah to sing her a song as she plaited Rebekah's hair or spun thread beside her or walked through the camp, looking at the work of the women and children and old men. Everyone looked up when Deborah came singing, and gave her a smile. And they smiled at Rebekah, too, and answered her questions, until she understood everything she saw going on, all the work of Father's household.

Rebekah was ten years old when Father lost his hearing, and her brother Laban was twelve. It was just as hard on him as it was on her, for as she had been Father's constant companion in the camp, Laban had been his shadow on almost every trip to visit distant flocks and herds where they grazed.

To Laban it was like a prison, always to be in camp because his father rarely traveled. And Rebekah was no happier. Once she would have rejoiced to have Father always near the home tents, but he was short-tempered now, and bellowed often for no good reason.

Everyone was ill at ease. But the work of the household went on, day after day, week after week. People get used to anything, if it just goes on. Rebekah didn't like the way things were, but she expected this new order to go on unchanged.

Until, a year after her father's deafness began, she happened to come up behind several of the servant women boiling rags, and overheard them talking about Father.

"He's an old lion, with all that roaring."

"A lion with no teeth."

And they started to laugh until one of them noticed Rebekah and shushed the others.

Rebekah told this to Laban, and at first he was all for telling Father. But Rebekah clutched at Laban and held him back. "How will you even tell him? And if you make him understand, then what? Should he beat the woman for saying it? Or the others for laughing? Will that make them love him better?"

Laban looked at her. "We can't let them laugh at Father behind his back. Soon they'll laugh in his face, and then they'll do what they want. Already the servants don't even try to tell Father half the things that happen. Pillel makes decisions all by himself that he used to never make, and Father knows it but what can he do?"

"We can pray to God for him to hear again," said Rebekah.

"And what if God answers us the way he answered Abram and Sarai when they prayed for a son? Can Father wait ten years? Twenty? Thirty?"

They knew well the tales of their father's uncle Abraham, the great lord of the desert, the prophet that Pharaoh could not kill, and how his wife Sarah bore him a baby in her old age.

"But what else can we do?" said Rebekah. "Only God can let Father hear again."

"We can be his ears," said Laban. "*We* have time to explain things to him. Let the men tell us, and *we'll* tell Father."

Rebekah had her doubts about this. She had tried talking to Father many times, speaking slowly so he could read her lips, and at first he had tried to understand her, but most of the time he failed, or got it only partly right, and the resignation in his eyes when he looked away from her and refused to try anymore made her so sad she couldn't even cry. "What, you'll press your mouth into his ear and scream?"

Laban rolled his eyes as if she were a hopeless simpleton. "Writing."

"That's a thing for city priests."

"Uncle Abraham writes."

"Uncle Abraham is far away and very old and spends all his time talking to God," said Rebekah.

"If the priests in the city can write, and Uncle Abraham can write, then why can't Father and I learn to write?"

"Then I can, too," said Rebekah, daring him to argue with her.

"Of course you can," said Laban. "You have to. Because as soon as I can, I'll be out with the men, and you'll have to be able to talk to Father, too."

For three days, Laban and Rebekah spent every spare moment together, working out a set of pictures they could draw with a stick in the dirt. Some of the words were easy—each of the animals could be drawn quickly, as could crops, articles of clothing, pots, baskets. Day and night were easy enough, too—the sun was round, the moon a crescent. Water was a bit more of a challenge, but they ended up with a drawing of a well.

"What if you want to say 'well'?" asked Rebekah.

"Then I'll draw a well," said Laban.

"What if you want to say, 'There's no water in the well'?" asked Rebekah.

"Then I'll draw a well, point to it, and then rub it out!" Laban was beginning to sound exasperated.

"What if you want to say, 'The well has been poisoned'?"

Laban pointed to his well drawing and then pantomimed gagging, choking, and falling down dead. He opened his eyes. "Well? Do you think he'll get it?"

"That can't be the way Uncle Abraham does it," said Rebekah.

"We aren't trying to write to Uncle Abraham," said Laban. "We're just trying to talk to Father."

"What if you want to say, 'I'm afraid there might be bandits coming but Pillel says they're just travelers and there's nothing to worry about but I think we should gather in the men and sleep with our swords'?"

Laban glared at her. "I will never have to say that," he said.

"How do *you* know?"

"Because I would just . . . I would just tell him that bandits were coming and bring him his sword."

"No!" shouted Rebekah. "The men would know it was you who decided and not Father. And they can't follow Father into battle anyway, so it would have to be Pillel in command at least until you're tall enough to lead the men yourself, and anyway the whole idea of this is to help Father keep the respect of the men, and if you aren't telling him the truth and letting him decide then they won't respect him or you and they won't trust you either and then we've lost everything."

It was obvious Laban wanted to argue with her, but there was nothing to say. "Some things are just too hard to draw," Laban finally admitted. "But you're right, we have to try."

"I think writing isn't worth much if you have to be right there to make faces or fall down dead," said Rebekah.

"There's a trick to it that we don't know."

"If priests who are dumb enough to pray to a stone can do it," said Rebekah, "*we* can figure it out."

"If we make fun of their gods, people in the towns will shut us out," Laban reminded her. It was one of the rules learned by those who moved from place to place, following green grass and searching for ample water.

Rebekah knew the rule. "I was making fun of the priests." She looked again at Laban's drawings in the dirt. "Let's show Father as much as we've figured out about writing."

"I don't want to show him until we have it right."

"Maybe he can help us *get* it right. Maybe he knows how Uncle Abraham does it."

"And in the meantime, how will I draw a picture of us not knowing how to draw pictures of things we can't draw pictures of?"

"If you draw something and he doesn't understand, then at least he'll understand that we don't know how to make him understand, and that's what we're trying to make him understand."

Laban grinned. "Now *you're* sounding like a priest."

Rebekah laughed. "The Lord is not made of stone, he is in the stone. The Lord is not confined by the stone, he is expressed by the stone. Since the Lord was in the stonecutter who shaped the image, the idol is both man's gift to the Lord and the Lord's gift to man."

Laban whistled. "You *listen* to that stuff?"

"I listen to everything," said Rebekah. Her own words made her think of Father, who could never listen to anything again.

"I listen to everything, too," said Laban. "But *you* remember it."

"That has to be the worst thing for Father," said Rebekah. "That he remembers being able to hear. Being at the center of everything."

"What, you think it would have been better if he had *always* been deaf? Who would have married him, then? Who would be our father?"

"Father would," said Rebekah. "Because Mother would have loved him anyway."

"But Mother's father would never have given her to a deaf man in marriage."

"She would have married him anyway!"

"Now you're just being silly," said Laban. "Would *you* marry a . . . a *blind* man? A cripple? A simpleton?"

"I would if I loved him," said Rebekah.

"That's why fathers decide these things, and don't leave them up to silly girls who would go off and marry blind, deaf, staggering fools."

Laban said this so loftily that she had to poke him. "But Laban, someday Father will have to find a wife for *you*."

"I'm not a . . . I don't . . . I refuse to let you goad me."

Rebekah laughed at his dignity. "Let's go show Father as much writing as we've got."

"I don't want him to see how bad we are at it."

"The only way to get better is to do it wrong till we get it right. Like you with sheep shearing."

Laban blushed. "You really *do* remember everything."

"I remember eating lots of mutton," said Rebekah. "I remember you wearing an ugly tunic woven out of bloody wool."

"You were only a baby."

"Come on," she said, pulling him toward the brightest-colored tent that marked the center of their father's household.

They did not clap their hands outside the tent, or call out for permission to enter—what good would it have done? That was one of the things Rebekah knew Father hated worst—the fact that people now had no choice but to walk in on him at whatever hour they thought their need was more important than his privacy. Or his dignity. He had tried keeping a servant at his door, but either his visitors ignored the servant or the servant kept out people Father needed to see, and besides, it was not as if the household could afford to keep a man away from his real work just to sit at the master's door all day. So Laban parted the tent flap and peered inside.

Father was going over tally sticks with Pillel. Because Rebekah knew that Pillel had just been to the hills south of the river, she knew that the sticks were a count of the main goat herd, and from the number of marks below the main notch she knew that it was a good year, with many new kids thriving. Last winter's rains had washed away dozens of houses built on land that had been dry through two generations of drought. But the hillsides were lush this spring, and the herds and flocks were fat and strong; and if there could be rains again this winter, they might not have to sell half the younglings into the towns for slaughter, but could keep them and grow the herds and become wealthy again, wealthy as in the days when Abraham had been a great prince whose household was so mighty he could defeat Amorite kings and save the cities of the plain.

Only she would trade such wealth and power, would trade even the herds they had, would give up the whole household and labor with her own hands at all tasks, hauling water like a slave and wearing only cloth she wove herself, if Father could only hear again.

Though of course that was a childish thing to wish, because if Father *could* hear, then he would have his great household and all his flocks and herds and there'd be nothing to fear. No, the way the world worked, you didn't trade wealth to get wholeness of body. It was when your body ceased to be whole that you also lost your wealth, your influence, your prestige, everything. It could all go away—*would* all go away, once something slipped. Everything we have in life, Rebekah realized, depends on everything else. If you lose anything, you can lose everything.

So do we really *have* anything at all? Was that what God was showing them by what he had allowed to happen to Father?

Only Father had *not* lost everything. Had not really lost anything yet. Pillel was still serving Father, wasn't he? And Pillel was keeping everything together.

But didn't that mean that now the herds and flocks and the great household belonged to Pillel? Out of loyalty, he served Father—but the men served Pillel. And there would come a day, surely, when Pillel would see the great dowry Father would assemble for Rebekah and wonder why his daughters had nothing like it to offer a husband, or when Pillel would look at Laban and wonder why the son of the deaf man was going to inherit everything Pillel had created instead of his own strong sons.

Why was she thinking this? Pillel would never betray them.

And yet how was it better that all of Pillel's labor, all his life, should belong to another man? Why *shouldn't* he be able to pass along great flocks and herds to his sons? Instead he would give them only the yoke of servitude, though his life's work had created great wealth. It was not fair to him, or to his sons. Any more than it was fair to Bethuel to be deaf.

A thought came to the verge of her mind. About fairness, about the way God deals with people. It was a thought tinged with anger and fear, but also with that thrill that came when she finally understood something that mattered. But as quickly as it came, the thought escaped her without her being able to name it, without her being able to *hold* it.

Wrong, Laban, I *don't* remember everything. The best things, the ideas that matter most, they slip away without my ever really having them.

Again the important thought verged on understanding. Again it fled unnamed.

Bethuel saw Laban and Rebekah because Pillel heard them and looked up and beckoned them to come all the way in.

"Ah, my children!" boomed Bethuel.

His voice was *so* loud, now that he was deaf. Though she knew he could not help it, it still made Rebekah a little ashamed when he boomed out his words at inappropriate times. Father could keep no secrets now.

"I'm done here," said Pillel. He rose, gathering up the tally sticks.

"The goats are doing well this spring," said Laban.

Pillel grinned. "The billies were frisky last fall."

"Or the nannies were too lazy to run away," said Laban.

Pillel glanced nervously at Rebekah. She hated it when people acted like that. Just because she was the daughter of the house and her purity had to be protected did not mean she was *blind* and did not know how lambs and kids and calves were made.

"You can stay," said Rebekah.

"No he can't," said Laban, annoyed.

"Only your father bids me stay or go," said Pillel mildly. "And he has asked me to leave."

Rebekah looked sharply at him. Father had said no such thing. But there were many things Pillel and Father were able to communicate without words—there always had been. A glance, a wink, a tiny gesture; they understood each other so well that words were often unneeded. Of course that had not changed with Father's deafness. But what was to stop Pillel from claiming that Father had told him something when it was merely Pillel's own decision?

Trust, that's what. Pillel had earned the family's trust, and just because he *could* lie did not give Rebekah any right to suppose that he would. When a man had earned their trust, he ought to have it, and not lose it just because a foolish girl noticed that he could probably get away with any number of small betrayals.

When Pillel was gone with the tally sticks, Laban wasted no time. He pulled back three layers of rugs to expose a patch of hard sandy soil. Rebekah watched Father as Father watched Laban draw his pictures. He grew more and more puzzled, and Rebekah could not help agreeing with him.

"What are you *drawing?*" she whispered. "This isn't anything we worked out together."

"I'm trying a new one," he said.

"Well *I* can't understand it."

Angry, Laban rubbed out the drawing with his sandal and began again. This time he drew the symbols that they had worked out for saying what was being prepared for dinner. The fire, the spit, the pot. Only this was absurd. They hadn't even been to the kitchen fires today. "Laban, what are you doing? We don't know what's for dinner."

"I'm not telling, I'm asking," said Laban. "What he *wants*. And then we can go tell the women."

He turned to Father, who was studying Laban's drawing with an odd expression. Laban waved a hand down within Father's field of vision, and Father looked up at his face. Laban elaborately mouthed his words.

"Dinner," Laban said, then pointed at the parts of the

drawing. "Food. Dinner. Kitchen. Cookfire. The pot. The spit. See?"

"If you use all the different words, how will he know what each picture *means*?"

Laban whirled on her. "If you think you can do better, give it a try!"

"Yes, I will," she said. Taking the stick from Laban's hand, she began her own drawing. She drew a tall man, a short man, and a short girl. She pointed to Father, Laban, and herself, then back at the drawings.

Father nodded. That was more than he had done with Laban's drawing, but she did *not* look at Laban lest he think she was being triumphant. He got huffy when he thought he had been shown up.

Rebekah rubbed out her pictures, then drew just the boy and girl, and this time the girl had a stick in her hand and under the point of the stick Rebekah drew a very tiny picture of the very picture she was drawing—the boy, the girl, the stick.

Father chuckled.

But Rebekah wasn't done. She drew a picture of an ear, then scribbled across it. Then a picture of an eye, and a dotted line going to it from the drawing the girl was making.

Then she knelt before Father and mouthed her words carefully. "I draw. You *see.* That is how you *hear* us." She touched the picture of the eye, then reached up and touched Father's ear. Then his eye, then his ear again. "You see, and that's how you'll hear."

Father shook his head.

He didn't understand.

No, he *did* understand. Because he wasn't just shaking his

head. He was smiling, then laughing, but it was a rueful, affectionate laugh, and he gathered Rebekah into his arms and then reached out for Laban as well and embraced them both. "My children, wonderful and wise."

"He likes it!" said Laban.

Father must have felt the vibration of Laban's voice, because he pulled back and looked expectantly at Laban's face.

"It's writing," Laban said. "Like Uncle Abraham."

Father wrinkled his brow—he didn't understand Laban's words. But it hardly mattered, since the next thing he said was, "It's writing. You're trying to write to me."

"Yes," said Rebekah, and Laban almost jumped out of his clothes in his excitement, jumping up and down, obliterating the drawings with his feet.

"But you don't do it with pictures of the *thing*," said Father. "You make pictures of the *sounds*."

Father reached out a hand. After only a moment's hesitation, Rebekah realized he wanted the stick and gave it to him. He thought for a long moment, then made three marks in the dirt.

"You make marks that stand for the *sounds* of the word," he said. "That's your name, Rebekah."

"It doesn't look like anything," said Laban.

Father didn't hear him, but explained anyway. "This mark is always 'ruh.' And this mark is always 'buh.' And this one is 'kuh.'"

He made three more marks. "'Luh,' 'buh,' 'nuh,'" he said.

"Look, your name and mine are the same in the middle," said Rebekah.

"But my name isn't 'luhbuhnuh,' it's Laban."

Father was studying their faces, as usual, and saw Laban's resistance.

"We just write down the solid sounds," Father said. "The ones that don't change. The Egyptians do it foolishly, and so do the Babylonians and Sumerians—the priests have a separate picture for every possible sound. Bah, beh, bo, bee, boo, bim, ben, ban—a separate picture. So you have to learn hundreds and hundreds in order to write anything. But we use the same mark for all the 'buh' sounds. 'Bah,' 'beh,' 'bo,' 'bee,' 'boo,' we just make this mark. 'Bim,' 'ben,' 'ban,' we make the same mark but we add this one, for the sound of the nose. See? Look, I'll show you."

Using just the marks from their names, he wrote them in several different combinations, then said the words. Sometimes the same two or three symbols stood for two or three or four different words at the same time. "But it doesn't matter," he said. "Because one word will make sense and the others won't. So you always know which is which. And if you don't, then you just add a word so we know which one you mean."

Rebekah's head was reeling. She started making sounds with her lips and tongue and trying to count them. "Kuh buh muh tuh chuh nuh guh luh . . ."

Father saw what she was doing and stopped her with a touch. "I'll show you all of them that I remember. I learned this when I was a boy, you understand. I haven't used it much since then. There was no one to write to, and nothing to read. I never taught it to you because it was so useless. I almost forgot that I had ever learned it." He laughed bitterly. "It was for sacred writings. Tally sticks are enough for counting goats and sheep, which is all I've ever needed. Abraham had all the ancient writings. Once he had a son, I knew his boy would have the holy birthright and there was no more need for me to remember how to write. Was my son going to be a priest? I never thought of using writing for something else. For myself."

Rebekah heard him, but her mind also raced in its own direction. "But this means we can write *anything*," she said. "If we can make the word with our mouths, we can write it down, once we know all the marks."

Father must have read enough from her lips to know what she was saying. "I'll teach them all to you, all that I remember. This is a *good* idea, children. You can write to me to tell me what I need to know. It's too hard to read lips. Too many sounds come from the back of the mouth. Everybody talks too fast. Or they shape their mouths so queerly when they're trying to talk to me. But this way—you'll give me my ears again!"

Then he frowned. "But I don't know if I should teach *you*, Rebekah."

"Why not?" she asked. Trying not to overshape the words. Trying not to say them too fast. Trying not to show how indignant she was at the idea of being left out.

Father calmed her with a hand on her arm. "No, you're right, Rebekah. It was always for the boys. Writing was part of the birthright. The keeper of the ancient writings had to know it. But now *we're* going to use it so you can ask me what I want for dinner. Of course I must teach you, Rebekah."

They set to work learning the alphabet. At first Father could remember only about two-thirds of the letters. But by the time they had been writing messages to each other for several days, Father remembered them all, or at least remembered signs that worked well enough. And as long as they all remembered the same signs for each sound, what did it matter if they were exactly the same as the ones Abraham used on the sacred books? Uncle Abraham was far away and very old, if he wasn't dead already.

Of course the servants and freemen of the household saw what they were doing and how these marks allowed Bethuel to speak aloud the words that others were trying to say to him. When Laban saw this, he tried to close the others out by rubbing out the marks when he was done, or concealing them from view with his body. At first Rebekah followed his lead and tried to keep the secret from the other children and the women who were the first to try to learn. But then she remembered how she had felt when Father suggested that he might not teach *her* how to read and write the letters.

Why should anyone be shut out of this? The next time Laban started trying to shield his writing from one of the servants, Rebekah challenged him and called the woman over to see what they were writing. "Don't you see?" she said. "We're not priests, trying to keep this a secret. This is for *Father*, so he can hear. It's better if *everyone* in the household can speak to him, isn't it? Every little child, every woman, every man. Because who knows when a bear might come into the camp, or a troop of bandits might be seen, and *everyone* ought to know how to come in and scratch a word in the dirt so Father has the warning."

Laban was still reluctant, though Rebekah could not think why. But after he saw that Rebekah was going to teach everyone in camp who wanted to learn, he gave up and joined in.

For many of the servants it was only a novelty, and they quickly lost interest without learning more than a few marks.

Some, like Deborah, tried to learn but never really understood; they ended up drawing pictures after all, and called it writing. But others, especially children, got caught up in the game of it, and soon many of them were making dirt scratches all over the campsite, so that you could hardly go anywhere without seeing something scrawled on the ground.

Which included some nastiness, too. Ugly words and mean gossip. Rebekah didn't like that, how people used these marks to be able to say cruel things that they would never have dared to say with their mouths so people would know who had said them. She was especially hurt at how often she found "Rebekah is ugly" and "Rebekah is stupid" among the words written in the dirt. Sometimes they were even scratched into stone so they couldn't be erased.

Who was writing such things? Who hated her? She looked at all the other children with suspicion for a while, wondering who it was who despised her but was too cowardly to say it to her face.

Maybe it was all of them.

And why just children? Could it be that this was what *everyone* thought in the whole camp?

Rebekah did not speak of these things to Father or even to Laban. Nor did she rub out the offending words, lest someone take satisfaction from knowing it bothered her. Still, it was not as if she could keep them secret from Father. After all, he was not confined to his tent, and now that so many people could write messages to him, he was out and about the camp more than he had been in many months. This was a blessing, the greatest blessing of all, Rebekah thought, because people could see that he was still the ruler of this house, the master of all things. But it also meant that he was bound to see the cruel words about Rebekah, too.

One day Rebekah found out just how seriously he had taken it when she heard someone crying out in pain and ran from the kitchen fires to see what was happening. Deborah met her, frantic with worry. "He's beating people! Make him stop, Rebekah!"

"Who?"

"Uncle Bethuel! Don't let him beat me, Rebekah. I've been very good!"

Deborah wrung her hands as Rebekah led her toward the cries. "Deborah, Father won't beat you." Deborah always took other people's beatings as if they were only a prelude to her own, though Father had never beaten Deborah and, in fact, rarely beat anyone. Whatever had happened must have been terrible.

A servant boy named Belbai lay naked and writhing on the ground as Father towered over him, thwacking him so harshly with his staff that each blow drew blood and Rebekah was certain that some bone was bound to break, if it hadn't already. "Father, what are you doing!" she cried. But of course he didn't hear her. So she ran to him and caught at his arm and clung so he could not strike again . . . clung until Father stood there, his chest heaving with anger and exertion, as she wrote her question into the dirt. "What did he do? You never beat children."

"*You* tell her what you did!" Father roared at Belbai.

Belbai, who was panting and sobbing in pain, could not speak.

Rebekah saw Khaneah, Belbai's mother, standing helplessly nearby. She dared not interfere with her son's punishment, and yet clearly it was unbearable for her not to be able to go to the boy. So Rebekah beckoned to her, and stopped Father when he raised his staff to drive her off. In a moment the woman was on her knees, cradling her son's head and shoulders in her lap.

Rebekah wrote in the dirt: "Will you kill him? Break his bones?"

"Yes!" cried Father. But even as he said the words, he stepped back, showing that he would not kill him, would not break his body.

"Forgive me," Belbai whimpered. "I never meant it."

"Never meant what?" asked Rebekah.

"Don't you speak to him!" roared Bethuel. "I won't have you speak to him! I'll tear off his ears before I let him hear your voice!"

That was when Laban arrived at a run from the bean fields, having been told of the commotion by one of the children. He demanded to know the cause, and Belbai, encouraged by the way his mother's arms enfolded him, finally said, "I was the one writing against Rebekah."

It was Belbai? Why him, of all people?

"You!" cried Laban. He seemed to explode with fury, and he stomped hard on the boy's ribs.

Belbai cried out and Khaneah shrieked, but no one raised a hand to stop him. Except Rebekah. "It was nothing but words," she cried. "He's been punished more than enough for *words*."

"I should have known it was him," Laban said. And he started to gush out an explanation, but Father stopped him and made him write it. Laban spoke slowly, writing each word as he said it.

"Last summer he saw Rebekah walk by and he said, 'A rich man is going to pay a lot to get that pretty one in bed.'"

Bethuel's eyes grew wide with rage, but it was not his anger that made Laban hesitate—it was Rebekah's presence that stopped him.

"Go away, Rebekah," Laban said.

"Not a chance," she said.

"I don't want you to hear this!"

"I should have heard whatever it is *months* ago." Then she wrote on the ground, so Father would know what she was saying: "I will hear this."

Father seized Laban's shoulder and pointed to the ground. Enough talking, *write.*

Laban resumed his account. After the phrase "get that pretty one in bed," Laban wrote, and said aloud: "If some lucky boy doesn't get there first."

Khaneah wailed in grief and Belbai hid his head in his arms. They both knew that he had said the unsayable, and what it would mean to them. Even Rebekah understood now. This was not just words.

Bethuel was furious, not least at Laban himself. "Why didn't you tell me at the time!" he roared.

Laban wrote, "That was before writing. I warned him that if he ever said such a thing again, I would tell Pillel and he and his mother would be sent away. He must have started writing bad things about Rebekah as soon as he learned how. Out of spite."

"I never meant them," cried Belbai. "I was angry at Laban."

"What did he say?" demanded Father.

Laban wrote down Belbai's words.

Father turned to Belbai with contempt. "Laban showed you and your mother mercy, and you were *angry* with him? Fool. And because you were angry at Laban, you wrote words to torment my daughter? Meanness on top of foolishness."

"But everybody knows how beautiful she is!" cried Belbai.

When his words had been written, Father spat upon them. "All my daughter knew was the words you wrote. I saw how they stung her, and how she held up her head in pride so no one could see she was ashamed."

Deborah listened to all this wide-eyed. "All this drawing, Rebekah, it was about *you?* Bad pictures of *you?*"

Rebekah had no chance to explain, for at that moment Khaneah, weeping, began slapping her son's face, so that it was from her that he cowered now. "This good man found me whoring for bread and took me into his house and took away my shame!" she cried. "But you are still the son of a whore!" She rose and forced him to his feet, though he was still bent over with pain. She shoved him away from her. "Out of the camp! Out of the camp! You have no place here!"

Then she ran to Bethuel and threw herself prostrate before him, and with her lips against his feet, she cried out, "You were merciful to me and my son, and we have repaid you with shame! We are the lowest swine who live in their own filth! We deserve to die, we deserve to die."

Laban started to write her words, but Father stopped him. "I know what she's saying."

At first Rebekah thought, How can he know? Does he hear through his feet? And then she realized: She is saying the only thing she *can* say. She is thanking him for not slaying her son for his disloyalty and ingratitude, for slandering his daughter and speaking of her as if she were any man's woman, a harlot. She is begging for mercy.

Father spoke to Laban. "Have Pillel give her three days' provisions, and let her take her clothing, and her son's clothing, and coppers for a room."

Laban was outraged. "Coppers!" he wrote. "If he touched Rebekah, would he get silver?"

Father slapped his son lightly across the face. "I will not have you face me down. I forgive you because you spoke in anger, on your sister's behalf. But if *you* had told me at the beginning, we would not have come to this day, and your sister would not have seen or heard any of this. So do not condemn me for showing mercy to Khaneah and her son, when you depend on my mercy as well." He reached down and took the woman by the hand and lifted her up. "If she returns to harlotry that is her choice, but let God never reproach me that she did it because I sent her away penniless."

Weeping, she clung to his hand and kissed it until he drew away from her. As soon as his back was to her, several of the servant women threw stones that landed at her feet. The message was clear. It was time for her to go.

Laban spoke to her. "Wait there, by that cedar tree, until I come to you with the coppers my father is giving to you because he loves God, and not because you deserve anything but stones from us."

Still weeping, she nodded, and shambled over to her son. Roughly she dragged him along behind her, heading for the cedar.

Rebekah saw no more, because Father took her by the hand and, gently but irresistibly, led her to his tent. Rebekah wanted to wait until she could calm Deborah down, for her nurse was still agitated, on the edge of crying. "Laban, explain it to Deborah," she called. She could see Laban forcing himself to calm down so he could soothe the poor woman, and then Father had her inside the tent.

He spoke to her haltingly, filled with shame. "That a daughter of mine should have suffered such things. Heard such things, and in my own house, and from the son of a whore."

Rebekah wrote in the patch of dirt they always kept open inside his tent: "She was not a whore in your household."

Father embraced her. "You are a child of mercy. But how will I ever erase his words from your memory? You remember everything, and so this ugliness will be inside you forever, poor child, poor child."

Rebekah let him hold her for a moment longer, until her question was about to burst from her. She pulled away from him, took the stick, and wrote:

"Am I really beautiful?"

Father chuckled, then embraced her again, so that her face was held against his belly as it shook with laughter. "I suppose you don't want to forget *everything* he said, do you!"

"You never told me," she wrote.

"What good does it do for a woman to know she's beautiful?" asked Father. "Did she cause it to happen? What if you got the pox, or some injury that marred your face? If you never knew you were beautiful, you would not grieve at the loss of that beauty."

"Did you command everyone else not to tell me?" she wrote.

"It was not their place to tell you," said Father.

A boy had been beaten and he and his mother had been

sent away because he had said something about Rebekah's beauty. Any servant girl could be pretty and she would know it because everyone would talk about it. But Rebekah was the daughter of Bethuel, so no one could tell her, no one could speak about her.

All these years, and I have not lived in the same world as everyone else. There are things people don't tell me, because of who my father is. It's like being blind. When it comes to things I can't see myself, I only know what people tell me.

Just like Father, in his deafness. Laban and I worked hard to make sure he was told everything. But nobody told *me*, and I wasn't even deaf or blind or anything. My whole future will be different than I thought it would be. Men will want to marry me, and not just for my dowry. Maybe a man will want me out of love.

For a moment she felt herself dazzled by the future. Beautiful! I might be mistress of a great house! I might marry a prince, a king!

And then she remembered Belbai, bleeding, staggering, his mother supporting him as she led him away. Belbai could easily have died today. For her. For his desire for her, for his anger at being forbidden even to speak of her. His mother was ruined again, after having once been saved. Father had been generous to Khaneah, but it did not change the fact that she once again was without protection.

Because Rebekah was beautiful.

Rebekah did not want to cry in front of Father. She pulled away from him and fled to her own tent, suddenly ashamed and afraid.

Alone in her tent, Rebekah threw herself onto the rugs and wept. In moments Deborah came in and lay down beside her, covering her with a comforting arm. "My poor baby! Did Uncle Bethuel beat you, too?"

"No, no, I'm all right. Father would never hit me. I'm just sad."

"Because of Belbai?"

"I'm sorry he and his mother have to suffer so much because of what he did."

"He shouldn't have made mean pictures of you."

"No, he shouldn't," said Rebekah. She patted Deborah's arm. "See? I'm all right now."

"No you're not," said Deborah. "You just want me to leave you alone, but I don't want to."

"Why not?"

"Because I don't want to go out there. What if Uncle Bethuel sends me away?"

"He'll never do that. As long as I'm here, you're my nurse."

"But the other women say you'll soon get married and go away and then I won't have any work to do and I eat too much, everybody says so. Uncle Bethuel can't afford to feed people who don't work."

Which was a common thing for Pillel to say. How could Deborah know that it didn't apply to her?

"Deborah, you're *family*, not a servant. You're my cousin."

"What if he sends me home? I don't want to go home. My papa is angry with me."

"No, he's not."

"He's angry because of the baby. I wasn't supposed to have a baby."

"You don't have a baby," said Rebekah.

"I know," said Deborah. "He died."

She said it so simply, as if it made her only a little sad. "I never knew you were married," said Rebekah.

And then she realized how stupid a thing that was to say. Who was the simple one? Deborah had never been married. Simple as she was, some man in her father's household—or perhaps some stranger—prevailed upon her when she was very young and begot a child on her. How could Deborah even have understood what was happening?

"I'll never get married," said Deborah. "Men don't want ugly stupid girls. They want pretty smart girls like you."

Suddenly Rebekah understood what it meant that all her life Deborah had told her how pretty and smart she was. Deborah was saying, without even realizing it, How unlike me you are. I'm ugly and stupid, you're pretty and smart.

"Deborah, don't you know? I don't want to be pretty. I didn't even know I was pretty."

"I always told you," said Deborah. "You're so pretty all the time."

"I wish I weren't," said Rebekah, her whole heart in the words. "I should take my knife and cut a deep scar right across my face and *then* nobody would be troubled about me." She even reached for her knife, though she had no intention of actually cutting herself.

Deborah did not know that, however, and clutched at her hand, clung to it, refusing to let Rebekah take the knife. "No, no, you can't, you can't! Not my little Bekah baby! Nobody can ever hurt you, not even you!" Deborah wept furiously.

"I know, I know, don't worry, I didn't mean it. Please, Deborah, don't be frightened, I won't cut myself, I just . . . *wish* something would happen so I could get away from my face."

Deborah laughed through her own tears. "How can you

31

get away from your face? Your face isn't even chasing you, it goes in front!"

"Why do I have to be beautiful? Laban isn't handsome. It isn't fair!"

"Laban is very strong and good," said Deborah.

Yes, that was the truth. A man didn't have to be handsome; nobody cared what a man looked like as long as he was mighty in battle or commanded a huge household. Laban was heir to all that Bethuel owned, and so he would be beautiful enough to attract every ambitious girl for many miles around. He could have his choice of wives. Even if Father picked his first wife for him, Laban could take whatever additional wives and concubines he wanted.

But even if she were extraordinarily beautiful, which she doubted, the choice of husbands would not be Rebekah's. Father would not force her to marry someone awful, but he would choose carefully for her, and whatever man he chose, that would be her husband for life. If she were ugly, then it would be ordinary men who sought her, men that she could easily persuade Father to turn away until one came who was decent and good that she could love. But being beautiful *and* the daughter of a prominent household meant that men of wealth and power would also be attracted to her, and Father would be tempted by the bridegifts they might offer, by the possibility of connection to a great house. He would not force her even so, but it would be harder to persuade him if he liked a man that she could not bring herself to love. It would hurt him, anger him, and Rebekah hated even to imagine such a thing. She had spent her life trying to keep her father happy. Whatever beauty she had would fight against her now, unless by some miracle the first great man who came to court her was also a man that she could love.

Not likely. She had seen plenty of rich and powerful men, and almost all of them were ugly of soul, greedy and grasping, bossy and mean-spirited. They smiled at Father because he was rich and powerful, but to their servants they were curt or surly or brutal, demanding always and praising never. Rebekah knew the truth—that as a man treated his servants, so would he treat his wives. Married to such a man as that, she might please him at first but soon he would grow tired of her, irritated at her ways, because such men were never pleased for long. She had seen the wives of men like that, shadowy women who lived in the small circle of their children and womenservants, finding such happiness as they could but always under the cloud of their husband's disdain or even, now and then, outright hatred.

Father would never choose such a thing for me. But he would choose a man who seems to be cheerful and happy, and that is the face that all men show to him, so how can he know the truth? How can he understand what marriage to one of his friends would be like for a girl like me?

"Rebekah," said Deborah. "You should pray to God to make you ugly."

Rebekah laughed. "God doesn't grant prayers like that."

"Yes he does!" said Deborah. "Father said that God made *me* ugly."

"You are *not* ugly, you silly goof. You're beautiful."

Deborah pursed her lips. "Everybody but you says I'm ugly, so who's the silly goof?"

Rebekah sat up and hugged Deborah tightly. "*They* are, anyone who would say that," she said.

"Are you happy now?" asked Deborah.

"Yes, I am. I'm happy."

"Happy as can be?" Deborah could never be happy until she knew she had cheered Rebekah up.

"Happy as can be." Rebekah showed her a big toothy grin—the grin that had always been the end of this childhood game.

"I'm so glad you're my little girl," said Deborah. "They would never have let me keep my little boy even if he hadn't died. So I'm glad they gave me you to nurse instead."

Rebekah had a sickening thought. When her mother died, and Rebekah needed a wetnurse to feed her as an infant, had they taken Deborah's baby away from her so that Rebekah could have the infant boy's place at Deborah's breast? Or was it simply a coincidence that Deborah's baby had died just when Rebekah needed a nurse?

If they took Deborah's little boy, was he still alive, perhaps? Or had they . . . could they possibly have . . . killed him?

No, no, they served God, all the descendants of Terah, and that meant that they did not sacrifice human beings and regarded all children's lives as sacred, even those born in bastardy. Those who served God did not take the lives of the innocent, certainly not for the mere convenience of the baby daughter of a powerful man.

Deborah's baby must have died, that's all. Perhaps God in his mercy took one child to himself so that Deborah could have the care of a little girl that she could stay with forever, instead of a little boy who would have been taken from her as soon as he was weaned.

"Poor Deborah," said Rebekah. "I didn't know you lost a baby. That must be the hardest thing in the world."

"I didn't lose him," said Deborah. "I took very good care of him. I always knew where he was and whenever he cried I fed him. God wanted him, that's all. Father didn't want my baby around the camp, he got angry whenever he saw me with him, so God took my little boy to his own house where he could love him all the time."

"Who told you that?" asked Rebekah. Whoever it was had been very kind to Deborah, to tell her a story so filled with comfort.

"Nobody had to tell me, silly," said Deborah. "That's just the way God is. Everybody knows that."

"God doesn't always do nice things," said Rebekah. She felt wretched immediately for saying so, and not just because Deborah looked so dismayed.

"God does only good things," Deborah insisted.

Although she already felt bad about it, Rebekah was in a defiant mood and refused to back down. "Not to me. It wasn't nice to make me beautiful."

"He gave you a beautiful face because you have a beautiful soul," said Deborah. "I heard Uncle Bethuel say so."

Rebekah realized at once what this had to mean to Deborah. Since she had been told God made her ugly, wouldn't that imply to her that it was because she had an ugly soul? It made Rebekah angry, to realize that Deborah had lived all her life with the sort of things being said right to her face that Belbai had written about Rebekah. Deborah should not have to believe such things.

"I'd rather be good than beautiful," said Rebekah, "and you *are* good."

"You're good *and* beautiful."

"I'm not either one," said Rebekah. "I'm not really beautiful, either, because I'll get old just like everybody else and if I get married I'll have babies and get fat and nobody will think I'm beautiful then. So beautiful is not something I *am*, it's just something I have to put up with for now."

Deborah reached out and touched her face. "You're my pretty girl," she said. "Always and always."

"I don't mind being *your* pretty girl. I just don't want some man to see me and think of me as *his* pretty girl. I don't want someone else to get angry and get sent away like Belbai."

"Then always stay in this tent with me!"

"If only I could."

"Just like during a storm, when the sand is blowing everywhere, you stay in here with me and nobody has to cry."

One of Rebekah's favorite memories was the first big sandstorm she remembered. It had begun terribly, with everyone running around the camp in a panic, tying things down, getting animals into the shelter of caves and tents. A dozen sheep crowded into the tent with Rebekah and Deborah, but from that moment on the memory was a good one, of Deborah singing louder and louder to outshout the wind outside, the feel of her arms around Rebekah triumphing over the horrible sound of a million grains of sand pelting against the tent walls. When the storm was over it took two hours for the men to dig out their tent entrance, but through it all Rebekah had never been afraid because Deborah had her arms around her and kept singing songs and saying, "God knows where you are, God knows where you are."

Maybe that was an exceptionally strong sandstorm, or maybe she was simply old enough not to have to hide in a tent, but there had been no more storms that drove her inside. Nowadays Rebekah just put on her veil, tied it at her neck, and helped the others get the animals to shelter and staked out long cloths over the beans and vegetables. The veil kept the sand out of her eyes without keeping her from seeing what she was doing, until the job was done and she could go inside a tent with the others.

She thought of all the women wearing veils during a windstorm and how no one could tell who was who until the veils came off. Women in veils were not beautiful or ugly. They were simply invisible, indistinguishable.

O God, she prayed at once, Is this what I should do? Thou gavest me the burden of prettiness, but may I not bear that burden in privacy by wearing a veil?

She wasn't sure what kind of answer God would give. At least she got no warning *not* to do it, and in moments she had Deborah helping her search for her veil.

"Is there a storm coming?" asked Deborah.

"I'm keeping storms away," said Rebekah. And now she had the veil in her hands, then over her head and tied at her neck. "Look, am I pretty?"

"Silly, of course you are," said Deborah.

"I mean, can anybody *see* whether I'm pretty?"

"Take off the veil so I can see."

"I mean with the veil *on*."

Deborah was a little impatient with her for not knowing. "Nobody can see anything with a veil on, of course."

"That's how I like it," said Rebekah. "I'm going to wear this always, whenever I'm out of my tent. So you won't have to fix my hair up anymore, because no one will ever see it."

Deborah burst into tears. "Why won't you let me fix your hair?"

"Of course you *can*," said Rebekah. "You just don't have to."

"But I want to."

"Then you will," said Rebekah. "Don't you fret."

"Take your veil off, then, so I can fix it."

"No, I'm going to wear this veil all the time, so get used to it."

"It's time to do your hair," said Deborah. "Don't be a brat."

So Rebekah took off the veil.

"Doesn't that feel better? Don't wear that silly veil."

"I will," said Rebekah. "Because that's what God wants me to do."

"Did he tell you?"

"He didn't tell me not to," said Rebekah.

Deborah thought about this as she ran a brush through Rebekah's hair. "You mean if God doesn't tell me not to fly, I can fly?"

"No, but I prayed and . . . never mind, Deborah. I'm *going* to wear the veil until I lift it for my husband."

"I hate wearing veils. They're heavy and they make me sweat."

"Me too," said Rebekah. "But I'd rather sweat than show my face."

"What else isn't God telling you not to do so you can go ahead and do it?"

Rebekah looked at her sharply, sure that this had to be ironic. But it was Deborah saying it, so there was no irony in it.

"I don't know," said Rebekah.

With her mind on God, as Deborah kept on brushing,

Rebekah began to pray silently, the words forming on her lips but making no sound. "Let me not marry a man who wants me just because I'm beautiful," she prayed. "Let me live my life with a man who cares nothing for beauty, but who serves thee. Like Sarai, the princess from the ancient lineage of Ur, who married Abram, the desert priest. Abram loved her through all the years that she was barren. Loved her even when she was old and had lost all her beauty. Let me be loved like that, by a man who will not replace me with concubines when I'm old and ugly. Let me be loved by a man who loves God more than me."

"So?" asked Deborah, when she was done.

"What?" asked Rebekah.

"You talked to God, what did he say?"

"I don't know."

"What did you say to him?"

"I said, If I am to have a husband, let him be a man like Abraham. And since there's nobody much around here, if I'm going to have a husband like Abraham, God will have to bring him to me, however far the journey is."

CHAPTER 2

Father hated the veil she wore, and for the first few weeks it was a struggle between them. But when he forbade her to wear it, she refused to leave her tent. When he commanded her to leave the tent—without the veil—she covered her face with her hands. When he commanded her to take her hands from her face, she sank to the ground and wept into the hem of her skirt, with Deborah bending over her, doubling the noise of her weeping with her own.

Finally he gave in, but not without a sermon about how it was an affront to God to reject the beauty he had seen fit to bestow on her.

Laban, though he ridiculed her veil, soon became her ally in the struggle with Father. It was Laban who finally persuaded Father that it was not worth the struggle, that in fact the veil would create an air of mystery.

"It will make people think we have something to hide,"

said Father. "Some disfiguring disease. Leprosy. Scars. Pockmarks. A steady drool."

In reply Laban wrote, "It will show she is modest and will not flaunt her beauty."

"It will show she is disobedient and self-willed."

"Only if you continue to forbid the veil. And how beautiful will she be, perpetually in tears?"

"Tears dry up," said Bethuel. "Even my tears for your mother."

"But sullenness and frowning only become hardened into the face," wrote Laban. "Like Pillel."

Perhaps it was the thought of Rebekah coming to look like Pillel that finally tipped the scale. In any event, Father laughed and told Laban to tell Rebekah that she could wear her veil, though perhaps she could substitute one of looser weave so she could see well enough to sew a straight stitch.

It wasn't long before some of the servant women began to dress *their* daughters with veils. Laban wanted to ask Father to forbid it. "They're mocking you, Rebekah."

"Perhaps they've learned that it's good not to tempt men to wicked thoughts," said Rebekah.

"Or else their mothers simply want people to think their girls are as beautiful as you."

Rebekah wanted to ask, Are they? Am I the most beautiful? But she recognized this as pure vanity and left the words unspoken. "I don't mind if people think they're *more* beautiful," she said, praying silently for God to help her make this statement true.

"More likely people will think the whole camp was scarred by the pox," Laban muttered. But when Father spoke to him about all this veil-wearing, Laban wrote what Rebekah had said. "Let it be known that our young women are modest, not vain like the city girls. Let it be seen as humility before God." And, once again, Father gave in.

"Armies may tremble before a man's mighty sword, but no man can stand before a household of women," said Bethuel. Often.

So passed the months and years, as Laban learned how to manage great herds and how to lead men in battle, and Rebekah learned how to manage a household, with all the weaving and cooking and planting and harvesting and preserving that filled each day from dawn to dusk. She learned to judge the ripeness of beans and the strength of thread, how to help a woman give birth and how to turn milk into cheese or ferment it into yogurt, how to make bread rise and how to season and cook a lamb so it would have the robust flavor of wild deer.

By the age of fifteen she knew the names of all the women and men of the household, and all the children, too, as surely as Father and Laban knew every bearing ewe and every new kid and calf. "The women and children are *my* flock," she once told Laban, when he seemed surprised that she bothered to learn the names of useless children. "Where do you think tomorrow's shepherds will come from? They're the children I teach to water and weed the garden. If they come to you knowing how to work hard and take responsibility even when no one is watching, it's because someone like me has done her job well."

Laban repeated her words to Father, to his friends, to everyone who would listen. "What woman has ever been as wise a mistress of a household as Rebekah? Her veil conceals a beautiful face, but her face conceals wisdom and virtue. So the veil, by hiding the distraction of her beauty, becomes the window to her soul."

When Rebekah learned that Laban was saying such things about her—not just in the camp, but in town when he went there to sell woollen cloth, cheese, and leather—she forbade him to praise her so immodestly. "All women do these things, foolish boy," she said—though of course he was three hands taller than her, with a surprisingly thick beard for a man of only seventeen years. "The only reason it surprises *you* is because you never saw our mother doing it."

"Well, there you are," he said, as if this proved his point. "You never saw her either, and yet you learned it."

"I saw what needed doing and did it," she said. "You'd think I had saved a kingdom or healed a leper or found a spring in the desert."

"All right, I'll tell people you're lazy and all your cooking tastes like dung, so nobody will marry you and we can keep you running things here forever."

"Yes, your wife would love to have me around all her life."

"I don't have a wife, and as long as you're here, I can't think of any reason why I should get one."

At which Rebekah rolled her eyes, since she knew and Laban knew that he had already fallen in love three times— with completely unsuitable girls, of course—and wherever he went, well-favored daughters were trotted out and their needlework shown to him and their cooking fed to him.

For that matter, whenever a visitor came to Bethuel's tent, he was fed Rebekah's cooking and shown Rebekah's workmanship—not just weaving and sewing, but fields of beans and vegetables, and stores of cheeses, smoked meats, and oils and wines that had been acquired in trade for the wovenwork of the women who toiled under her guidance. But Father knew better than to try to show *her*. Instead, the visitors merely glimpsed her, veiled, as she went about her business. And because she did not have to hear what was said about her, she was able to pretend that she did not know it was said, or that many a visitor's main business in Father's tent was to offer fine gifts for him to pass along to her. Father always declined the gifts, of course, but he turned their visits into profitable trade when he could. He did not trouble her with tales that would only make her upset.

But now that she was of a marriageable age, it was inevitable that one of the supplicants would so please Father that he would begin to think that perhaps this man or that one might be a good son-in-law.

Through it all, however, Rebekah grew less and less interested in the prospect of marriage. Didn't she already have all the work of a wife? Except the actual bearing of children, and she'd helped with enough births to know just how pleasant *that* could be. She loved children and was good with them, but there was no shortage of children among the servants in her father's household, and if she wasn't the mother of any of them, she was, in a sense, the mother of all, since she ruled over the household women and all the children still at breast or knee. So what would marriage bring her, except the pain of childbirth and the loneliness of being taken away from all she knew and all she loved?

In her husband's house she would be a stranger. She had no experience with that. She had seen how it was for new servants brought into the house, men who had to prove themselves by the strength of their arm and their way with beasts, women who had to earn their place by more subtle contests, and who even then could never rise within the hierarchy of the household the way new men could. Naturally, as wife she would be at the head of the household women—for even if her face had been ugly as a toad's back, Father would have seen to it her dowry was enough to place her as first wife. But Rebekah knew perfectly well that being nominal head and actually being the leader of the women were two different things. Here, she had grown up among the women, pampered because she was the youngest, the daughter of the house, and motherless as well. Finally, after Father became deaf, she asserted herself as mistress of the house of Bethuel and the women understood that she needed to take that role. They did not resist her. But she had always known these women and they knew her, too. She was never, not for a moment of her life, a stranger.

"I don't want to leave home," she told Deborah.

Deborah nodded wisely. "It's hard to leave home, even to go to your uncle's house."

"But you did it," said Rebekah.

"There was a baby who needed me."

"There's none who need *me*."

"There will be, silly," said Deborah. "That's why you *get* married, so you can have babies you can *keep*."

"What kind of man will marry me, Deborah? A man from a great herding household? Then I'll always be pitching a tent and packing it up again, or if they settle down near a town, they'll have a house there, and what do I know about tending a place with hard walls and a roof, and neighbors living just steps from the door?"

"Maybe you'll marry somebody like your father, who stays in one place but lives in a tent."

45

"There's hardly anyone like Father."

"I've never been to a town," said Deborah.

"You haven't missed a thing," said Rebekah.

The few times she had gone into a city, she had not liked it. The hearty stink of animal dung, the nauseating smells of human waste and rotting food, the acrid odors of tanning and dyeing. And the crowds—the jostling, the noise, people shouting and cursing or even cheerfully greeting each other without seeming to care that dozens of strangers could hear them bellow. Yet perhaps the hardest thing for her in town was the lack of a horizon. Walls everywhere, blocking your view—to Rebekah it was like perpetually being trapped in a canyon. She had been trained all her life to keep in mind where she could run, if danger threatened—bandits, a lion, a bear. True, lions and bears generally stayed out of villages, and the large towns kept a wall, but when the wall failed, when a town fell, what had been built as their protection became their trap, leaving the townspeople at the mercy of marauders with no hope of escaping into the open. Cowering in their houses, that's what all the town people were doing, however bold a face they might wear in the street.

"If you love your husband," said Deborah, "then you won't care if it's a tent or a house. That's what they all say."

"*If* I love him."

"Why wouldn't you, if he gives you babies?" asked Deborah.

"Not every husband is good," said Rebekah. "It's not just about babies. You've heard the stories the women tell."

Tales of the kind of master who beat everyone, not just the servants, but his own children, his own wife. Who could stop such a man? Or the man who was insatiable, constantly bringing new women into the household and casting his seed about in strange beds and strange places, so that his wife could never be sure that there would not be dozens of would-be heirs ready to contest the right of her own children to inherit. And when a husband had a new favorite among his women, there were tales of wives persecuted, mocked, even driven from their homes as the husband who had sworn to care for her looked on indifferently.

"*Your* husband would never treat you badly," said Deborah. "Uncle Bethuel would never let him."

"Father won't have any say about it, once I marry a man."

Deborah laughed. "If Uncle Bethuel hears that your husband treats you wrong, how long do you think he'll wait to come get you back?"

"How would he hear?" asked Rebekah.

Deborah thought about that. "I forgot. He's deaf." Then: "You could write to him?"

"And who would carry the letter?"

"I would."

"And how would you do it if my evil husband forbade you?"

"I'd go anyway."

"And what if he caught you and beat you?"

"Then as soon as he was through beating me, I'd go again."

Rebekah believed her. "No, don't say that," she said. "I'd never let you suffer like that for me."

"I'd never let *you* suffer from a bad husband. I'd tell Uncle Bethuel no matter what."

Only then did it occur to Rebekah that Deborah assumed she would go with her when she married. And of course she was right. What else would Deborah do? It was the only job she was trained for, to care for Rebekah. And Rebekah would never have the heart to refuse to take her along. Yet in a new household, would the other servants be kind to her? Understand her slowness of speech and thought, her inter-mittent memory? No, Deborah would be taunted and teased, and Rebekah, being new, wouldn't have the power to stop them. If she tried, they'd only tease Deborah more mercilessly behind her back.

One more reason, as if she needed one, for Rebekah not to marry anybody. Not unless God chose him.

In all her anticipation of troubles to come, she did not think of the hardest problem until it actually faced her.

His name was Ezbaal. He was a youngish man, no more than thirty, who had inherited his wealth when his father was killed by thieves in the streets of a town where he had gone to trade. Ezbaal had been only eighteen at the time, but he already had the respect of his father's men, so they followed him in seeking vengeance on the city that had failed to keep the old man safe. Ezbaal took the town by stealth and forbore to slaughter all the inhabitants only when they produced a huge treasure as blood-price, along with the heads and hands of the thieves who had slain his father.

Yet, though his manhood had begun in bloody justice, along with that tale it was said that he ruled his household with wisdom and mercy and patience beyond what anyone could expect from a man so young. It was with admiration that Ezbaal's name was spoken in all the desert camps, and even though, for obvious reasons, Ezbaal shunned settled life, he had good relations with most of the great desert families and shared water rights in so many wells that it was said he could travel from Elam to Egypt, from Sheba to Hurria, without having to fight for water or go thirsty for a day.

Ezbaal had called upon Father before, when Rebekah was seven or eight years old, and she remembered seeing him from a distance, this man of legend who seemed so young compared to Father, but who strode with purpose and greeted all without fear or boasting, as if he counted himself the equal of any man, yet took all men to be his equal in return.

Now he came again, but not with his great household to share water for a season in the nearby hills. No, this time he came with only a small entourage, enough men to make robbers think twice before attacking them on the road, and, surprisingly enough, three women. The camels they had with them were not enough to be a serious trading caravan; the cattle were not enough to be a herd. They could only be gifts for Bethuel.

He might have come like this if he needed Bethuel's help in war, but there was no rumor of war, and he would not have brought women. Ezbaal had come with marriage in mind.

The whispers flew through camp like swarms of summer flies, buzzing everywhere so there was no escape. "Bethuel can't say no to *him*." "Rebekah has to fall in love with him at once!" "They say he married years ago but she died in bearing her first child, who died as well, and the poor man has been grieving ever since." "He's so rich he doesn't need to marry for a dowry, he can marry for beauty, he can marry for love."

Gossip also centered around the women who came with Ezbaal. One of them, it was agreed, was almost certainly his mother, and as the afternoon wore on, the other two were rumored to include the mother of Ezbaal's dead first wife,

Ezbaal's sisters, his aunts, his great-grandmother, or the high priestess of Asherah from any of several famous cities, who was coming along to test Rebekah's purity and bless any marriage that might ensue. Of course the three women actually with Ezbaal could not be *all* these things; Rebekah could not think of why he would have brought them along at all.

Rebekah was not one to wait for rumors, however. Soon after Ezbaal's party had been seen and a messenger sent, who ran back with word that Ezbaal begged hospitality and that his company included fourteen men and three women, Rebekah took Laban aside and asked him who the women were and why they had come.

"They're here," Laban said dryly, "to look behind the veil, you dolt."

Ah. Of course. Father would not display her to Ezbaal like a cow, but a man like Ezbaal would not marry a mere rumor or mystery. Rebekah's face would have to be seen by someone that he trusted. And if it was a woman—or three women—willing to view her face in privacy, she could have no possible reason for objecting.

She felt a thrill of fear at that. After all, just because a servant boy and her own father and brother had declared her to be pretty did not mean that she would be beautiful in the eyes of a man who had wandered half the world and seen all there was to see. She could imagine his mother or aunts or whatever-they-weres coming back to him and saying, "You might as well marry the veil, because you'll be wanting to leave it on her through the whole marriage," or, "She's pretty enough, for a girl of the desert, but in a world where true beauty can be found, why should you settle for this?" And he would leave without asking for her hand in marriage, and then she could take off the veil, for no one would think her truly beautiful again. "She might have been beautiful as a girl, but womanhood did her no favors," that's what they'd say of her.

And after all these years of vanity—for what was this business with the veil, she realized now, except the sheer vanity of thinking no man could look upon her face without being driven mad with love?—it was exactly what she deserved, to have mystery replaced with pity. And Father would be teased when he visited the towns, about how he always did better business when he kept his goods in a sack than when he put them on display. Perhaps they would have to strike the tents and move far away, to a land where the shame of Rebekah's exposure would not have made them figures of ridicule.

"You do still have a face under that thing, don't you?" Laban asked, though of course he had seen her face many times. She did not wear the veil inside her father's tent, because she knew it offended him and, at least with Father and Laban and the oldest, most trusted servants, there was no fear of her beauty—her *reputed* beauty—causing disturbance.

"All but the nose," she said. "It kept snagging on things and I finally cut it off."

"You'll be all the prettier, I'm sure," said Laban. "I understand they're growing their women without noses in the cities of the coast. They don't cook as well because they can't smell the food, but it's better for kissing. You don't have to turn your head."

He was rewarded by being hit on the shoulder with a spoon, at which he retreated, laughing.

Despite her fears, Rebekah couldn't help getting caught up in the excitement in the camp. Though she thought of marriage only with dread, she also knew that it would come, sooner rather than later, and to have Ezbaal ask for her hand would be about as high an honor as she could aspire to. If he came with the offer of a bridegift instead of a demand for a dowry, that would be a sign of true favor from God, for such a thing happened only to great women, like Sarai, who was a king's daughter when Abram darkened the whole plain around Ur-of-the-North with the vast herds he brought to her father when he married her.

It was foolish to compare herself to the incomparable Sarah, for she was a woman of legend. Yet could she not also hope, in some secret place in her heart, that she, too, might be part of a legend, even if it was only a small one?

To be the wife of Ezbaal. . . . All would envy her. All would honor her. And he was a just man, fair in all his dealings, so she would have nothing to fear at his hand, and her children would be well treated. Her sons would be raised to excel in herding, husbandry, and war; her daughters she could raise with grace and skillful hands and willing hearts, and see them placed in good homes with good men, because they would be well dowered. All her future looked dazzling, if he asked for her hand, if Father said yes.

So what was it that made her feel a sick dread inside at the thought of going away with him? Was it nothing more than the excitement and nervousness any girl should feel at the coming of a husband and lord—her suitor and lover? The fear of rejection when the women saw her face?

No. She had those feelings also, and knew them for what they were.

Not until she wrote his name in the dirt with a stick did she understand what made her sick with dread to have him come. It was the last two syllables of his name. Ba'al. The word only meant "lord," and there were many who still said that it was just another name for the God of Abraham. But Rebekah knew that Ba'al had long since ceased to be another name for God. Instead he wore the face of a hundred graven images in cities and villages throughout the land, and it was to these images that the people prayed. And the priests were not priests of God, but rather priests for hire, telling people, not how to live clean from sin, but rather that doing whatever they wanted was no sin at all, as long as they made their sacrifices to Ba'al.

Was Ezbaal's name the one given him by his parents, or did he choose it himself? If he chose it, then it meant he was a pious man in the worship of the false god; and if his parents chose it, it suggested *they* had been pious, and would he not also show respect to them by worshiping the god they named him for?

How could she marry a man who did not serve the God of Abraham?

She could not go to Father, for from the moment Ezbaal arrived, Father was with his noble visitor. And because Laban was at Father's side almost constantly, writing for him so the conversation with Ezbaal could go smoothly forward, she could not talk to her brother, either. It would do no good to discuss this with Deborah—what would she know? What could she do?

So Rebekah went to Pillel.

It was not a thing lightly done. Pillel was unfailingly courteous with her, but she always sensed in him a coldness, something held back, as if he had not decided yet whether to like her or not. And since she had taken to wearing the veil, he had virtually stopped talking to her at all, except where the business of the camp required that he speak to the chief of the women. But now, at the very least, she had to get a message discreetly delivered to Father, and who else could do that?

Pillel was, as always, in the midst of work, supervising the slaughter of two calves and four lambs for the feast that night. Already drained, cleaned, and skinned, the carcasses were disjointed and quartered before being spitted, since there wasn't time to roast them whole. Rebekah, too, had been busy, preparing four disused firepits that were only brought back into service when a large company visited or in time of drought, when unusual numbers of animals had to be slaughtered and their meat preserved. But she left her women tending the fires and came to stand beside Pillel with her head downcast, saying nothing but by her presence demanding attention.

He turned at once from the man he was speaking to. Indeed, he turned so abruptly he left his own sentence unfinished. Rebekah knew this was as strong a rebuke as Pillel could give her—by treating her visit with exaggerated importance, he was demanding that her business be important enough to be worth so much bother.

Well, annoyed you may be, Pillel, but this message must be delivered.

"I need to speak with you privately," said Rebekah.

He made as if to leave with her at once. She would not have that.

"As soon as you have finished disposing of the business at hand," she said, then stepped aside and bowed her head again, to wait for him. It left him no choice but to finish giving instructions to the servant he had been talking to, and to watch as dripping haunches, shoulders, loins, and heads of the beasts were spitted.

Rebekah saw that he was not instructing the men to take the meat to the firepits, and became annoyed. "The firepits are ready for the spits," she said. "The fires are banked and tended, and the women know their work."

At once Pillel waved a hand and the men holding the spits took off at a run.

Why was Pillel so annoyed with her? It was not unheard of for her to need to talk to him in the midst of his work.

He turned and gazed at her with a face devoid of expression.

"Pillel, there are rumors that the visit of Ezbaal may have something to do with me."

He said nothing.

"I need to know," she went on. "Is his name a just one? Does he worship Ba'al?"

"I know nothing of his gods," said Pillel.

"Nor I. Nor, I think, does Father," said Rebekah. "So Father might need to be reminded that his daughter will never serve Ba'al or any other god of stone."

Almost at once Pillel's face changed, from one unreadable expression to another. Rebekah could not begin to guess what went on in her father's steward's mind.

"If you could find a discreet moment," she said, "to remind him of this, before he agrees to anything that would be impossible for me to fulfill . . ."

She left the words dangling.

Pillel nodded, then raised one hand a little. It was a familiar gesture—the one he used whenever he thought Father was making a decision without having thought everything through. It was at once obsequious in its slightness and firm in its negativity.

"I have never heard my master speak against Ba'al," said Pillel.

"Why would he?" asked Rebekah. "But he takes part in no worship of Ba'al or Asherah, and gives no tithes to their priests or temples. Everyone knows he worships the God of Abraham."

"Forgive me for saying it, but as far as I'm aware, no one outside this camp knows that."

"Well, of course he doesn't announce it, but Abraham is his uncle, and our family is the family of the birthright."

"Which will pass to one of Abraham's sons," said Pillel. "What has that to do with Bethuel? If he wanted it known that he served Abraham's god, would he not have said so to all he meets, as Abraham does?"

For a moment Rebekah wanted to blurt out, Have you met Abraham? Face to face? What kind of man is he? Has he really seen the face of angels?

But there was a more important matter here than her curiosity. Pillel was resisting her and she did not yet know why.

"Pillel, regardless of what Father has or has not said, he cannot give me in marriage to a man who would expect me to join him in worshiping Ba'al or Asherah. I will serve the one true God and only him as long as I live, and the man I marry must do so also."

Now Pillel looked truly shocked. "Your father will not be happy to hear such a defiant tone."

"I'm not being defiant in saying that," said Rebekah, becoming annoyed. "I'm being obedient. Pillel, you have served my father all my life, and you don't know that we are true to the one true God?"

Pillel actually looked confused. "I knew that you stayed aloof from the priests of the cities and paid no tithes to them, and I knew that your gods were small images so that they could be carried around with you—"

Those wretched little god-images! Rebekah wanted to scream in frustration: Father always ignored her when she suggested that they shouldn't use them, and Laban laughed at her for being so particular, but the images *did* confuse people. "Pillel, those images are only to help the servants understand that our God is not the same god they worship in the cities, and to help them think of the true God when they pray."

"I am one of the servants," said Pillel. "And all gods are God."

"All gods are *not* God," said Rebekah. "Only God is God, and we do not worship an image."

"I see my master Bethuel bow down before stone images to pray," said Pillel, "and I bow behind him, and his son and daughter bow beside him also."

"But the stone is *not* God." She could not contain her frustration any longer. "I *told* Father that nothing good would come of his using those images. Just because great-grandfather Terah made them does not make it right or good. It only confuses people—the way it's confused you."

Pillel looked at her coldly. "I am not the one who is confused."

"Go to Father and tell him what I said," Rebekah replied. "You'll see who is confused. I will not bow down to the image of a false god. I wish I had never bowed down to an image at all, because the true God needs no images."

"How can I go to my master and tell him that his daughter refuses to worship with her husband as I have seen her worship with her father all her life?"

"Now that I have told you," said Rebekah firmly, "how can you *not* tell him?"

As if explaining things to a little child, Pillel said, "A woman worships the gods of her father and then she worships the gods of her husband."

"After all these years in my father's house," said Rebekah, in a tone just as condescending, "you still remain a stranger who does not understand what he sees."

She should not have said it. It could only hurt him and make him angry, at a time when she did not need anyone working against her.

"Pillel," she said at once, "I'm sorry, I spoke falsely and in anger."

He did not reply at all.

"You are not a stranger here."

"Of course I'm a stranger," he said. "The line between family and servant is always clear in my mind and I have never been confused."

"But not a stranger. I only meant to say that if you think we actually worship the stone images Father keeps, and if you think he would have me marry a man who would require me to worship false gods . . ."

"I know what you meant," said Pillel. "But I don't know how to say what should be obvious to you without giving offense."

"Say it and I swear I will not be offended."

"Mistress," said Pillel, "I have worked beside your father longer than you have been alive, and I swear to you that it is you, not I, who does not understand what your father worships, and what he will expect of you."

His words stopped her cold. Was it possible that he was right? Didn't Father reject the gods of the cities and towns? Did he think that the images he prayed to were actually somehow God himself and his Servant or Son, rather than being mere depictions, puppets they used when they acted out the story of creation?

It was too great a mystery to be sorted out. How could Rebekah have come to understand what she understood, if Father believed something so different? Who would have taught her? Of course the way she understood things to be was the way things really were. It was Pillel who was wrong.

But he meant no harm by resisting her—indeed, by his lights, he was trying to save her from embarrassment.

"Say this, then," she told him. "Say that he must talk to me before promising anything, because I must be able to worship God all my life, in the way that God must be worshiped."

"I will say what my mistress requires of me."

"All I need is for him to talk to me before he gives his word."

"And if he gives his word without talking to you?" asked Pillel. "And Ezbaal turns out to be a fervent worshiper of Ba'al and Asherah who requires his entire household to bow down to them and dance and celebrate before the images?"

"Then Father will either break his word or he will have to live on, knowing that he sent his daughter to live with a husband who will hate her, because I will never bow down or dance or sing or tithe or do any kind of worship before an image of Ba'al or Asherah. Before I did such a thing, I would die."

A smile came to the corners of Pillel's mouth. "It is easy for a child to speak of dying before obeying. But when the father of your children demands that you—"

"I will bear no children to a man who does not serve God," said Rebekah.

Pillel's face darkened. "You may be sure," he said, "that I will report this conversation to your father."

"That is all I ever asked of you," said Rebekah.

Pillel made no move to leave.

"Well?" asked Rebekah.

"Well what?" asked Pillel.

"Aren't you going to go tell Father what I said?"

"There is no urgency," said Pillel. "They can't begin discussing you until after they've feasted, and almost certainly not until the next morning. I'll take an opportunity to speak to him privately, before the matter can come up."

That was all she had ever asked him to do, but now it sounded like a threat. Pillel clearly thought less of her for this.

Was he right? Had she somehow misunderstood what Father believed?

With no one else to turn to, she finally resorted to talking with Deborah. After the meat was roasting, Rebekah left the women to do their work and returned to her tent for Deborah to dress her hair and help her into her finest clothing. No matter how things turned out, if she was to be seen she had to look her best so as not to shame Father.

"Deborah," said Rebekah, "what do you know about God?"

"He made everything," said Deborah. "He is king of the whole world. Even the lions and bears."

"You know they have gods of stone in the cities. We never bow down to those."

"No, never," Deborah agreed.

"Do you know why?"

"No," said Deborah, wonderingly, as if she sensed she were about to be let in on a great secret.

"No, I mean really, *do* you know why?"

Deborah looked puzzled and thought long and hard. "Because we have better gods here?"

Better gods. The stone images Terah made. But then what else would a simple-minded woman like Deborah think? She could not possibly understand the complicated reasoning that allowed Bethuel's house to bow down before stone images of God while refusing to bow down before stone images of Ba'al, who was, supposedly, the very same God, merely with different priests.

For that matter, you didn't have to be simpleminded for the distinction to seem meaningless. Once you knelt before an image of stone, the stone began to be your god, and not the God the stone supposedly represented. It was that simple and always had been. That was why Abraham did not claim Terah's images along with the birthright. He knew the images were false by their very nature, and could never be anything else. The keeper of the birthright knew that every stone of the earth showed the power of God, but none could contain his image.

Father has been wrong, just as his father was wrong, and Terah before him.

How do I know these things? How can I be so sure? If my father is wrong, then who taught me the true religion that I feel here in my heart? Not my mother, surely—none of her words, no sound of her voice remains in my memory. Not my nurse—Deborah understands nothing. How did I learn these things with such certainty that I know I'm right even if both Father and Pillel stand against me?

From Abraham.

From a man she had never met. All she had of him were stories, what he did, a few things he said. The way he faced death at the hands of a priest of Pharaoh in Ur-of-the-North, and God sent an earthquake to knock down the idols of the temple and save his life. The way he refused any reward when he saved the kings of the cities of the plain, lest anyone think that these kings had made him rich, for the only wealth he had was what had been given him by God. The way he trusted in the promise of God that he would have children as number-less as the sands of the sea, as the stars of heaven, even though his wife was as barren as a dried-out stick. The way he refused to take the gods his father had carved to represent the God of heaven and his Servant, by whose word all his creations were made.

She had learned her religion from the stories of Abraham and Sarah, and then assumed that her father understood things the same way. And he did! He had to! He was not a fool, he had to have learned the same things from these stories that Rebekah had. Pillel was wrong. Father would agree at once when he was reminded that no marriage could be entered into without protecting her right to worship the God of Abraham, and him alone.

"You don't look happy," said Deborah.

"I'm worried a little, that's all."

"If he doesn't make you happy, I don't want you to marry him, no matter how rich he is," said Deborah.

"And I won't, either," said Rebekah. "If he doesn't make me happy."

"Oh, silly," said Deborah. "You're not like me. You're a good girl. You'll do what your father says."

Rebekah left her words unchallenged. Time would tell whether she was a good girl or a bad one.

She was not yet fully dressed when Laban came to her tent. Hurriedly, she and Deborah pulled the finest gown over her head and then admitted him.

"Who's writing for Father, if you're here?" asked Rebekah.

"Pillel," said Laban. "Not a patient writer. He keeps leaving out words and letters."

Pillel would have the opportunity now to tell Father what Rebekah had said. Whether he chose to do it or not would be another story.

"It must be an important errand," said Rebekah, "that brings you here and leaves Father to decipher Pillel's writing."

"You are not going to serve the dinner in Father's tent," he said.

This would be a sign of great disfavor, ordinarily, but Laban was smiling a little, which told her that it must not be bad.

"You're going to be too busy dining with Ezbaal's grand-mother, his mother, and his sister."

"Not serving them? Dining with them?"

"You're to instruct our women to serve the same meal in both tents. And not the worst cuts of meat, either. Your meal is to be almost as fine as the one laid before Ezbaal."

"Let me guess," said Rebekah. "I'm not to wear the veil."

"Not inside your own tent," said Laban. "Not when the only people who will see you will be other women."

"Too late to try for a case of the pox, isn't it?"

"Don't worry," said Laban. "You're ugly enough to frighten a goat into giving sour milk."

"That's a relief," said Rebekah.

"Frankly," said Laban, "I think the women will hate you."

That would solve everything, wouldn't it? But she still couldn't bring herself to hope for it. "Why will they hate me?"

"Because next to you, they look like she-camels."

"On a long journey, a man would rather have a good camel than a pretty woman."

"Listen, my little lamb, there is no journey *that* long." With a laugh, Laban ducked back out of her tent.

"May I stay to see the fine ladies?" asked Deborah.

"Of course," said Rebekah. It still bothered her, sometimes, that the woman who used to scold her when she was naughty—and still did, sometimes—had to ask Rebekah's permission to stay for company. But of course she had to ask, because sometimes the answer was no, and Deborah truly did not have the judgment to make such decisions on her own.

The food was prepared, if not perfectly, then as best it could be on short notice early in the spring, when they were still living from last year's harvest. Rebekah took her place on a rug in her tent, with Deborah tending to the flap. A quick instruction to a serving girl, a longer wait during which Rebekah tried to decide whether she wanted to make a good impression or a bad one, and then her guests were there, clapping their hands outside the tent.

Deborah opened the flap and admitted them; Rebekah rose to her feet to greet them with kisses. The grandmother introduced herself as Ethah and promptly seated herself in Rebekah's own place—but of course the old can do what they like. Ezbaal's mother did not let go of her shoulders after their kisses, instead holding her at arm's length to look closely at her face. "You put a veil over *that?*" she said.

Rebekah only smiled in a way she hoped was enigmatic, and said, "What name should I call you?"

"You must call me Mother, of course," said the woman.

Whereupon Rebekah resolved to call her by no name at all. She would not be tricked into intimacy so easily as that.

She turned to greet Ezbaal's sister and found the woman to be different from the other two—taller, as tall as Rebekah, but with her hair so arranged that it served almost as effectively as Rebekah's veil to hide her face. The woman's hands trembled, and she could scarcely bring herself close enough to kiss Rebekah's cheeks. What—someone here who was even more nervous than Rebekah? Why? *She* was not being examined by women who were deciding on her worthiness as a bride.

Or was she?

For the first time it occurred to her that there might be more to this visit from Ezbaal than merely to see if Rebekah might be an appropriate bride. After all, there were two marriageable men in Bethuel's household, too. Laban, of course, was too young to be married to a mature woman like this. But was it possible that Ezbaal had brought his sister with an eye to trying to entice Bethuel to marry again?

It *was* rather odd that Father never married again after Mother died, thought Rebekah. Rich men often took several wives, yet Father had married only the one woman. Why hadn't anyone brought a sister or daughter to visit him before?

"And what is *your* name?" asked Rebekah. "Or am I to call you sister?"

"Never that," said the woman in a voice that sounded husky, as if she had been weeping. "Call me Akyas."

The word meant "rejected" and it could not possibly be her name. But whatever game these women were playing, Rebekah would take it all in stride. She had a game of her own, and now that she had met them, she decided to play it. She did not want to marry into a household dominated by these women. The falseness of the mother, the rude presumption of the grandmother, and the strangeness of the sister—what place would there be for her in their household?

They conversed about nothing for a little while—the journey, the good winter rains this year—and then the food began to arrive. The women said nothing, of course, either to praise or criticize the food; indeed, they ate in virtual silence and took only small portions, except for Akyas, who ate nothing at all.

Finally, though, the grandmother, Ethah, began quizzing her. The test was underway.

"Who really cooked this food?"

"Why, the servants, of course," said Rebekah brightly. "Don't you have servants do the cooking in your household?"

"I meant which of the servants chooses what will be served, and how?"

"No servant, Ethah, but the daughter of the house."

"No child your age can do that sort of job," said Ethah scornfully. "The servants would mock your youth as soon as you turned your back, and do what they wanted."

"Perhaps your grandson can ask my father how he chooses and trains his servants," said Rebekah. "In all my life I have never seen servants behave as you describe. Does the bean paste displease you? I see you have barely touched it."

"Too spicy," said Ethah coldly. "Which is to be expected, when you let servants do it—*they* don't have to pay for the spices, so what do they care?"

Rebekah immediately sent the serving girl for simple bean paste. "I fear that I'm the careless, wasteful one," said Rebekah. "Perhaps in my desire to make a good impression, I used too much spice and marred the dish."

"No, no, dear," said "Mother." "I find it nearly perfect."

"Then you must tell me how I can improve it, so that someday I might earn your judgment of perfection."

"But I haven't the faintest idea of how to make it better," said "Mother." "You use a kind of bean we never grow or cook with."

"The meat's too good," said Ethah, complaining again. "What kind of woman serves this quality to the women? It should have been reserved for the men, if you knew your manners."

"But this *is* the second-best meat," said Rebekah. "If you prefer, though, we can trade this dish with the servants—I would not be ashamed to have you see what we serve to them. My father and my brother understand cattle, so I can hardly do ill when cooking meat they raised and slaughtered."

Did Akyas laugh softly, or merely stifle a belch? She continued to say nothing, which was beginning to irritate Rebekah.

Still, it was obvious that the grandmother's grumpiness was being exaggerated, perhaps as a test of Rebekah's patience and grace. And "Mother" was being just as unnaturally nice, to try to win her over. So far, Rebekah might very well have made an excellent impression. It was time to put a stop to that.

"I hope you don't mind that we did not offer any portion to the gods," said Rebekah. "But I don't believe that Ba'al or Asherah are anything more than stone images, powerless to answer prayers, and the true God asks for larger sacrifices than to spill a bit of this and that at every meal. Besides, it spoils the rugs."

"We do it over an altar dish," said Ethah testily. "You might have provided one for *us* to use."

"But in my tent there is only one God," said Rebekah brightly. "I will have no mockery of the true God by permitting others to be worshiped here."

Ethah smiled triumphantly at the others, as if she had just won an argument. "Mother" faltered a bit, but bravely tried to smooth it over. "All gods are the same God, in the end, don't you think?"

"The living God is the only God," said Rebekah. "All the imitations are simply a way for priests to maintain control over the poor and ignorant."

"Now we see she's filled with rage!" cried the grandmother.

"Why should I rage?" said Rebekah. "I speak only the simple truth. I have no cause to be angry with those who do not know the truth. I pity their ignorance, and seek to help them understand that the God of Abraham is the only true God."

"God of Abraham!" cried Ethah. "Yes, the one who told him to take his favorite son up the mountain and sacrifice him!"

"That is not true," said Rebekah. "Abraham has spent his entire life fighting against the monstrous practice of sacrificing human beings to these false gods."

"But to the 'true' god he'll sacrifice his own son, is that it?" asked Ethah. "Don't you tell me it's not true—my grandson is a good friend of Abraham's firstborn, Ishmael, the one who was cheated out of his inheritance when that runaway priestess Sarah had the wretched little baby Isaac, no doubt by some kind of sorcery, which is probably why Abraham wanted to kill it. Ishmael heard the story from his own father. It happens that at the last minute Abraham turned coward and sacrificed a ram in his son's place, but he had Isaac all tied up and ready for the blade!"

So the story originated with Ishmael. Of course it was not to be believed. Ordinarily, Rebekah would keep the peace by seeming to agree with her guests and keeping her own opinion to herself—but today that would not serve her purpose. "There you are," said Rebekah. "Just one more example of the lies Ishmael tells in order to make it seem that Abraham was wrong to choose Isaac over him."

"Have you ever met the old man?" asked Ethah.

"No," said Rebekah.

"Well, *I* have, and I tell you that he's a bloody-handed old hypocrite, who pretends to hear from his god, but he's just using that lie to get people to do what he wants."

"You have met Abraham," said Rebekah with a smile, "and I have met you."

The words hung there, as each of them understood the unspoken completion of the thought—that having met Ethah, Rebekah chose to believe in Abraham.

"So this is the woman who wants to be the bride of my grandson! A girl who insults her betters to their faces!"

"But I do not want to be the bride of your grandson," said Rebekah. "Nor has anyone asked me to be his bride."

"Don't pretend to be such a fool as not to know why we are here!" cried the old woman.

That was when Akyas finally spoke. Or, rather, laughed—a low throaty chuckle that silenced everyone until she reached over and patted Rebekah on the knee. The touch chilled her. So did the laugh.

"Let us share in the jest," said "Mother."

"Of course Rebekah knows," said Akyas. "She is acting this way because she wants us to hate her. If we take an ill report to Ezbaal, and he withdraws his offer, then she never has to have an argument with her father over the question of marriage."

"Do you mean this girl has already made up her mind not to marry my grandson, without even having met him?"

"Ezbaal is twice her age," said Akyas. "Even though *we* understand his worth as a husband, who could expect a child of this age to know what a husband looks like? She dreams of dashing young boys. Probably she already has her eye on some completely unsuitable shepherd. Girls this age always do."

Rebekah almost spoke out angrily to deny this, but realized in time that, just as she had been playing a game with them, Akyas was playing a game with her. So she said nothing and did her best to keep her face a blank.

"See?" said Akyas. "She has control of herself—she wants to answer, but says nothing."

"I think you're putting too good a face on her," said the grandmother. "You're so eager for this match that you can't possibly see anything but virtue in the girl."

"But I'm not eager for the match," said Akyas. "If it happens, so be it, I'll join in the rejoicing. But I know something of unhappy marriages. Why should I wish such a thing on either my brother Ezbaal or this girl?"

What could this sudden show of sympathy mean? Rebekah continued to hold her tongue, unsure what the others might read into anything she said.

"What is the real issue here, girl?" asked Akyas. "Is it that you simply don't want to marry at all? Ah, yes—this has to be it—you want us to reject *you*, but from then on, any man whom your father brings, you'll compare him to Ezbaal and say, 'This one is not as good as the first one you brought.' Until you finally find one that *you* favor. It gives you an excuse to control your own marriage. Is that it?"

"You give me credit for too much cleverness, and too little wisdom," said Rebekah. "I trust my father to find a good husband for me. If it be Ezbaal, then I will rejoice. As long as I can continue to worship the Lord God of Abraham, and no other god, I will be content."

"You will be content," said the grandmother, "if your husband only beats you once a week. What do you think marriage *is?*"

"If that is your sad experience," said Rebekah mildly, "then I hope my marriage will be better than yours."

Ethah glared at her for a moment, then turned to the other women and smiled pleasantly. "I think," she said, "that we'll report that Rebekah is charming and beautiful, but too young for the match. So we'll betrothe them and take her with us, train her to be a loving wife, and hold the marriage when we find that she is ready."

"And when will that be?" asked Rebekah.

The old woman smiled beatifically at her. "When you bow your head and speak submissively to your betters."

"Ah, that's a relief," said Rebekah, adopting the same tone of exaggerated cheerfulness. "I feared it would be when I was as hard and withered and bitter as you."

Ethah clenched her teeth a little, but she maintained her smile. "It will be a pleasure teaching you modesty."

Rebekah turned to "Mother." "Did she train you in the way she promises to train me? Is that why you are so fearful, so eager to keep the peace? Did she beat you? Or merely humiliate you into submission?"

"Enough," said the grandmother. "Whether it's a careful plot on her part or she's really as rude and ignorant as she seems, it hardly matters. I won't have my grandson's life plagued with a girl like this."

"The choice is his," Akyas reminded her. "He has never been ruled by you, or by his mother either."

His mother, she said. Not simply "Mother." So she and Ezbaal might be siblings, but not by the same mother. And Akyas spoke of knowing the bitterness of a bad marriage. There was a story here, and Rebekah could not help but wish she knew it.

"Girl," said Akyas, "you put on a brave face. Perhaps it is true that all you care about is whether you can worship your god. So . . . what if we told you that Ezbaal is not concerned about whom you pray to? That you can marry him and he will not interfere with your private worship?"

Rebekah tried to find the trick or trap in what she was saying. "How can you speak for him?"

"I don't speak for anyone," said Akyas. "I only ask you, what *if* those were the terms?"

"Those who truly worship the Lord God of heaven do not

worship any other god, or even allow others to think they worship an idol."

"So you will not join in the festivals of Ba'al," said Akyas. "If Ezbaal consents to that, you have no further objection? We would then see your sweet obedience, and not this defiance?"

"I owe you only the courtesy of a hostess, not obedience, madam," said Rebekah. And then realized that by speaking this way, she was showing a sweet and, yes, obedient attitude.

"That is what I hoped," said Akyas. She turned to the others. "We have indeed unveiled her here," she said. "Veil after veil, if I see aright."

"If you think I'll forget what she said here today . . . ," said the grandmother.

"I think," said Akyas, "you'll remember only that if she comes home as Ezbaal's bride, she will be mistress of the camp, and you will show her proper respect, and she will show the same to you. Is that not so, Rebekah?"

"The grandmother of my husband, and his mother also, and his sister, will all have nothing but respect and love and true service from me," said Rebekah.

The grandmother laughed bitterly. "Fifteen years of loneliness have made a peacemaker of you, Akyas."

"A powerful woman makes the best partner to a powerful man," said Akyas. "It is only weak women and weak men who don't understand this."

Rebekah saw the other women bristle at this, but they said nothing to contradict her. This seemed remarkable to her, to say the least. Why would they endure having Ezbaal's sister speak to them this way, implying they were weak? There is more between these women than meets the eye, she thought.

Was Akyas her ally? Or merely her cleverest enemy? There

was something in the solution she had offered that seemed like a poisoned sweet. She would be free to worship God as she chose, and would never be called upon to take part in the worship of Ba'al—what more could she ask than that? And yet she knew there was something wrong with this. Akyas was about to triumph over her, and she did not know how.

"You are so gracious, lady," said Rebekah to Akyas. "Yet you speak of unhappy marriage. Surely you could not have been unsuccessful in marriage, having such grace as yours?"

"You see this girl?" said Akyas, as if proud of her. "Now she examines *us!*"

"Tries our patience, you mean," muttered the grandmother.

"At our ages," said Akyas, "we should have stored up quite a lot of *that.*" She rose to her feet, and the other women followed her lead. Again a sign that she, the youngest of the three, was really the leader of this group. Why?

Rebekah rose. "I fear my poor food has displeased you. You've hardly eaten."

"On the contrary, your meat and drink are delicious," said "Mother." "Whoever taught you to cook did well indeed."

"I could have wished the *sauce* to be a bit less spicy," said the grandmother, making it clear by her tone that she was not speaking of the sauce at all.

"It was the sauce I liked best," said Akyas. "I wish I could have had it every day." Then, suddenly in a hurry, she turned her face away and seemed almost to flee the tent, she moved so quickly. The others followed.

As soon as they were gone and Deborah had secured the tent flap behind them, Rebekah sank to the rugs, trembling. "Oh, it was awful, awful."

"I don't understand," said Deborah. "Did they like the food or not?" She knelt beside Rebekah and put her arms around her. "I thought it was *so* delicious."

Rebekah buried her face in her nurse's shoulder. "Oh, Deborah, it wasn't the meal, it was me. I failed completely."

"Failed? Oh, you mean . . . Ezbaal won't marry you?"

"The opposite! I thought I was winning by making the grandmother hate me. How was I to know it was the *sister* who was the leader? And she *liked* me. I can't think why, I was as horrible as I could possibly be without actually spitting on anybody."

"Spitting! Better not, I taught you not to spit when you were little."

"Then I'm glad I didn't forget your lesson," said Rebekah. In truth, though, she wanted very much to spit on something. The marriage plan would go forward, and even though it seemed Ezbaal was giving in on everything she cared about, she knew the marriage would be wrong, that she had overlooked something important.

"My little girl," said Deborah proudly. "You have grown up just as I hoped you'd be. Pretty and clever . . . and you don't spit."

Rebekah pulled away from her, looked at her face to see if she could possibly have meant those words sarcastically. But no, there was nothing but beatific happiness in Deborah's face. She was incapable of irony. It was Rebekah's own guilty conscience that put barbs into Deborah's words.

You have grown up just as I hoped you'd be, Deborah was saying. And that was it. A child growing up as she was taught. That was the loophole, the twist, the trick in the deal Akyas offered her. Ezbaal might let Rebekah worship no other god but God—but nothing had been said about the children they'd have together. He would raise them up to pray in the high places and dance in the groves, enemies of God. What would it matter to her then, that *she* could pray to God, that *she* was pure of the defilement of idolatry, if her children were polluted from the cradle up?

I hoped that by making them hate me, I would spare myself an argument with Father. But since that plan has failed, I will have that argument, and I will win it, because I will *never* marry a man who would teach my children to love any god but God.

And once Father realizes what a marriage to Ezbaal would mean, he would never dream of requiring such a thing of me.

But after what Pillel said, Rebekah was not sure of this at all.

Please, God of Abraham and Sarah, she said silently. Please fight for me. I haven't the strength to stand alone, if all are against me.

CHAPTER 3

It was after dark when at last Rebekah was summoned to Father's tent—a servant's whisper at her tent door, so as not to waken anyone else in the camp—and by the time she hurried outside, no one to be seen.

We will do this in stealth, in darkness, in silence, thought Rebekah. The marriage plan will unravel, but there will never be a quarrel that Ezbaal might hear.

Father, Laban, and Pillel were all waiting in his tent, their faces barely visible in the light of a single lamp that flickered with every movement of an arm or leg that might start the wick bobbing in the oil. Laban greeted her with a raised eyebrow, though what he meant by it Rebekah could not guess. Pillel was made of stone. But Father . . . could it be tears shimmering in his eyes?

The lamp had been set on the exposed dirt where people wrote things to Father. Pillel handed her a stick polished smooth by the grip of many hands. But Rebekah wrote nothing, for she knew that Pillel and Laban would have already discussed the issues with Father, and she dared not speak until she knew where Father stood.

"Ezbaal will let you serve God. A generous man, I think," said Father. "His women gave him a good report of you. He asks to marry you, and I have said—"

"No!" cried Rebekah. Could he possibly have given consent already, without speaking to her first?

He could not hear her, but he could see her face and knew what she said. "I have said that I will find out what is in your heart. You will find no nobler, braver, richer, stronger man in the world than this one. But now that I am faced with losing you, I find that it's a bitter thing indeed to watch you go. No man has had a better daughter, and I will feel impoverished and lonely without you in my camp."

"Then you'll be happy," she wrote, "for I won't marry him."

"What?" asked Laban. "Have you lost your mind?"

Pillel said nothing, but she could feel his contempt for her just the same. Pillel believed that everyone should fulfil his role and keep to his place—certainly *he* did—and he had no use for those who refused, as she was refusing.

"Rebekah, you have to marry sometime," said Father. "You have children of your own to bear, your own household to govern now. I've kept you here too long."

Her previous words were still there in the dirt, and now she added, "Because he will never let me raise my children to serve God."

Father's expression darkened. "Ah, God, now in my old age thou sendest my own words back to me."

Rebekah did not know what he was talking about. "What?" she wrote.

Grimly Father shook his head, and then spoke carefully, choosing his words. "When I was a younger man, I thought I would be another Abraham. I learned to read the holy writings, I felt the birthright like an angel leaning over my shoulder. I could not tolerate the slightest impurity—wasn't it vital that I prepare my household to be the dwelling place of the Lord?" He interrupted his own story and looked at Rebekah. "The way you are now. So sure that you know what the will of God must be."

Rebekah wrote in the dirt: "I know what you taught me."

To her surprise, Father snatched the stick out of her hands and scratched out her words so vigorously that a cloud of dust rose within the tent. "The kingdom of God is not a walled city," he said, "with guards to keep strangers out and citizens in. The kingdom of God is an open tent, with room in the shade for all who seek shelter."

Rebekah reached again for the stick. "And when the wind blows?" she wrote.

"It was just a parable!" Father said impatiently. "It doesn't have to be correct at every point! I'm teaching *you*, or have you forgotten who is the father here?"

These words left Rebekah trembling. She would never be disrespectful to her father, and yet her father was trying to tell her that she should marry Ezbaal, and she knew—she *knew*—that she could not obey.

How did she know? she wondered. How could she be so certain? All day she had thought of reason after reason why the marriage must not happen, and then as the reasons were stripped away, a new reason came into her mind, but always with the same foregone conclusion: She must not marry Ezbaal.

Was this nothing but a young girl's fear? No, she knew it was not. She had never been timid about doing what must be done, and even though she dreaded marriage for many reasons, she also knew that it was her duty, and she knew there could never be a better match than this one. It was an honor to her family that Ezbaal had come to them, and it would bless her father's house to be tied to such a man as he. And she knew she had nothing to fear from him, compared to many other possible husbands. Life in Ezbaal's house would be good—even with his crotchety grandmother constantly criticizing her. She would win the old woman's heart in due time. This marriage was a good one; there could not be a better one. She was not afraid.

And yet she could not say yes. Why not? What was holding her back?

She closed her eyes and spoke silently to God. Is my father right? Can I teach my children to love thee even though their father will worship other gods?

Immediately she felt herself filled with a sense of emptiness, as if the spark of joy within her had fled.

O God, she thought again, it will embarrass my father to refuse this great man's offer and cost him many good things. It might make an enemy of Ezbaal. How can I refuse something so important to my family? It is my duty to my father to marry Ezbaal.

This time the very strength of her body fled, leaving her feeling faint, her eyes momentarily darkened.

"O God, don't let thy spirit flee from me!" she cried aloud.

Father, watching her, saw that she spoke without writing,

and demanded of Laban and Pillel, "What? What did she say?"

But Rebekah made no move to reassure him, for she now understood that she was in a dialogue with God. And then, having realized this, she realized that she had been in this conversation all day. Each time her last reason for refusing Ezbaal was taken away, a new one came with even more certainty, and yet she had never once thought, till now, that this very certainty was part of the answer. When God speaks in a woman's heart, she realized, he fills her with courage to do his will. That is why I have been in such torment today. God is trying to lead me in a path that neither my family nor Ezbaal's family can see.

Lord God of Abraham, she said silently, tell my father what you are telling me! Let me not be alone in this!

She looked into her father's eyes, seeing his expression of concern for her, and saw that there was something else as well. He was as torn as she.

God had already spoken to him and showed him what was right.

She knew it with utter certainty, and so she boldly wrote, "You already know what God wants me to do. Why do you try to persuade me to choose between God's will and yours?"

Pillel reached out a hand and took the writing stick from her. She looked at his face—as passionless as ever—but knew that he was angry, or he would not have, in effect, forbidden her to speak more to her father.

Laban was not so restrained. He laughed. "What, you think you're a prophet now? Able to see into the mind of God, and Father's mind as well?"

But Rebekah turned away from them and faced her father,

staring into his eyes and daring him to deny what she knew he knew.

At first he was defiant, meeting her gaze angrily—but he said nothing, even though he opened his mouth as if to speak. And after a long silence he looked down at the ground where she had written her challenge.

"Yes," Father said. "I know that you can't marry Ezbaal. Even though I will never find you a better marriage than this one, I have known from the moment he arrived that you could not be happy in his house."

Pillel and Laban both recoiled from his words. "What's going on with you two?" said Laban in a whisper.

Pillel also whispered, but he meant her to hear. "I see now that you *do* control him."

Control him? What could Pillel possibly mean by that? Had there been some rumor that somehow she ruled over her father? But of all people Pillel had to know such an idea was absurd. She didn't have time to deal with him now, though.

She knelt up, reached out, and took her father's hands in hers, bowed over them, and kissed them. Then, taking the writing stick, she answered him. "God will provide a husband for me, if I am to marry."

Pillel reached for the stick and wrote in large letters, "Ezbaal will make a dangerous enemy."

Father frowned. "Just because a man is disappointed in love . . ."

Pillel wrote quickly. "He goes home. Rumors fly. He's embarrassed. He gets angry. He needs to restore his pride. He looks for chances to hurt you. The wound festers."

Father shook his head, but Rebekah knew that Pillel was right.

"Soon the slightest offense becomes a pretext for war," the steward wrote.

"He came for a marriage," Rebekah said to Pillel. "So let him go home having made one."

Pillel looked at her as if she were crazy. "Who else would be worthy to marry Ezbaal?"

Father slapped lightly at Pillel's hand. "Write, don't talk. I want to hear this."

Rebekah took the stick from Pillel. "Ezbaal brought his sister, the one who calls herself Akyas," she wrote. "She was married once, but no longer, and you are also unmarried."

Father laughed. "Me?"

"Tell him your daughter is too young to marry, you're not ready to let me go. I never had a mother's training. But you want the families to be united."

"I know nothing about this Akyas," said Father. "Her name even *means* that nobody wants her!"

"She's the sister of Ezbaal," said Pillel, and Rebekah wrote his words.

Then she added her own. "She's something of a beauty, if she doesn't hide behind her hair. And very smart. And strong."

"Then let her marry Laban!"

Laban loudly said, "No!"

"She's a grown woman," wrote Rebekah. "It would be like Laban marrying his mother."

Father laughed, but she could see he was considering it. He looked at Pillel.

Pillel took the stick. "If Ezbaal says no, then you are matched, refusal for refusal. No shame."

"But what if he says yes?"

"So what?" wrote Pillel. "You already have your son and heir. If you hate her, let her have her own tent and pay no attention to her."

"You have a bleak view of marriage," said Father.

Pillel said nothing.

"Let me think," said Father. "All this talking—all this waiting for you to write—it makes me tired."

Rebekah got up at once and kissed her father, then embraced him tightly. He could not hear her voice, but she knew he would understand how she was thanking him. He was not going to make her marry Ezbaal. He was even considering taking a wife he didn't want, just to spare her the unhappiness of having children with a man who did not serve God.

Rebekah was the first one out of Father's tent, and suddenly she found herself being shoved forward—and not gently, either. She turned around, furious, to find that Laban was just as angry. "How dare you! You selfish halfwit!"

"How dare I what?" she said. "I didn't hear *you* volunteering to marry Ezbaal's sister!"

"Do you know what it would mean to me, to have Ezbaal's sons as my nephews? We could have raised our sons together to be friends, and who would stand against our families through all the grasslands?"

"Who cares?" said Rebekah. "If they don't serve God, they're no different from any other desert herdsmen."

"They'll serve God, under one name or another."

"I can't believe you would say something that ignorant."

Pillel stepped between them. "Your voices can be heard."

They both knew that it was disastrous in a negotiation to let your opponent know what you really wanted. They fell silent at once, but Laban gave her one last look of distaste before he stalked off toward his tent.

Rebekah looked at Pillel, but he, too, was already walking away. Whatever he thought of her, at least he had agreed that her idea of Father marrying Akyas was a good one. No matter what stupid plans Laban might have had—easy for *him* to plan, *he* didn't have to do the marrying right now—she had found a way to obey God without causing the family to have an enemy.

Back in Rebekah's tent, Deborah had been dozing, but she woke up when Rebekah came inside. "What, what? Tell me!" she demanded.

Rebekah put her finger to her lips. "We have to speak very quietly. Voices carry at night, and Father has a lot of negotiation to do tomorrow." She sat down beside Deborah and leaned in close. "I won't have to marry Ezbaal."

She expected Deborah to be delighted, but that would have been too simple. "You mean we don't get to go off together and have babies?"

"Someday we will," said Rebekah. "When God wills."

"Oh all right," said Deborah. "But don't make me wait forever. I want to hold your babies and take care of them."

"You'll have plenty of chance to do that."

"How?" said Deborah. "Everybody said there was no better husband in the world than Ezbaal, so who will you marry now?"

"Hush now, everybody might say that but it doesn't make it true. A man who doesn't serve the Lord can't possibly be the best husband for *me*."

"You could teach him," said Deborah.

"Hush, now, hush, I need to sleep. And aren't you just a little bit glad we don't have to leave home right now?"

Deborah shrugged fretfully and turned over to go back to sleep.

Rebekah lay down on her bed and stared upward into the darkness above her. Everything had worked out after all. She had figured out a way to serve God and still keep the family safe and Father happy. The curse of being pretty and having a rich father wasn't so bad if you were also smart enough to figure things out.

She was just dozing off with these thoughts spinning in her mind when all at once she realized what she was actually saying. At once she leapt from her bed and knelt in the tent, looking upward toward heaven. "Oh Lord," she said, softly and miserably, "is there anyone more foolish and ungrateful than I am? All this was thy doing, and not my own at all. Thou gavest me the courage to say no to the marriage, and thou didst soften the hearts of my father and Pillel so they could hear me. Surely the plan that came into my mind was also thy gift, and here I was being proud that I was so clever. Forgive my unworthiness, Lord, forgive me and please, please keep making things work out right. Please make it so Ezbaal doesn't get angry, and please don't make Father marry Akyas if she would be awful to him or something. Because if somebody has to be unhappy, let it be me, and not Father."

She wasn't sure if her prayer made up for her vanity a moment before, but she couldn't think of anything else to say, so she lay back down and, after a while, slept.

PART II

UNVEILED

CHAPTER 4

Rebekah was surprised how Father fretted about the wedding, constantly finding some pretext to summon her to his tent to ask the same questions, over and over.

"I don't expect her to be pretty," Father said for the fifth or tenth or twentieth time. "I'm not a boy and she's not a girl. But why won't they let me see her?"

Rebekah didn't even bother to answer anymore. There was no point in scratching the same letters into the dirt. Laban joked that they ought to have engraved all their commiserations in stone and then simply pointed to the appropriate phrases. "It would have saved time."

"And when it's time for *your* wedding," Rebekah added, "we could reuse them."

"*I'm* not going to marry some girl I've never seen," said Laban.

"Oh, I know," said Rebekah. "But of course we can't let her see *you* in advance."

"That's not fair," Laban said. "Father says I can't beat you with a stick, and anything less won't make an impression."

But with Father there was no joking. "If she's not ugly or scarred or deformed, why keep her veiled until the wedding?"

Rebekah started to write an explanation, but Father waved away the stick. "You think I won't know what you're going to say? You were veiled when he was offering to marry you, so I had to agree to marry Akyas the same way. But I've agreed now, so what's the big mystery?"

Again Rebekah started to write, but only got as far as "His mother and grandmother and . . ."

"But it's completely different!" Father said. "He had *three* women examine you, and they got a good look at your face. You said yourself that her face was half hidden under her hair."

Rebekah wrote, "She's not a leper."

"Oh, good. I always wanted to marry a non-leper."

Rebekah almost wrote a sharp retort, but she knew better and stayed her hand.

"I know what you were going to write. I'm deaf, so I can't be too fussy."

That *was* what she was going to write. But she had to pretend it wasn't, so instead she wrote, "A link with Ezbaal's family is a good thing, and . . ."

"And I had to agree to let her worship her own gods, because they had agreed to let *you*."

She wrote: "It's all my fault, I know . . ."

"It's not your fault. It's Pillel's fault, with all his talk about making an enemy of Ezbaal. Suitors get rejected all the time, and it doesn't make them enemies!"

She rolled her eyes. The answer to that one was very long and tedious to write, and Father already knew it by now.

"Don't roll your eyes at me."

So she flung her arms around him and kissed him hard on the cheek.

"What was *that* about?"

She parted from the embrace and took his cheeks between her hands. "You are a wonderful father who saved me from a marriage that would have made me miserable."

"You're talking too fast for me to read your lips."

"I love you."

"Yes, well, you should. The sacrifices we make for our children. The things we give up, so that they can be happy."

And with that she could leave his tent again, knowing that she'd be summoned back in no time.

Truth to tell, she was puzzled by this business of Akyas marrying Father with a veil on. For all her reassurances to Father, she had to agree with him that it was strange. If Ezbaal was retaliating for the fact that Rebekah had been kept veiled, it was petty and spiteful of him or else he had a mean sense of humor. And if he wasn't, if there really was some reason to keep Akyas veiled, then it wasn't right to keep it from Father. A man had a right to know whom he was marrying, didn't he?

But when she said this to Milchah, one of the old servant women, she only laughed. "Foolish girl," she said. "No man ever knew whom he was marrying, and no woman either."

"You may not know what kind of spouse they'll be, but at least you should know if they have a missing nose or something."

"What difference does it make? Two days after the wedding, his bride might be set upon by a lion and be so badly mauled that she has no nose, and no ears either, and then what, does he send her away?"

"Some men would."

"It takes a lot more than that to make a good man send away his wife."

"There won't be a lion."

"Oh yes there will," said Milchah. "Not the kind that growls. The lion of days, that nibbles at you and paws you every hour like a cat playing with its prey, but so gently that you don't feel it until one day you look at your husband and he's as sunburned and wrinkled as leather that got soaked in the rain, and you suddenly realize, I must look like that, too."

"But that's different. A husband and wife go down that road together."

Milchah looked at her with a sudden intensity. "Not always," she said.

"What does *that* mean?"

Milchah hesitated, then shook her head. "I'm an old woman, and I forget which stories are fit for children and which are not."

"I'm not a child, and I can hear *anything*."

"Compared to me everybody's a child, and some stories are not worth hearing."

"I'll go through the camp telling lies about you," said Rebekah.

"You're such a baby," said Milchah. It was an old game between them, which never changed, even after Rebekah took her place as mistress of the household.

"I'll tell them that you always add too much salt to the pot because you've completely lost your sense of taste."

"I'm not going to tell you anything important, foolish girl. But I did once hear a story about a bride who secretly taught her children to make offerings to a god that her husband hated, and one day he caught her and was so angry at the deception and the disobedience that he divorced her on the spot and drove her out of the camp."

"If that's a warning, you can be sure that's *precisely* what I would have done if they had made me go ahead with my marriage to Ezbaal."

"Make of it what you will," said Milchah. "It's time for my nap."

"What? Have I made you angry? Really, not just playing?"

"I'm always annoyed when young fools only hear what they want to hear."

"I heard you, Milchah, I always listen."

"Would you *really* have defied your husband, knowing that you were bound to be caught someday, and then you'd never see your children again?"

Rebekah *hadn't* thought through the story very well. "But . . . when Father sent Khaneah away, she got to take Belbai with her."

Milchah gave a sharp laugh. "Your father was sending *Belbai* away, and besides, Belbai was *not* your father's son. Do you think for a moment the head of a great house would let a disobedient wife take *his* children with her when he sent her away?"

"I never thought of that," said Rebekah.

"That's why God hasn't let me die yet," said Milchah. "So somebody can say something sensible to you now and then."

"That's why a woman shouldn't marry a man who doesn't worship the same god."

"Oh, now you're full of all kinds of wise rules, aren't you?" said Milchah. "What if her father promised that she'd be obedient, but he didn't tell *her*?"

"Father would never do that, so it won't matter to me."

"Yes, you're lucky that your father understands just how important a religious difference can be," said Milchah. But there was something nasty in her tone. Rebekah understood at once.

"Father came to his senses as soon as I reminded him of how important it is to raise my children in a house where only the God of Abraham is worshiped."

"And he loves having you speak of the God of Abraham," said Milchah, getting even nastier.

"But . . . that's the only true God," said Rebekah.

"But his *name* isn't 'the God of Abraham.'"

"I've never been told his true name," said Rebekah.

"And still it doesn't occur to you that maybe your father would rather you spoke of 'the God of Bethuel'?"

"Father never said . . . he always—"

"All those stories of Uncle Abraham," said Milchah. "And Lot. All the famous boys. And here's Bethuel, trying to serve God as best he can, and even his own daughter says 'God of Abraham.'"

"If you're trying to make me feel bad, you're doing a good job of it."

"Don't feel bad, Rebekah, everyone does it. And now that your father's deaf, he never has to hear it. Maybe he thinks of *that* as a blessing. But now, please, don't you have something to do to prepare for the wedding?"

"I've given everybody their tasks."

"Well, give yourself one and go do it, because I need a nap."

The conversation with Milchah made Rebekah all the gladder that she had obeyed the will of God and refused to marry Ezbaal. And she wondered again what Father was getting himself into with this marriage. What if Akyas had children? Father had given her permission to worship her gods as long as she did it in private, but she could imagine Akyas defying him and insisting on taking her children with her to town for the festivals of Ba'al and Asherah. Akyas had a sharp tongue, and she knew her own mind. *That* would be interesting, watching the two of them go at it, head to head.

Rebekah thought back to the way Akyas had acted the one time they conversed, during that supper in her tent. She was a sharp one. She kept her face hidden, but she saw everything and understood many things that couldn't be seen. And wasn't she the one who had come up with the trap that Rebekah almost fell into?—You can worship the God of Abraham, all right, but not a word was said about her children. Sly. Clever. Stubborn. It made Rebekah admire her strength, but also it made her afraid for Father. Akyas could be a difficult woman. Why was Father so worried about her *face?* It was a lot more useful to know how Akyas conducted herself in an argument.

Milchah was right. The lion of days would ruin beauty, but not right away. What about the bear of quarrels? There was nothing gradual about *that* beast. Father had a mighty roar, and when he was furious he could stay his hand but not his tongue.

Of course, it would be hard to sustain an argument with

him now, when all Akyas's words would have to be scratched into the dirt.

What am I worrying about? Why should they argue? Akyas was married before, wasn't she? She knew what could go wrong in a marriage, and she would be on her guard to make sure it didn't happen again. Hadn't she said as much, that night in Rebekah's tent?

Still, Rebekah couldn't stop worrying about Milchah's warning during all the days of preparation for the wedding. Father had taken a great deal more thought and care about finding a spouse for Rebekah than Rebekah had taken about finding a spouse for *him*.

Finally, on the night before the wedding, with all the preparations done, Rebekah found that she could not sleep for worrying about Father and Akyas. She lay awake looking up into the darkness above her bed, and it occurred to her that on the night before the wedding, she was hardly likely to be the only one awake. In fact, in the stillness of night she could hear men's laughter in the distance—Laban would be there, no doubt, and Ezbaal, too, celebrating with Father and commiserating with him on his loss of bachelorhood. Not to mention making ribald jokes, or so the women said the men did whenever they were alone together.

But what were the bride and her women doing?

The thought came into Rebekah's head that the person most certain to be awake was the bride-to-be.

Akyas. Rebekah's stepmother-to-be, who would certainly expect to rule over the women in Father's household. Tomorrow, as soon as the words were said and the earthen bowls were dashed back upon the earth, Rebekah would lose her place.

She should be either worried or relieved, but she was not aware of either feeling in her heart. She had done her duty when there was no one else to do it. Now it would belong to another woman, and Rebekah could easily return to her proper role as child of the house. As simple as that.

What an absurd thought, she realized. Nothing would be simple. She had no idea what it was like, to be daughter of a house ruled by a wife. Would she be pampered or scolded? Rebekah tried to think back on what Akyas had said and done during their all-too-brief supper together. That conversation was all about what kind of wife Rebekah would make, and the only other attitude of Akyas's was a bit of cynicism about marriage. There was nothing in what Rebekah remembered of that night to guide her in how Akyas might regard a stepdaughter who had once ruled in a wife's place.

And yet Rebekah *still* felt no fear. This woman would have the power to make her life miserable, and yet she felt nothing but peace at the thought of having her come into the family. That was very odd. Surely she should feel *something.*

Should I have called upon her? Akyas was in seclusion, Ezbaal's man had announced, and would not see anyone until the wedding. Instructions had been given by intermediaries. It was hardly a circumstance conducive to making visits to the tent of her temporary hermitage. And yet Rebekah knew that whether or not she should have called upon Akyas before, she certainly should do so now.

At this hour?

Why not? It wasn't that late.

Rebekah rose quietly, so as not to waken Deborah—who slept heavily in any case, gently snoring in her corner near the doorway. Covering herself with a simple robe, Rebekah slipped out into the cool air of a summer evening in the high grasslands.

No sooner did she begin to make her way toward Akyas's tent, however, than she felt a sudden dread. What could she do that was more foolish than to defy the bride's seclusion and waken her at some awful hour of the night?

Rebekah turned back to the tent, wondering what she could have been thinking even to consider such a course of action, when all of a sudden the fear left her and she again thought: But that's absurd. It isn't that late, and Akyas will be up, and why shouldn't the daughter of the household come to her to welcome her in advance? It would be a gracious thing to offer, anyway, and if Akyas didn't want her to come in, she had only to refuse to admit her at the door.

Rebekah turned again and strode boldly toward the tent of Ezbaal's women. At once the dread and doubt returned to her, but she paid it no heed, refusing to let foolish fear stop her from the right course of action. Soon she arrived at the tent door, and yes, a light flickered dimly within. Not wishing to clap her hands at this quiet hour—for who knew how many people would think it was *their* tent into which someone desired entry?—Rebekah merely snapped her fingers several times.

At once someone touched her arm. Rebekah whirled to see a stern-looking man looming over her, holding a lamp inside a pierced jar. Of course Ezbaal had set a guard to watch over the women's tent!

Rebekah waited to be recognized, but then realized that was stupid. She had not been seen without her veil by any man in Ezbaal's party, so how would this poor fellow recognize her? Indeed, if she had been thinking straight, she would have worn her veil—in fact, she could not think why she had forgotten to wear it, since it had been second nature to her for years to put it on whenever she ventured outside, day or night. Yet tonight she had forgotten it, and so would not be recognized.

All this thought passed in a moment, and she was about to begin to explain who she was when the man's expression changed to one of embarrassment.

"Ah, mistress, no one told me you were abroad tonight," he whispered. "But why wouldn't you simply go in?"

His seeming recognition of her confused him. Had Akyas and the other women described her *so* carefully? And why should she simply walk in? "Am I expected, then?"

"You are careful, mistress," he said with a shy smile. "I hope I passed your test." Then he backed away into the darkness, taking the faint lamplight with him.

Different households trained their servants in different ways, apparently. What was there to do now, but simply part the flap and go inside?

The lamp flickered from a low table, and before it a woman knelt, praying to an image—of Asherah, Rebekah supposed, since it was obviously of a woman—while on two of the three sides of the tent, two heaps of blankets and the slight sound of breathing showed where Ezbaal's mother and grandmother no doubt lay asleep.

Rebekah was surprised that it was prayer that kept Akyas awake, and not conversation with the other women. But they were older, and had seen many a wedding, so no doubt they needed their sleep in order to make a good showing in the morning.

After a moment, Akyas—for Rebekah supposed it was

she, from the slightness of her figure and the fullness of her hair; and who else of the three would be awake the night before the wedding?—finished her prayer, touched her forehead, kissed her fingers, then dipped them into a tiny bowl before the idol and anointed the statue's head and breasts and hips. Only then did she turn to see whose entry into the tent had made the wick of the lamp flicker and move within the oil.

Her eyes widened in surprise. So Akyas had been expecting to see someone, but not Rebekah.

Rebekah dared not speak loud enough to be heard across the tent—she did not want to waken the others. So she made as if to leave.

Immediately Akyas beckoned to her, insistently, as if she would brook no argument. Rebekah came quietly across the rugs—fine thick rugs, heavy for the beasts to carry, but just what Ezbaal was bound to provide for the women of his house. Akyas lifted the lamp and held it between them. So quietly that her breath did not make the lamp's flame flicker, Akyas said, "I hoped that you would come."

That might be true enough, thought Rebekah, but it didn't change the fact that she had been expecting someone else. "I would have come sooner," Rebekah answered, "but I did not know if your seclusion . . ."

Akyas waved her hand dismissively. "Let's go outside to talk. Old women sleep lightly."

"I heard that," murmured Ethah.

"And thereby proved me right," said Akyas softly.

"Get out, you pack of hooting baboons," Ethah said; and then, almost as a continuation of the same sentence, she snored.

Akyas, laughing silently, led the way out of the tent. When they were well away from any one tent, Akyas spoke quietly. "I wish you could have met Ethah under better circumstances. She has quite a sharp sense of humor."

"Or you have," said Rebekah, smiling. Dim though the nearly moonless night might be, her eyes were used to it by now, and she could see that Akyas's face was not just pretty in the way people thought, but also lively and intelligent. "I'm so glad I came tonight, though I was afraid you wouldn't want me."

"Afraid?" asked Akyas, laughing softly. "You walked right into my tent."

"But your man outside told me—"

"It's all right," said Akyas. "As I said, I hoped you would come. Ezbaal suggested that I stay hidden and veiled, partly I suppose out of pique—he didn't like having to bargain for you sight unseen—but I thought it would make everything simpler, too. The hardest part of my seclusion has been not seeing you."

"You flatter me."

"Not at all. I thought I might gain you as a sister, but will you mind too much that I will have you as daughter instead?"

"Not too much," said Rebekah with a smile. "I was the first to suggest to Father that there was more than one way to tie the families together."

Akyas reached out and brushed a wisp of hair out of Rebekah's face. "Who tends your hair?"

"Deborah, my nurse."

"You still have a nurse?"

"I was so young when my mother died, Deborah is the only mother I knew. She's also a kinswoman, and just a bit feeble-minded. She serves me well, and I plan to keep her with me all my life."

"You're loyal, then."

Why did Akyas still seem to be measuring her? "Loyalty begets loyalty," she answered. "Deborah would die for me. I'm the center of her life."

"So you have not been wishing for a mother."

"I see mothers all around me. I don't see how they treat their children differently from the way Deborah treated me. I think what I've missed isn't so much a mother as having a wife in my father's life. I see the other women with their husbands, and I think, was my mother like this with my father? Or like that? A nag? A scold? A cowering slave? Or a friend, a strong companion? Trusted or mistrusted? Things I'll never know."

"But haven't you heard stories about her?"

"No one speaks of her," said Rebekah. "When I was little, and I asked, they said Father didn't like to have her spoken of. I suppose it made him too sad."

"And what did *he* say?" asked Akyas.

"He just . . . didn't answer, when I asked about her. But he got such a sad look on his face, so far away and regretful, that I learned not to mention her. Until his deafness, he was always with me, and I think I made him happy. I thought of that as my job in the camp, the way other women cook or farm or spin."

"And after he became deaf?"

"I took my place as head of the women. He needed that more, since even *my* presence made him unhappy then."

"You write to him, so he can understand you."

"Yes. Laban and I tried to invent how to do it but we got it all wrong. He taught us the writing of the holy books."

"I can't write, you know," said Akyas.

"But of course I'll teach you."

"Isn't it a holy language? I serve Asherah. You know that, don't you?"

"If I didn't before, I do now," said Rebekah. "But no, the language is just . . . the common speech of every day. The letters aren't holy, only the books."

"Ah. Religious things can be so complicated. You never know what a man will get prickly about."

"And Father will let you worship Asherah?"

"In private. That was worked out in advance."

"And what about your children?" asked Rebekah, thinking of the problem she had faced.

To her consternation, Akyas laughed aloud, catching herself at once, but continuing to laugh silently, as if this were the most amusing question in the world. Finally she spoke. "I think it is safe to say that any children I have with Bethuel will grow up loyal to his god."

His god. Well, there was one person, at least, who didn't call him the God of Abraham. But hearing it said that way made it sound as if God were just one god among many. He wasn't the god of Bethuel, he was God. But of course he wouldn't seem that way to Akyas. This was going to be complicated. To have someone in the camp who didn't speak of the Lord as if he were the only living God.

"And that doesn't bother you? That your children will not serve Asherah?"

"I made my peace with Asherah long ago. If a woman has

to choose between her children and her god, I think the children are the better choice."

Rebekah looked away. It was not the choice *she* had made. Or . . . no, it rather *was* the choice she made, wasn't it? Not to marry a man at all if he might make her face such an awful choice.

Akyas touched her arm. "My dear child, I didn't mean to hurt you. Ezbaal will make some girl a wonderful husband, and he will have strong and mighty sons. But I saw that night at supper that you were not the one for him."

"Oh," said Rebekah. "I thought you had decided I *was* for him."

"I did. I did decide that, because I wanted you with me. But it was selfish of me. I was thinking that perhaps I could help you to be happy in spite of the problems that might arise."

"So you liked me, even though I was so awful to everybody?"

"I liked you *because* you were so awful to everybody. And that wasn't why I didn't think you should be with Ezbaal. I simply . . . I know the kind of man Ezbaal is. He will have many children. In fact, he already *does* have many children. No wife, mind you." Her mind made a sudden turning. "I've heard that Bethuel has been chaste ever since your mother . . ."

Rebekah blushed. She had never thought about that aspect of her father's life. It was rather as if all the flirting and affection she saw between women and men were something for ordinary beings, while Father was above all that.

"Of course you wouldn't monitor what he does in his travels," said Akyas.

UNVEILED

"In all my life," said Rebekah, "he has never done anything to cause dissension in the camp."

Akyas blinked twice, and then apparently understood how obliquely but fully Rebekah had answered her question. "So there is no woman in the camp who will especially resent my coming."

"They will all be equally delighted," said Rebekah. "And I suppose they'll be glad not to take their instructions from a mere girl."

"You're hardly a mere girl any more. You're old enough to marry, after all!"

"I'll always be a child in this camp. No one doubted my authority, mind you, but most of them had seen me as a naked baby and they didn't . . . well, they didn't ever come to me for counsel, if you see what I mean. Orders, but not advice. Everyone was my teacher. And that was good. I think I know every kind of work done in our camp."

"Which guarantees that when you do marry, it will probably be to a town man, where almost nothing you learned will be useful," said Akyas wryly.

"Was that a joke or a curse?" asked Rebekah.

"A memory," said Akyas.

"Ah. Your first husband was a man of the city?"

Akyas looked off into the distance for a moment. Rebekah knew the look. Akyas did not want to talk about her unhappy marriage. She could hint about it, so that people would know that she was not a woman who had reached this age without a husband, but what made the marriage so awful was not to be discussed.

"Rebekah," said Akyas. "Tomorrow, will you stand with

105

me? To write my words for him? Since he can't hear my voice."

"But that's Ezbaal's place," said Rebekah.

"It's whoever's place I say it is," said Akyas. "Ezbaal is my brother. Do you think Laban would dare thwart you if you wanted *me* to stand beside you at *your* wedding?"

"But my father is still alive, so that wouldn't be Laban's place."

"I need an interpreter," said Akyas. "Someone we both love and trust, to stand between him and me."

"Then I'll do it," said Rebekah. "Though I will *not* go into the marriage tent with you."

Akyas laughed. "No, there are some things that a deaf man has to do for himself, without interpretation."

"Why would you . . . why do you say that you love and trust me?"

"Because I do," said Akyas. "And that's all the explanation you're going to get, because . . . well, because you've never met you, if you see what I mean, so you don't know how easy it is for someone to love and trust you."

"I hope you're right," said Rebekah. "Because Ethah and . . . 'Mother' . . . didn't find it all that natural."

Akyas laughed again. "Oh, you're a delight. 'Call me Mother' indeed. But she . . . simply has to be intimate with everybody the moment she meets them. But of course that means she's never really intimate with anybody, since everybody is at exactly the same level of intimacy, the stranger and the longtime friend and the family member, all the same. She's not Ezbaal's mother, you know. Or mine. She was simply Ezbaal's father's senior wife at the time he was murdered. His real mother died giving birth to him."

"I had no idea."

"Ezbaal is a loyal man. Once you have a place in his life, he's loyal to you forever. Unless you betray him, of course, and then . . . well, he makes a marvelous friend. If he takes you under his protection, you are as safe as you can be in this world of wild beasts and marauding men."

And on they talked, about Ezbaal, about husbands, about city life, about the places she'd seen, all kinds of things, until it was so late that they were both yawning, and not for the first time, and Akyas finally said, "My dear child, my dear young woman, my dear *friend*, your coming to me tonight was the kindest thing anyone could have done for me. You were the answer to my prayer, in fact."

That made Rebekah a little uncomfortable, since of course Asherah didn't exist and therefore couldn't have answered anyone's prayer. But . . . maybe God heard the prayers of those who believed in false gods, and counted their faith as if it were faith in him, until they learned better. "Well, you were *not* the answer to my prayer," said Rebekah.

For a moment Akyas looked taken aback, so Rebekah hurried to finish her sentence. "You were the gift that God gave me without my even having to ask. Because *he* knew I needed you, even if I didn't know it myself."

A smile spread across Akyas's face. "Oh, you have a silver tongue."

"If I do, I must have got it from my mother, since Father's as blunt as a camel's snout."

Akyas laughed at that. "Good night, Rebekah. I'm gaining so much more than a husband tomorrow. Will you . . . even though I wasn't here to raise you, all these years you were growing up, will you let me pretend that I was? Will you let me think of you as my true daughter?"

"I hope I prove worthy of your thinking of me that way," said Rebekah.

"And I hope I prove worthy of your thinking of me, some-day, as your mother."

Rebekah kissed her cheek, and in so doing realized for the first time that they were exactly the same height. How could she ever think of a woman who was never *bigger* than her as her mother? She remembered most of the women in the camp as being giants compared to her, when she was a child.

But that wasn't really what Akyas wanted, was it? She wanted reassurance that she would be welcomed in her proper role in the household, and not be resented by the woman who had been the ruler of women before she came.

So she answered with the words that would reassure Akyas while still being truthful. "I don't really know what it's like to have a mother," she said, "but with your help, perhaps now I can learn."

Rebekah insisted on walking her to her tent. "I've walked these paths for years, in darkness and light. There's not an insect here that I don't already know by name just from the buzz."

"Then I'm glad I have you for my guide."

They said their good-nights at Akyas's tent door and parted with another kiss and an embrace that surprised Rebekah by its intensity. She returned to her own tent, to her own bed, feeling glad that she had dared to go and visit Akyas.

CHAPTER 5

There'd been many a servants' wedding in Rebekah's life, but those were simple affairs. Those that were wholly sworn to Father could not marry without his consent. He always gave it, with a prayer and a blessing, and the couple would move in together and that was that. The servants who were sworn for a set time could marry as they wanted—but still needed Father's permission to set up a tent within his camp, so it amounted to the same thing. He usually gave them a good rug for the marriage bed. What the hirelings did was their own affair, because of course their families didn't dwell in Bethuel's camp. Still, there was always some kind of celebration among the servants, and the gift of a kid or a lamb for the feast.

None of this had prepared Rebekah for a wedding of the ruler of the household. Everyone came into camp except those needed to protect the distant-grazing flocks and herds, and there were guests from the nearby towns and villages, too.

There were enough animals roasting to deplete the herds of many a lesser lord, and Father offered a sacrifice to God in a most solemn ceremony at dawn, so that the smell of cooking and burning meat filled the air like heavy incense, though there was plenty of that, as well.

Through all of this, Ezbaal was prominent, his laugh heard everywhere, his smile given to everyone. He hardly left Father's side, which of course meant that Laban had to stay with them, to write down Ezbaal's words. Father enjoyed every minute of it, and when Laban and Rebekah talked about it during one of Laban's rare moments of freedom, he said, "Father said a couple of times that Ezbaal reminds him of his own youth. But I think it's that Ezbaal is the kind of man Father *wishes* he had been."

"Or the kind he wishes *you* were," Rebekah suggested helpfully.

"But I already am," said Laban with a grin. "Far and wide my enemies quail at the mention of my name."

"Fortunately, you have no enemies," said Rebekah, "so we'll never know."

At last, when the sun was halfway to noon, the actual ceremony began. Father made a great show of giving a bridegift of a substantial number of animals to Ezbaal, following which Ezbaal gave a dowry for Akyas of equal value. In fact, though numbers were not mentioned, Rebekah was quite sure that the dowry was not just equal in value, but consisted of precisely the same animals that Father had just given to Ezbaal. The difference was that now the animals belonged to Akyas, though of course they would be mingled with Father's herds, and the ownership would matter only if, for some reason, the marriage ended and Akyas went away.

Not until these matters were taken care of did the women start singing an old song that served as the signal for Akyas and her two female companions to emerge from their tent. Akyas was veiled exactly as Rebekah was, and there was murmuring at that, though by now everyone had known she was going to do it.

The women came to stand beside Ezbaal, who then made a grand show of stepping over to Father and bringing him to stand in the place where he had been. Laban came with Father, and now Akyas beckoned to Rebekah to come and stand beside her, writing stick in hand so she could write whatever Akyas said, just as Laban had been writing Ezbaal's words. Rebekah suspected that the speeches might have been much longer and more eloquent had it not taken so much time for each word to be written down.

The words of the ceremony were simple, Father vowing before God to protect and provide for Akyas and her children as long as he lived, and Akyas vowing to serve him and his children with perfect love throughout her life. Rebekah noticed that she did not swear in the name of any god at all, no doubt to avoid giving offense by mentioning a false god in Father's camp.

When the oaths were all taken—Rebekah having written the words of Akyas's vow in the dirt—Ezbaal gave a great cry, of the kind shepherds give that can be heard a long distance in the dry desert air. Then he turned to Father, and Laban wrote his words as quickly as he could.

"Bethuel, it's done, and you've been a patient man to wive her wrapped in a veil. But now it's time for you to see the face you've vowed to keep with you throughout your life."

By the time Laban wrote "face" in the dirt, Bethuel had

caught the drift and turned expectantly to look at Akyas. But Akyas leaned down to Rebekah and whispered, "Ask your father to read *all* the words Ezbaal just said."

Rebekah rephrased it a little. "Your bride hopes you will read all of her brother's words"—so the request wouldn't seem so peremptory.

Father dutifully turned and read the rest—which consisted of the reminder that he had vowed to keep her for life. He looked a little puzzled, and Rebekah understood why. It seemed odd for Akyas to insist on reminding him of something so obvious. It could only make Father worry about what must be wrong with her, that she would insist that he was bound. What difference did it make, in a world where a man could divorce his wife merely by saying so and sending her away, regardless of any vow that had been given?

"My word is given and I will stand by it," said Father. "You have nothing to fear from me."

At that, Akyas turned to Rebekah. "Since my veil is coming off, my dear daughter—for now I may call you that truly, may I not?"

"Yes, of course," said Rebekah.

"Since my veil comes off, isn't it time for all faces to be seen? Ezbaal asked me to ask it of you, but in truth I would have asked you anyway. For my sake, won't you take off your veil first?"

It wasn't an unreasonable thing to ask—after all, Ezbaal was now Rebekah's uncle, and there was no reason to hide her face from him. So Rebekah was surprised at how reluctant she felt to unveil in front of everyone like this. Hadn't she run around this camp all her life, unveiled, until the last couple of years? It wasn't as if she loved having the thing over her face.

But it felt almost like stripping herself naked in front of strangers, to reveal her face with everyone watching like this.

Yet she could not refuse, so up came her hands despite her reluctance, and in a moment she was handing the veil to Deborah, who quickly straightened Rebekah's hair before she turned back to face the company.

There were low whistles and murmurs from Ezbaal's company, topped at once by Ezbaal's booming voice, shouting, "Bethuel, you fraud! *This* is the face you swathed like a leper? Look at her—between her face and the sun itself, who can say which shines with more beauty!"

Rebekah blushed at the extravagant compliment.

Akyas leaned down to her. "I had no idea he was going to embarrass you like that," said Akyas. "But he's not one to contain his feelings, and you are truly lovely in the light, my child. Ezbaal embarrasses you because he feels so keenly the loss of his chance to wed you."

Ezbaal was not finished. "If all the worshipers of the god of Bethuel had daughters like this, all the other gods would soon be out of business!"

This was coming perilously close to blasphemy, but Laban dutifully wrote the words for Father, who smiled and said, "It was never *my* choice to veil her, my brother Ezbaal."

"But it was definitely my choice to veil Akyas," said Ezbaal. "For hers is the only beauty that can be fairly said to approach that of your daughter."

"Hush now, Ezbaal," said Akyas. "You will raise expectations that I can only disappoint."

Rebekah hurriedly wrote those words for Father to see, even as Akyas reached up and removed her veil. She turned and gave it to "Mother," then turned back, as Rebekah had done, to face the whole group. Rebekah, of course, caught these movements only out of the corner of her eye, until she had finished writing. And when she looked up, it was not at Akyas—whom she had already seen unveiled on two occasions—but at the onlookers, who were strangely silent.

Indeed, Rebekah was surprised to see that some of Father's servants had actually turned their backs, and most of the rest were looking at the ground as if they could not bear to look at Akyas. What could possibly be wrong? Rebekah turned to look at her, and still could not fathom their response. Akyas was far more beautiful in daylight than she had been by lamplight. With her hair pulled back from her face, the shape of her face was full and gently rounded, with lips shaped to smile and eyes filled with silent delight. She seemed, in fact, to be oblivious to the embarrassment of Father's servants, and by her expression one might think that they were reacting with the kind of appreciation that had greeted Rebekah's unveiling.

Father, too, was looking at the ground, and Rebekah knew from his posture and expression that he was either very angry or deeply embarrassed. Or both.

Meanwhile, Laban stood there with his eyes so wide with surprise that he might have been looking at some divine apparition. He kept looking from Akyas to Rebekah and back again, until finally he laughed nervously and said, "Come on, Rebekah, you have to have noticed."

"Noticed what?" asked Rebekah.

"The two of you," said Laban. "I mean, you're as alike as two ewes."

Whatever *that* meant, since shepherds prided themselves on knowing each sheep from all others in the flock.

Rebekah felt Akyas's arm around her shoulder, and Akyas's voice near her ear. "Do you think she's grown up to look like me, Laban?" asked Akyas. "I see much of her father in her as well—it has only made her prettier, I think."

What did she mean by *that*? She spoke as if she were . . .

"I don't know what I've done, Ezbaal," said Father, his voice low and grave, "to deserve such a bitter prank as this."

"This is no prank," said Ezbaal. "When her husband cast her out for no greater sin than praying for Asherah's protection over her daughter, she eventually came to my father, who quietly adopted her as his daughter—as my sister. It was all handled with discretion—we wanted no fight with a man as powerful as her husband was, especially with the mighty Abraham as his near kinsman. She came with me as my sister, with no other purpose in mind than for her to catch a glimpse of her beloved boy all grown now, and the girl she gave birth to fifteen years ago now in the first bloom of womanhood. It was you, not I, who proposed marrying her."

Her beloved boy. The girl she gave birth to. Rebekah had never seen her own face—therefore she was the only person in the camp who could not have known how much they looked alike. But the guard last night—he must have taken her for Akyas in the darkness. And all the servants here—how many of them had been with the household longer than Rebekah had been alive? Most of the adults, anyway. They had all known that Rebekah's mother was not dead. That Father had sent her away, that somewhere in the world she was still alive, even if they had not known exactly where. And not one of them had told her. Not even Milchah, though now it was obvious that it was Father's marriage to Akyas—to *Mother*—that she had been speaking about.

As soon as Laban had finished writing Ezbaal's words, Father turned on him with barely contained fury. "You could have told me who she was when I first broached the matter."

"You didn't ask me who she was," said Ezbaal. "You spoke of her as my sister, and my sister she is, as she has been for more than fourteen years. Akyas is the name *you* caused her to take."

"'Rejected one,'" Laban murmured as he wrote Ezbaal's words. His stick moved so quickly now that his letters were barely legible and crossed each other haphazardly.

"I gave her no such name," said Father, when he at last reached those words.

"No, you merely made them true," said Ezbaal. "Well, do I take it that for the second time, you renounce your vow? For the second time, you send her away? But this time in full view of her children?"

Laban was still writing, but then began to falter, and suddenly he was sitting on the ground, bent over and weeping loudly.

Rebekah could not have named what *she* felt, but it most certainly did not lead to weeping, not like Laban was doing. She took her stick and wrote savagely in the dirt, "You lied to me."

Her movement must have been bold enough to draw every gaze, though the only one that mattered was Father's.

"Yes," said Father. "I did, and commanded that all the others do it, too. They dared not disobey, even among themselves. Blame no one but me."

Akyas's voice came softly from behind her. "All these years I have longed for you, dreamed of you, and now I see that you have grown up better and dearer and with more courage and wisdom than even a mother's love could imagine."

But Rebekah was in no mood to hear such things. She whirled on Akyas and hurled words at her like stones. "A mother's love! You lied to me too, from the moment you first entered my tent. Is that why you came? To mock me?" Rebekah turned to look at all the others from the camp. "And you!" she cried. "All of you, tut-tutting about how sorry you were my mother was *dead* and how nice it would have been if she had *lived*. All of you *liars,* and me the only one who didn't know the truth!"

Several of the women were weeping; others stared at the ground. Only Pillel met her gaze steadily, as if defying her to tell what they *should* have done.

She knew she was being unfair. But they had all been unfair to her.

"I didn't know," said Laban miserably. "I was lied to as much as you."

"What are you saying!" Father demanded. "Tell me what you're saying!"

Rebekah deliberately drew her foot across Akyas's vow that she had written in the dirt, and replaced it with letters boldly and angrily gouged. "Why bother to tell you, when you'll only make up your own version and make everybody else tell it for fifteen years?"

She was still writing when he began to answer, a note of pleading in his voice. "It was a terrible thing to take your mother from you, but all I could see was that she was going to raise you to believe in Asherah, at least a little, and you can't believe even a little in Asherah and still believe in God at all. You needed a mother, but you needed God more. Do you think I wanted to send her away? Do you think I haven't longed for her every day for fifteen years? Every time I saw your face, I saw *her* and hated myself for sending her away, but every time I saw how you love God and serve him, I knew I had done right."

She wrote again, but the anger was dissipating now, leaving her merely . . . tired. Dry. "That doesn't explain why you lied. That wasn't for God, that was so I wouldn't blame you. It was *cowardly.*"

"I, I, I," said Laban. "You talk as if you're the only one they lied to, the only one who lost your mother."

"You're a boy," said Rebekah impatiently. "You don't need . . ." But the look on his face stopped her. Obviously the words she was about to say were deeply wrong. He *had* needed his mother. And as he collapsed again into weeping, she realized that judging from her fury and his sobbing, he was the one most deeply hurt by this.

And maybe he was. Because she, at least, had Deborah all her life.

At the thought of Deborah, she turned to see the dear simple soul standing there with tears streaming down her cheeks. Rebekah walked to her, put her arms around her.

"Everybody's mad," said Deborah, "and I don't know why."

"This is my mother," said Rebekah. "She isn't dead after all."

"But . . . where *were* you?" Deborah asked Akyas.

Before Akyas could make any kind of answer, Rebekah turned to Father and spoke to him—as if he could hear her, and perhaps, without knowing the exact words, he could read her face. "Yes, Father. Where was she?"

Rebekah leaned her head on Deborah's shoulder—for Deborah was still half a hand taller than Rebekah and probably always would be, judging from Akyas's height. "But then, I *did* have a mother," she said. "It was no fault of yours, Akyas, but *this* is the woman who fed me and washed me and dressed me and dried my tears and taught me to be kind and fair and . . . *honest.* I wondered about you, but I didn't miss you the way Laban seems to have, because I had Deborah."

"Pillel!" shouted Father. "Come and write down what everybody's saying!"

"I had a mother," said Rebekah. "But now I wonder what I'm going to do for a father. Because the old one turns out to be a liar who took my mother away from me in my infancy and never had the courage to tell me what he did!"

Though he hadn't heard her, the anguish in Father's face told her that he understood the kind of thing she was saying. She turned to Akyas, who looked scarcely less upset than Father. "As for you, I know you truly love me, because you went to such great lengths to make sure that I found all this out here, today, with all these people looking on. What a fine story this will make, told around every campfire between Hurria and Egypt."

She stepped forward to meet Ezbaal's gaze—Ezbaal, who still seemed quite pleased with himself. "As for you, I thank God I was saved from marrying the kind of man who would set up such a cruel joke as this, played on two children who never did you any harm. How proud you'll be to tell about this jest to all your friends."

Ezbaal's face grew suddenly grave. "I was thinking only of reuniting your father and mother. It was not a jest. And the story will not be told to anyone, not by me or any man of mine."

Pillel was writing for Father now. "No one will speak of this," Father said determinedly.

"Everyone will speak of it," said Rebekah to Ezbaal. "Neither of you has authority over the people from the villages. And even in your households, no one could resist telling. It would be cruel of you to punish them for it." She turned to Deborah. "Come with me to our tent, will you, Deborah? I'm tired of all this company. And now that Father has a wife to govern the women of the camp, I don't have any duties. So I'll have plenty of time to sit in the dark and figure out just which parts of my childhood were true and which were false."

Only Laban broke the silence that fell as Rebekah and Deborah walked away. "You big selfish baby!" he called.

She tried to ignore him. He was distraught. Emotional. Nothing he said would be true.

"They didn't plan this to hurt *you!* They were all doing the best they could to do the right thing, only there was no right way to do it!"

She whirled to face him, and this time turned her fury on him, the one person she had spared before. "*I'm* the big selfish baby? Go dry your eyes, Laban, and tell me who the baby is."

It was a terrible, unfair thing to say, and she hated herself for saying it as soon as the words were out of her mouth. She *was* being a big selfish baby. Laban had told her the truth—the only one in her life, it seemed, who ever had—and all she had done to him, to anyone, was to lash out and try to hurt everybody as much as possible. She was ashamed, and yet at the same time she was frustrated that she had not hurt them more.

Surely there must have been something she could say that would tear their lives to pieces the way they had shattered hers. Something that could make them all feel as empty and foolish and worthless as she felt right now.

Deborah parted the tent door for her, and before Deborah could get inside herself, Rebekah had thrown herself on her sleeping rugs and burst into huge, wracking sobs. Mother, Mother, Mother, she said silently, perhaps murmuring the words sometimes, too. Mother. Mother.

After a while, Deborah came and patted her arm. "I'm not really your mother," she said. "I wish I had been. But then they might have taken you away from me."

Rebekah finally turned her thoughts to the sufferings of someone who was not herself. Deborah, who grieved for her lost little boy all these years, all fifteen years of Rebekah's life. Akyas must have grieved for me the same way. And Father, did he also grieve for the wife he lost? He had said so, many times. Was that true, then? He sent her away, but loved her still, missed her, mourned for her.

Sent her away for *my* sake.

The bitterness flooded her heart again, driving out all other feelings. That was the most galling thing about it—that Father had sent Mother away . . . for *her*. That can't be true. Father can't have been that stupid. Did he really think she wouldn't be able to tell the difference between the living God and gods of stone and wood? Between the God of Abraham and a silly god like Asherah?

"You're the only one I can trust, Deborah," Rebekah murmured.

"Everybody loves you so much," said Deborah. "Nobody would ever hurt you."

How odd, that this statement could be the truth, and yet somehow they had all managed to conspire together to do exactly that. To hurt her so deeply that as she lay here on her bed all she could wish for was to die, so she didn't have to live in a world where something like this could be done to her, and there was nothing she could do about it. Fifteen years stolen from her, broken and deformed and misshapen by loss and lies. Her whole life so far. And no reason she could think of to ever leave this tent again. Whom could she look in the eye? Who could speak to her, and she would believe them?

Only God.

And now that she thought of him, she couldn't help but ask him: How could you let such a thing as this happen? It was all done for *your* sake, wasn't it? And you stood by and let them tell me these lies and never whispered the truth to me, not even in my dreams. You could prompt me left and right when it came to strategies that would keep me from marrying a man who might raise my children to worship false gods, but you couldn't just once say, "By the way, Rebekah, your mother isn't quite as dead as people have led you to believe."

She rolled over on her back, the tears suddenly dried, her heart empty.

The words of her own bitter, hateful prayer stung her to the heart.

I turned down the noblest man among all the great houses of the desert, and all for exactly the reason Father sent Mother away. What would I have done, if Ezbaal had agreed to let me raise my children to worship God, and then I caught him teaching my sons to sacrifice to Ba'al? I couldn't divorce him, the way a man could divorce a woman. I would have had to stay and watch and hate him for leading my sons away from the truth.

That was the choice Father faced. And there he was, and Mother, too, watching me make *exactly* the same choice Father had made. What did Mother think, when I refused to marry Ezbaal for precisely the same reason Father sent her away?

She knew the truth. And yet she still went through with the wedding. Still wanted to have Father as her husband again. It wasn't just so she could see her children again, either. She could have told Rebekah that first night who she really was, and Rebekah would have arranged for Laban to come also and find out the truth. In her rage at Father, Rebekah might even have crept off to go live with her in Ezbaal's household, not as a new bride, but as a long-lost daughter. But Akyas did not handle things that way. She did nothing to undercut Father's authority. Indeed, she went to great lengths to make sure Father was married to her before he found out who she really was.

It could only mean that she forgave Father. She had seen how firmly Rebekah was committed to serving the God of Abraham, so that Father's victory was complete, and yet she still wanted to return to the marriage.

There are desires here that in my anger I did not think of. Laban, for all his grieving, *he* saw it. But Rebekah the fool, all I could see was how they lied to *me*, how *I* had been betrayed, how *I* was humiliated. Me? *Mother* was the one who humbled herself. *Father* was the one the trick was played on; his shame was far greater than any I might feel.

Ezbaal must be so grateful that God saved him from being married to a brat like me.

"Would you like some supper?" asked Deborah.

"What?"

"You've been asleep," said Deborah. "They've all come to the tent—your father, your mother, Laban, several of the women, even Ezbaal. But I wouldn't let them in because you were asleep and I thought you needed to rest. You looked so peaceful lying there."

"How can I have been . . . I've been awake the whole time, thinking about . . ."

"Were you just pretending? You're really good at it, then, because I shook you and you never seemed even to know it."

Rebekah felt her cheeks. Dry. Her eyes were still tender from crying, but her eyelashes were caked with dried-on tears, and her clothes damp with sweat and wrinkled from lying on them.

And she *was* hungry.

"Yes, I'd like to eat."

"Good!" said Deborah. "There's an awful lot of meat. The whole wedding feast!"

"They went ahead without me?" She felt stupid as soon as she said it. What did she expect, that the whole feast would be put off until she woke up from her nap and gave them permission to proceed?

The feast had gone on. Which meant the wedding was considered valid. Father hadn't renounced it because of the deception. Father and Mother were married. Again. After fifteen years. After my whole life. I will finally know what it's like to have my own mother with me.

What an odd way God has of answering prayers you didn't even know enough to ask.

CHAPTER 6

Everyone was being so careful of her that Rebekah feared she might live the rest of her life confined to her tent, with no one but Deborah to speak to. Finally, by nightfall, she realized that having lashed out at everyone, if things were to be set to rights she would have to begin.

She began at the beginning. With Father.

Yes, he had lied to her. But that did not erase the love he had surrounded her with, the trust he had shown her. It did not change the fact that he had also needed her, when she and Laban reopened the door of language to him. One lie did not undo a lifetime of love. One lie, told over and over again, did not become a thousand lies. It remained the one, looming ever larger until it threatened to crush them all, but still only one, undone in a single moment of truth.

She clapped outside his tent, in case someone was with

him who might hear. And, yes, the flap was opened by Akyas. Mother.

"Oh, Rebekah, thank you for coming. He can't sleep. You have no idea how unhappy he is."

"I know how unhappy I am."

"You were right, Rebekah. To set up a grand moment of unveiling—it was wrong. But Ezbaal and I were afraid that if we told anyone in advance, Bethuel would send me away. We needed his oath first, in order to have a hope of restoring our family."

"Believe me, Mother, I've thought this through a hundred different ways, and bad as this was, I couldn't think of a better one."

"This wasn't my plan, you know. When I came. I really did come here in order to see you. To see what you had become."

"Well, you saw me at my finest today."

"You have a sharp tongue, that's sure. You found exactly the words to shame everybody."

"Now that I've got the punishment down, I need to work on the part about judging fairly."

Akyas embraced her. It still felt awkward to Rebekah. Their bodies didn't meld together out of long custom the way hers did with Deborah's. Still, it was a start. It felt natural to call her Mother. Nothing false about it, the way it had been when Ezbaal's stepmother tried to get Rebekah to call her by that title.

"Do you want to be alone with him?" asked Mother.

"No," said Rebekah. "I'm glad you're here. It's where you should have been all along."

"That doesn't make it easier to have me there when you talk to him."

"But it makes it right." Rebekah studied Mother's face, looking for some trace of the bitterness she must feel about all her years in exile—the bitterness that filled Rebekah's heart. But then, Mother had had fifteen years to get used to what had happened to her.

Mother smiled at her. "Pillel said you were unusually wise for a child."

"*Pillel* said that?"

"Well, actually he said, 'for a girl.'"

"Was that back when he was still hoping he could get me married and out of here?"

Mother laughed. "So you don't think he likes you, is that it?"

"Was he steward before? When you were here?"

"Yes. Face like stone. And a hard judge. But if he praises you, it counts. He said you were wise. And he said it this afternoon, while you were in your tent."

"After I ranted at everybody."

"I think he was trying to reassure me and Bethuel that we hadn't created a monster."

"Let's not rush to judgment on that one. I'm still angry, you know. And all the other feelings. I haven't forgiven anybody. I'm just too tired to cry any more."

"Speaking of crying: poor Laban. He hasn't shown his face since the wedding, either. I suppose he thinks it isn't manly, to cry like that. But it was about things that happened to him as a child. A motherless child. That's who was crying today, don't you think? The child, not the man."

"Whoever it was, it's Laban who has to live it down," said Rebekah. "But I'll never goad him about it, if that's what you're asking."

"Think of all the years I've missed, of the two of you together. Did you quarrel all the time?"

"Not much," said Rebekah. "Teasing, but little quarreling. I think we clung to each other a little. Not like half the children in camp, who spend their days screaming, either from joy or rage."

The inner curtain parted, and Father came into the front room of the tent. "I wondered why there was a cold draft," he said. "Come inside and let the tent flap close."

At once the conversation between women ended, and both of them sat down with Father. Rebekah took up the writing stick and began to form letters in the dirt patch. She started to apologize, and Father reached out and held her wrist. "No," he said. "You have nothing to apologize for."

Rebekah wrote, "You didn't hear half of what I said."

"Believe me," he answered, "I've had every word of it repeated to me since, and even though you weren't very generous in your reading of events, you weren't wrong, either. You never have to apologize for telling the truth."

Rebekah snorted and wrote, "Come now, Father."

"All right," he said. "Half the apologies we have to make in life are precisely for telling the truth, but right now, anyway, don't waste time apologizing to me. I'm the one who has to apologize to you."

She agreed completely, of course, but out of courtesy started to protest that he didn't need to. Again he stopped her. "It's late, and I'm a tired old man with a new bride, so let me get straight to the point. I owe you an explanation. More important than a mere apology. You need to know why your father would do the things I did."

Rebekah nodded, set down the stick, and turned to face

him more directly. She would listen, answering with her face instead of written words.

"I loved your mother more than anything or anyone in the world, until you and Laban were born," said Father. "And then a strange thing happened. It brought me closer to her than ever, but there could be no doubt of it—I loved my children more than my wife, more than anything. And I feared for you, all the things that could go wrong. All the dangers in the world. Wild animals. Marauders. Disease. Famine. Storms. Things I could protect you from, and things I could do nothing about. You could fall in a stream and drown. You could climb a rock and fall. Whatever I did, wherever I went, there it was in the back of my mind, this constant worry about you. I never felt that about your mother. She was a strong, wise woman, even if she *was* city-born, and she had taken to life in the camp quite naturally. So I didn't worry about her. I knew she'd be all right."

Father took a deep breath. "But your mother never understood God. She worshiped with me, as a good wife should. But she couldn't see why it was any of my business that she worshiped other gods as well. Especially Asherah. It drove me mad sometimes. I wanted so much for her to understand that the God of heaven is real—so real that you don't have to pretend to see him or make an image to look at."

Rebekah refrained from looking at the little gods that sat on a low table in the corner.

But he must have seen her stop herself from glancing that way. "Let's not have that argument again, not right now," he said. "Let's just say that even as I took every precaution I could against all the other dangers in the world, the one thing I feared most—that you would grow up without respect for the true and living God—the greatest danger to you came, not from some outside threat, but from your own mother."

Rebekah glanced at Mother to see how she was taking this. Maybe having her present wasn't such a good idea. But she didn't seem to mind hearing Father say these things.

"We argued about it. Back and forth. Wasn't I going to dedicate my children with the priests in the city? She finally gave up with Laban, figuring that it was men's business, whether he was to be presented before Ba'al or not. But when it came to you, she wouldn't let the question rest. 'She must be presented to Asherah.' 'Asherah needs to know her name.' And I wouldn't let her take you. And then one day I came in when I was supposed to be away for the whole day, and found her with a priestess she had smuggled into the camp, along with a tiny figure of Asherah to which they were in the midst of presenting you. Of course I was furious, at the deception, at the offering to an idol, and at myself for not realizing that just because I said a thing didn't mean it was going to be obeyed. If God's commandments are disobeyed all the time, why should I expect mine to be treated with more respect?"

Again Rebekah looked at Mother. But Akyas continued to gaze steadily—no, raptly—at Father's face. Had she truly forgiven him completely for all this? Or was she merely pretending, so that she could be back with her family? And what about that very issue—Rebekah well knew that Mother still worshiped Asherah and had brought an idol into the camp. Was Father going to tolerate it? Father was talking about these issues as if they were ancient history, but it seemed to Rebekah that the same problems remained even now.

"I couldn't see a solution," Father went on. "At the

moment, in my rage, I declared our marriage over and ordered her to pack and leave, taking her dowry with her."

"It wasn't much of a dowry," said Mother. "My family was poor. It was my face that won me such a husband. My face and my prayers to Asherah."

Father was watching her. Rebekah made as if to translate, but Father shook his head. "She was beautiful, but she still thought it was her goddess that had brought her a rich husband."

Rebekah laughed. "Fifteen years apart, and he still knows just what you're going to say? You don't need to learn to write."

Mother laughed. "I wish."

It was the laughter that got to Bethuel. "All right, tell me what was said that made you laugh."

When Rebekah had written out her summary, Bethuel chuckled, too, but rather grimly. "Well, I'm wrong as often as I'm right, and half the time I'm right, I think I'm wrong, and half the time I'm wrong, I think I'm right, so what do you do? Anyway, all that night before she left, I went back and forth in my own mind. I was not too proud to rescind the divorce and take her back. I didn't want her to go. I loved her desperately.

"But it came down to this: I had to know you would be raised to love and honor God. And with your mother here, I could never be sure. It wouldn't take much to raise doubts in your hearts—the very fact that she didn't believe the same things I did would be obvious even if she never said a thing. I realized that it had been a mistake to marry a woman from the city, no matter how much I loved her. You have to choose a wife who will teach the most important things to the children when they're small. Little children live in their mother's world, not their father's.

"So as much as I loved your mother, I did what had to be done. I sent her away. And much as I've missed her, as hard as it has been for you and Laban, I still think that was the right thing. Laban's a good boy, a true servant of the Lord as I've tried to be. But you, Rebekah, your faith goes beyond that. I think God speaks to you. I think that's why you say things that are wiser than you should ever know, at your age."

Still Mother sat there, not arguing as he declared himself to be right in their ancient, family-wrecking argument.

Mother caught Rebekah's glance. "He's right," she said. "If I had raised you, I would have taught you to serve Asherah while pretending to serve your father's god, just enough to keep him happy."

"But you still pray to Asherah."

"I do," said Mother. "Because she's the only god I know. This God of yours and Bethuel's, I don't know him. He doesn't know me."

"But he does," said Rebekah. "Don't you see that he brought you here just now because—"

"Please, let's not discuss this now," said Mother. "You'll have to write everything for your father and we'll never be done."

Rebekah sighed and wrote a brief explanation for Father. "You have plenty of time to discuss all that," said Father. "All of this is just trying to lead up to why I didn't tell you the truth. That *is* the sticking place for you, isn't it? The bone you just can't chew up."

Rebekah wrote, "I understand that you didn't want me to hate you."

"No, no," said Bethuel. "Oh, well, of course I didn't want you to hate me, but I would have borne that as the consequence of my choice, if that's what it took. No, I had to lie to you so you wouldn't grow up hating God."

That hadn't occurred to Rebekah.

"Your mother, driven away from her home because she wouldn't worship God. No, worse, because she wouldn't worship *only* God. Would you hate your father? No, because your father was merely obeying the Lord. It's God you would be angry at."

"Eventually I would have understood," she wrote.

"And eventually I would have told you," he said. "But what was the day? When would I know it was time to tell you? That's when I turned coward. I could have told you when you were old enough to start leading the women of the camp. Surely there was no reason to keep the secret any longer then. But it was easier to let things go on as they were. I didn't want to see the hurt and anger that . . . that I saw today."

Father sighed. "But all along, I was punished. Surely you understand that, Rebekah. Because I missed her. She was the joy of my life, and I had sent her away. As you grew, though, you were so much like her. You had her face, her voice. And the way you could outtalk anybody!"

Mother laughed. "Oh, that's not *just* from me."

Father did not hear her, of course. "Rebekah, I loved you for yourself, but I also loved you for the echo of your mother in everything you did. And then that wagon fell on me in the stream, and I lost my hearing, and then I understood that God was not going to let me go unpunished for taking your mother from you."

"It wasn't God," said Rebekah, "it was an accident."

"It was my own words," said Bethuel. "When your mother was leaving, I acted very stern and calm—now *that* was a *lie!*—and I said to her, like this terrible curse, 'Your voice shall never again be heard in my house.' It was meant to be a curse on her, for having deceived me about Asherah. But instead, when my hearing was taken away from me just before your voice changed and became womanly—became like your mother—well, I realized that I had cursed myself. Your mother's voice was going to be heard in this camp, whether she returned or not, because you were going to sound just like her, the way you looked like her. So I had to go deaf, don't you see? So my curse would be fulfilled."

"Do you think God keeps a tally of such things?" asked Rebekah. "I think he has better things to do."

"What do you think the priesthood is," said Father, "but the power to bind in heaven with words said here on earth?" He shook his head. "Now your mother herself is back, and yet my curse remains. I will never hear her voice again."

Rebekah knew that the priesthood didn't work that way, but she couldn't see any point in arguing with him any further. The sadness in him seemed like a weight, bending his shoulders. But Mother leaned out and took his hand and kissed it, and some of the weight seemed to lift again.

"She forgives me," said Bethuel. "She disagrees with me about God, but she agrees that if I was going to raise you to serve him, she could not have been here. Now she can't change what you believe—she isn't even going to try."

"Your god blesses you," said Mother. "Even though he doesn't know *my* name, he's a good god for you."

"We see the world differently," said Father. "But we agree

on the most important thing—that you and Laban are at the center of it."

Rebekah picked up the writing stick. "I wish you had trusted me more," she wrote. "I would have served God anyway."

"You don't know that," said Father. "You never know what *would* have been. And besides, when I made these decisions I didn't know what kind of child you were going to be. And maybe you wouldn't have become the woman you are, without Deborah and without your dependence on me and Laban, which you would never have had, not the same way, if your mother had been here. You are today what you became because of choices in your past. If those choices had been different, how can you be sure you'd be the same person now? No, our lives have taken their course. We can't change where the river flowed yesterday. We can only choose where it will flow today."

There were a thousand things she might say, arguments against his decision, complaints about how he himself didn't actually live by those wise words, but was constantly trying to outguess the past. The truth was, however, she did not want to argue. She just wanted to have peace in her family. So that she could get to know her mother as well as she knew her father and brother. So they could be whole.

That's why she smiled and hugged her father and kissed him and wrote to him words that were only true by intention: "I forgive you. You did what you thought was right." And then the words that were true indeed: "I'm glad my mother is here. I'm glad that we're all together now."

There were kisses and tears and embraces for a little longer, and then she left.

But not to return to her tent in the darkness. No, there was one more apology she had to make.

Laban did not respond to the clapping of her hands, but she was not about to let that stop her. She pulled open the flap of the tent, intending to go inside and *make* him listen to her apology. But even before he could have seen who she was, his voice came roaring out of the tent: "I forbid you to come through that door!"

Startled and a little afraid at the pain that was still audible in his voice, she pulled back and was about to go back to her tent when she realized that she could not, could *not* let him go to sleep tonight still hearing her foolish words in his mind.

So she went to the back of his tent and, careless of how dirty it would make her clothing, not to mention her face and hands, she wriggled under like a snake.

If he heard her he gave no sign. It took a while for her eyes to get used to the darkness—he had no lamp burning, and it was full night, with only a tiny bit more moon than there had been last night. At best all she could make out was a faint silhouette, and even that she found by listening for the sound of his breathing.

"Laban," she said, "I need to talk to you."

"I told you to stay out," he said gruffly. But not shouting. That was a good sign—that when he knew who it was, that it was Rebekah, he did not yell at her.

"Actually," she said, "you forbade me to come through the door."

"And you figure crawling under the tent wall makes you obedient?"

"Perfectly."

"For a sister."

"Absolutely."

"I can't show my face out there, Rebekah. Never again as long as I live. If I could dig a deep enough hole, I'd bury myself so I could skip the whole funeral step. I want to die."

"Nobody thinks ill of you for crying, Laban."

"'Who's the big baby?' Someone said that, and it was true."

"A stupid person said it," said Rebekah. "Even though you were weeping, *you* were the one speaking sensibly to me. *You* were the one trying to understand and be fair to everyone, trying to get me to stop saying such cruel and unjust things. Not only that, but you were the only one *brave* enough to try to talk to me. Everybody else wanted to run away from the ravening she-bear."

Laban laughed, but it was still pretty grim sounding. "That's not what they'll remember."

"Who cares what they remember? In the morning, I'll come by and we'll go out together. If anybody teases you or even looks at you funny, I'll beat him to a pulp. I'll . . . tear his arm off and beat him with it. I'll rip his head off and spit down his neck. I'll—"

"Enough!" cried Laban. "How do you think it will restore my dignity here, to have my sister beat people up on my behalf?"

"I have to take Mother around and let her know what all the women are doing. And then we have to teach her to read and write. And meanwhile Father needs someone to write for him. We can't afford to have you stay in your tent."

"You can do the first two, and Pillel does the last."

"Laban, I'm going to go off and get married someday."

"When somebody *better* than Ezbaal comes along? In thirty years?"

"And *when* I go—"

"Ha!"

"You will be the heir to everything and someday you'll have to rule this whole camp. Now, how will you do that if you're still hiding inside your tent?"

"I won't be by then," he said.

"So you're planning to come out."

"Someday."

"When?"

"Someday . . . when the slop jar fills up."

Rebekah laughed. "So you'll come out with me tomorrow?"

"Yes," said Laban. "I take it you're speaking to Father?"

"Oh, I never stopped speaking. I think I spoke pretty continuously through the whole second half of that marvelous wedding."

"Several townspeople died of old age, had their funerals, and were buried while you were talking."

"And you need to get to know your mother. She's really wonderful."

"She looks so much like you."

"Or the other way around. But you look like her, too."

"Not so much."

"You'll like her, Laban."

"You got to talk to her before the wedding."

"Yes, but I didn't know I was talking to my mother. She saw me acting like a self-righteous little prig even *before* the grand unveiling this morning. And she liked me anyway."

"Well, that changes everything," said Laban. "If she likes *you*, then she's bound to like *me*."

"My point exactly." She sat down beside him and put her arm across his shoulders.

"Oh, Rebekah."

"Oh, Laban," she said, imitating him just a little.

"The choices you make can change people's lives," he said. "Father did his best, but everybody in camp has to live in the world he shapes for us."

"We shape it together."

"But you and I have been pretty powerless."

"Up to now," said Rebekah. "We thought the adults had everything under control. Now we know the truth—they have no idea what they're doing, either."

"That's something. At least we know we're as qualified as anyone."

"But I've learned something," said Rebekah.

"A remarkable thing, for someone who never stops talking."

She squished his shoulder till he squawked. Not that it hurt him that much, just that he knew she would squish until he did. "I tell you this, Laban. There is never a good reason to lie to someone who loves you and depends on you. Never."

"I'm with you on that."

"I will never, never lie to someone who trusts me. That's what I've learned from Father."

"But people who trust you are the only ones you *can* lie to," said Laban.

"So I guess I've given up lying forever."

"Now I can find out the answer to all your deepest secrets."

She laughed. "Now that I know what a *real* secret is, I realize I've *never* had one in my life."

"You've had one," said Laban.

"What?"

"That stupid veil. You're not going to wear it anymore, are you?"

"Why should I stop?"

"Because, bonehead, *Mother's* face is going to be on display everywhere, and since you look just like her—"

"She's *much* prettier."

"Since you look *exactly* like her, there's really no point in hiding."

She gave in with a sigh. "I suppose you're right."

"Of course I'm right. I'm always right."

"Ah, there's the Laban I know and love."

"It's the Laban *I* know and love, too," said Laban.

"The next few years are going to be interesting," said Rebekah. "Having a mother and all. I'm looking forward to it, aren't you?"

"Not as much as I was looking forward to having Ezbaal as a brother-in-law."

"I'll try to find you another just as good."

Laban's tone turned serious. "I really *am* looking forward to it. You know the real reason I'm afraid to come out of the tent?"

"Because you're afraid Mother won't like you when she gets to know you."

"Yes." Then he apparently realized he didn't want to admit that. "No, that's not it."

"Yes it is," said Rebekah. "And I can promise you—she'll make allowances for the fact that you're a boy and stupid, and she'll like you fine, just as Father and I do."

"You always know how to buck a fellow up, Rebekah."

"I spread sunshine wherever I go."

"Then why is this tent so dark?"

Rebekah didn't answer, except with a hug and a kiss on his cheek. Then she stood up. "Is it all right if I go out through the door?"

"I insist on it."

"I love you, Laban. Always and forever."

"Always and forever. Whatever you need from me, even when we're both old and feeble, I'll make sure you have it. That's a solemn vow."

"I'll take you up on it," she said.

Then she returned to her own tent, eager to sleep and get this awful day behind her. And yet, awful as it had been, angry as she still was about having been cheated out of years that could never be restored, she realized she was also eager to wake up in the morning and begin her new life, not as a wife, but as a daughter to this woman that God had finally restored to her, even though Mother did not believe in him. For if God's hand wasn't in it, how could all these things have come together as they did?

PART III

CHOSEN

CHAPTER 7

Never in Rebekah's lifetime had the camp of Bethuel been happier than in the days and months after Mother's return. Everyone seemed to sing when they weren't talking, and the talk was filled with laughter; yet everyone worked as hard as ever, and with the year's good rains there was plenty of pasturage and so they prospered.

Was it this way, everyone so constantly cheerful, before Mother was exiled? Rebekah suspected not—back then, there would have been tension, with Mother sneaking around to worship Asherah and Father laying down the law. No doubt some of the servants back then had disliked her for disobeying Father, while others probably resented Father for trying to keep Mother from worshiping the god she loved best.

Now, though, the euphoria reminded Rebekah of the time she found a lost doll. It was a foolish, poor thing, a toy made for her by Deborah with little care for workmanship, and played with by Rebekah when she was a toddler with no sense of just how much torture the cloth and seams of the doll could withstand. In time she had wearied of it, set it aside, and forgotten it.

Then, when she was about ten years old, she happened to be rummaging through a pile of guest-rugs in search of one suitable for a noteworthy visitor, and what should she find between two rugs near the bottom of the stack? Her old doll, mashed flat by the weight of the rugs, still threadbare and seam-tattered.

Rebekah had no use for dolls by then, being much too busy with the real life of the camp, and she had stopped caring about this one long ago, or it would never have been lost. Yet in the moment of finding it, it became a treasure. She pulled it out and ran to show Deborah and then Father, rejoicing. She put the doll in a place of honor in her tent, where it remained even today, the emblem of her childhood.

Mother's return was something like that, Rebekah believed. She had become the lost treasure, found again. And, like the doll, her mere presence was cause for everyone to celebrate. It was not Mother herself, but the finding of her, the restoration of what was lost.

Oddly, though, Rebekah had no such feelings. Mother, after all, had not been hers the way the doll was. She had no memories of old times with her, no sense of recovering what she once had.

Instead, Mother was the woman she had first known as Akyas, the enigmatic stranger who fascinated her and yet frightened her, just a little, if she was honest with herself. Mother remained a mystery even now. She had once shattered her marriage and lost her children because of her devotion to

Asherah, but now she never gave any outward sign of being anything but completely content with Father and Father's God. Rebekah knew she had arrived with a small statue of Asherah and assumed that she still had it. But perhaps not. Perhaps that night before the wedding, when Rebekah came upon her praying to Asherah, she had been bidding the god farewell. Perhaps the statue went home with Ezbaal's women.

Or perhaps not. Was it possible that she kept it in the very tent where Father came to her in the night? And if she did, how did Father feel about it? If he knew of any god-statue— other than the two that he used to represent God and his Servant-Son during solemn occasions—he gave no sign of it. There was no outward conflict at all. Mother and Father got along perfectly.

Rebekah was not about to jeopardize *that* by asking any questions about what Father knew or didn't know, or about what Mother did or didn't do.

The first days after the wedding were busy. While most of the adult women remembered Mother, she did not remember them as perfectly, certainly not the names. After all, she had lived in another household all these years, and could not possibly have remembered the names of fifty women she never expected to see again. Yet it couldn't help but hurt those she did not remember. So Rebekah stayed near her throughout the first few days, ostensibly reporting to her on all the work that was being done, but actually reminding her of the women's names and telling her of marriages, of children born, of deaths, of children grown up and gone.

Then there was the matter of teaching her how to read and write. What children learned quickly came harder to adults; Rebekah already knew that. But Mother had a hard time paying attention. Much as she needed to know how to talk to her husband, she kept getting distracted during lessons, and for the first few days refused to endure the drilling and testing that Rebekah had put the servants through when she taught them years before.

Perhaps if Rebekah had been in awe of her, as giddy as the other women were whenever Mother was with them, she could never have solved the problem. But Rebekah was not in awe. In fact, she was more than a little disappointed that Mother wasn't . . . well, wasn't *serious* about learning.

"I'll tell you what," Rebekah said. "Since you aren't interested in memorizing the letters, I'll assign one of the servant women who can read and write to stay with you whenever you're with Father."

"What?" said Mother. "What are you saying? I have to learn this!"

"Yes, you do," said Rebekah. "But this isn't something you can assign to a servant to learn *for* you. You have to do the work yourself, and actually learn it by paying very close attention and practicing it over and over."

Mother was quite taken aback. "Did I come here to have my daughter speak to me like this?"

Rebekah was annoyed that Mother so instantly appealed to a relationship that in fact they didn't have. "Did you come here to waste my time with lessons you don't care enough to pay attention to?"

"What is it? Why are you angry at me?" asked Mother. "Is it because I've taken your place among the women? I hope you don't think I'm going to supervise every detail of what they cook and how they weed the garden and . . . I think if they're well trained they can do all those things themselves."

What did this have to do with the matter at hand, Rebekah wondered. "Mother," she said, "I'm perfectly happy to have you supervise whatever you want to, or not supervise whatever you don't want to. In fact, I'm not even talking about that. I'm talking about learning to read and write so you can *talk to Father.*"

"There you go again, getting that impatient tone with me, as if I were a servant. I'm not, you know."

The last thing Rebekah wanted to do was fight. "Apparently I can't talk to you about this without offending you," said Rebekah. "There are the letters, all written in the dirt. As long as you don't sweep that patch, you can keep referring to them until you know them. Good luck." She got up and headed out of Mother's tent.

"It's very rude to walk out of your mother's presence without her permission," said Mother.

"It's also rude," said Rebekah, standing at the doorway of the tent, "to ask me to teach you a skill that I have and you don't, and then pay no attention and make no effort to learn it."

"I *am* making an effort," said Mother. "Just because I'm not learning it as quickly as you'd like doesn't mean you should just give up."

"All right, then," said Rebekah. "What's the sound of the first letter in the list?"

Mother looked down at the letters in the dirt. "How should I know which one is first?"

"It begins on the right side of the top row."

"I don't know what sound it makes."

"But I've told you."

"But it takes time."

"No, Mother. It doesn't take *time*, it takes *practice*, and every time I try to get you to practice you start talking about something else and the lesson stops. At this rate, you will learn to read sometime after I bring my own grandchildren to come visit their ancient great-grandmother."

Mother looked at her in consternation and then laughed. "Do you talk like this with everyone?"

"No," said Rebekah. "In fact, I don't talk like this with anyone. I'm sorry, I don't know why I get so impatient."

"Neither do I."

"No, that wasn't true. I understand exactly why I get so impatient. I'm trying to do what you asked me to do, and you won't let me do it."

"And I'm trying to use this time alone with you to get to know you, to *chat* with you, and you insist on repeating these same things over and over again. Ah ah ah ah ah. Buh buh buh buh buh. Duh duh duh duh duh."

Mother's mockery of the letter-sounds was too funny, and Rebekah burst out laughing. Mother laughed, too.

"Sit down," Mother said. "I'm going to be here a long time. I'm not going to be able to memorize this whole list the first day. It's *you* I want to memorize. *You* that I want to get to know."

Rebekah sighed and sat down. "But don't you see, Mother? This *is* who I am. I'm the person who gets the job done. I plan it out, I work hard, and I don't let anything distract me until I've accomplished it. So in your effort to find out who I am, you are not letting me *be* who I am."

"You don't sit and gossip with the women?"

"They're *women*, Mother. I'm a girl. I'm also the master's daughter. So they don't sit and chat with me. They either consult me respectfully about the work, or if they feel at ease with me, they tease me like a girl. Or give me lectures about things I'll need to know."

"But that *is* gossip."

"Mother, you came into this camp as a bride. I came into it as a baby. They'll always see me as a baby. They'll always see you as a woman."

"In other words, you don't even know *how* to chat with me."

"I didn't know that's what you were doing. I thought you were bored with the lessons."

"And I thought you were lecturing me like a particularly stupid servant, making me do something over and over until I finally do it to your satisfaction."

"Except for the 'particularly stupid' part, yes, that's exactly what I was doing."

"Then let's teach each other," said Mother. "You teach me how to turn these scratches in the dirt into words, and I'll teach you how to gossip. I'll tell you all about my life in the past fifteen years, and you tell me all about yours, until by the end of a few months we actually know each other, like good friends."

"I can't believe I spoke to you the way I did," said Rebekah.

"You're not used to having another woman in the camp who isn't trying to fit in with your plans."

"I'm not really bossy," said Rebekah.

"No, but since all the women you've had dealings with have to obey you, even if they also love you, you've never learned how to talk to an equal."

"I don't think you want me to talk to you the way I talk to Laban."

"I think I'd rather have that than your lecturing tone or your impatient tone or your 'I'm going to go do something useful until you're ready to do things my way' tone."

This stung. Was that all that she saw in Rebekah? If I'm bossy, Mother, it's because I had to take charge of things here. If I'm not skilled at being a grownup lady, it's because I had no one but servants to learn from.

Or was that just an excuse? Maybe she's right, and this is who I really am.

"My dear sweet daughter," said Mother, "I can see that you're offended and I didn't mean to. I admire your strength. You've had responsibilities at your age that I never had—for one thing, Bethuel's mother was still alive and inclined to run things until shortly before you were born. So even as a wife I didn't do as much as you do. You're strong and you're smart and even when you're lecturing me, you're clever about it and funny and—I *do* love you and I'm *not* disappointed in you. I just wish you weren't disappointed in me."

"I'm not!" cried Rebekah, feeling all the more upset because she knew that Mother had hit right on the peg: Rebekah was, in fact, disappointed.

"Don't fib to your mother," said Mother.

"I'm not fibbing," said Rebekah. "And anyway, you haven't known me long enough to tell when I'm lying and when I'm not."

"On the contrary," said Mother, "you get the same faraway look in your eyes that *I* always get when I'm covering something up. It's a dead giveaway. You look too much like me, child. You have too many of my mannerisms."

"I'm not disappointed in *you*," said Rebekah, trying to be truthful. "I didn't expect you, so how can I be disappointed? I just don't know how to be a daughter, so I suppose I'm disappointed in me."

"Then let's just be patient with each other's way of doing things. I'm not as methodical as you are. You're not as chatty as I am. So I'll try to be a little more hard-working, and you try to make room for a few of my digressions."

And that's what they did, clumsily at first but gradually with more skill as time went on. It was the first time in Rebekah's life that she had to get used to somebody new, and it occurred to her that when she married somebody and went away, she'd have to go through this whole process, and not just with one woman, but with a whole household, not to mention a husband and all his kin.

If I can't learn to get along well with my own long-lost mother, I have no hope of getting along with a mother-in-law.

Over the days and weeks they *did* get along better and better, until everything between them became quite smooth. Mother did learn to read and write, and not all that slowly. And she and Rebekah did tell each other all kinds of stories. Rebekah learned to listen to Mother's stories the way Mother listened to hers—constantly thinking of some experience or story of her own to come back with. And now that she thought about it, this *was* the way other women gossiped, trading stories—and sometimes competing with them. Oh, you think *that* story of a miserable childbirth is bad? Well, let me tell you the awful things that happened to *me*. Rebekah had never been part of such conversations and so she didn't understand the skill it took to come up with a story that seemed appropriate to the conversation. But with Mother it was an art, and Rebekah at first admired, then envied, and finally emulated her.

As a result, Rebekah found herself using the same techniques with the servant women in the camp, and to her surprise they accepted her completely as part of their gossip circles while they weeded or kneaded or wove or spun. They hadn't shut her out of their conversations. She simply hadn't known how to join in.

Now it seemed like the easiest thing in the world, to talk like a woman. But up to now, she realized, she had only known how to talk like a man. Not that men didn't gossip. But in all those years of going everywhere with Father, Rebekah had learned how to explain things clearly, how to give orders that felt like requests and requests that could easily be carried out. She had learned how to get right to the important matters and lay them out in perfect order. Which had nothing at all to do with actual adult conversation—but in the old days, whenever Father had settled down to converse with grown men, that was when she got sent out of the tent or away from the fire, because they wanted to be able to tell stories they didn't want a little girl to hear. No wonder she had never learned how to gossip!

Still, it had not been a simple matter of Rebekah's lack of skill or her misunderstanding of her mother's motives. As the months wore on, Rebekah realized that when it came to leading the women of the household, she was very good at the ceremonial things and superb at giving encouragement and making everyone feel that she knew and cared about them. But Mother had no skill or, more to the point, no interest at all in the day-to-day workings of the camp. What Rebekah noticed by second nature—you can't let this woman season the beans,

CHOSEN

you can't trust that woman to stitch a seam that doesn't unravel, you have to let this other woman keep her children close at hand because she gets too fretful when she can't see just where they are and what they're doing—Mother didn't notice and didn't care when Rebekah pointed it out.

In fact, Rebekah found that she was still doing most of the work she had done before Mother came, and gradually the women learned that while they loved talking with Mother, if there was serious work to take care of, it was Rebekah they needed to talk to. The only exception to this was if the serious matter was trying to find a way to persuade Father to change his mind about some decision he'd made. Rebekah had always answered such attempts by reinforcing Father's decision and helping the women to reconcile themselves to obeying him. But Mother listened with great sympathy and then promised to "see what I can do."

Whether she actually discussed the matter with Father or not, the damage was the same. The women came to see Mother as their ally against Father. Sometimes she could get him to change his mind—all well and good. And when Father didn't change his mind, well, they could hardly blame *her*. She was still looking out for their interests.

What made this particularly bad was that it made it so the women of the camp now defined their interests as being different from the men's. Instead of everyone feeling that they played a part in the overall work of keeping the household running smoothly, with everyone's needs provided for, they began to think and talk as if the men were off doing meaningless tasks—"What do they do, anyway? They just watch a bunch of sheep"—while the women were working harder than the men would ever understand.

It was a division in the camp.

Maybe it wasn't terribly harmful—after all, the men and women still did their work. But there was less respect than there used to be, less of a sense of everyone being part of something larger than themselves. People who used to be proud of their own work were now resentful that they had to do it.

And it all came back to Mother.

When Rebekah tried to talk to Laban about it, though, he didn't understand. "It's always been that way," he said. "The men have always joked about how the women get to sit around and gossip while they have to go out in all kinds of horrible weather and live with the stink and the manure and the bugs and the bad food, and then when they get home they have to do all the really hard jobs that the women have saved up for them."

"It may have been that way among the men," said Rebekah, "but it was never that way among the women."

Laban only shrugged.

So Rebekah had no choice but to watch, doing what she could to encourage people to understand and even agree with Father's decisions, while Mother went about inadvertently giving them reasons to grumble and feel put upon.

The one time she tried to discuss it with Mother, the whole conversation got turned around and Mother ended up trying to teach Rebekah the wisdom of the way she did things. "You see, Rebekah, the wife—especially the first wife, which is what you will definitely be—has the responsibility to be her husband's softer side. He lays down the law—'It will be thus and so!'—and then she helps people live with the rules by listening to them and trying to help them feel that someone cares about their feelings. Of course I don't actually tell most of these things to your father. He isn't going to change his mind because the decision is actually necessary. But I provide a way for them to let off steam, you see?"

And for about a day, Rebekah did see. Mother had been so convincing that Rebekah believed that she must have been wrong all along, and what Mother was doing was actually better.

But by the end of the next day, having seen the griping and discontent that Mother left in her wake—never directed at her, of course, but only at Father—Rebekah knew Mother was hopelessly wrong.

Knowing it was one thing; doing something about it was another. Mother *was* the wife, and Rebekah merely the daughter, and that was that. All she could do was the same thing she had done when she learned that she had grown up within a huge monstrous lie: She vowed that when she had a household and family of her own, it would *never* be that way. She would never set herself up as the "nice one" while painting her husband as heartless and unloving. Just as she would never lie to her family.

You don't have to repeat the mistakes of your parents, that's what Rebekah decided. That's why you *have* parents, so you can avoid their errors when you start your own family.

Rebekah liked Mother, and loved her too. Admired her, enjoyed her company, learned from her, laughed with her—it was a very good friendship.

But within a few weeks she found herself spending more time with Deborah. Even though Deborah was a little hurt and huffy about how Rebekah had been ignoring her since Mother arrived, it still felt good to be with somebody who she actually knew and who knew her. Even though Deborah was a little slow-witted, all her habits had long since been adapted to accommodate Rebekah's, and Rebekah had long since learned how to respond to Deborah. Conversations with Deborah were never scintillating—but they were always comfortable and familiar.

Gradually, though, life settled into its new pattern, and all in all, it was a good one. Everything went smoothly, more or less, and if there was more grumbling among the women, there was also more laughter and singing, so perhaps it all evened out.

The one thing that seemed to have changed for good was the matter of suitors showing up to try to bargain for Rebekah's hand in marriage. Prior to Mother's arrival, there had been someone every week or so. Since Ezbaal came and went, there was not a one. If Father noticed it, he said nothing, and of course Mother did not know how it had been before.

Laban, as always, said exactly what was on his mind. "What do you think, silly girl? If you turned down Ezbaal, who else is going to think they could succeed where he failed? And if he rejected you, then who is going to quarrel with his judgment?"

"*I* think it's just because I stopped wearing that veil. Once they could see my face, all the mystery was over and I'm just not as pretty as people thought I was."

"*That's* not it," said Laban. "I mean, if they aren't coming here in the first place, the problem can hardly be the way you *look*. Though I'd get rid of that goiter if I were you."

"I wanted to, but Father said you're the only son he's got, so you have to stay."

"Listen, Rebekah, they'll start coming back. And even if

they don't, I'll get one of my friends in the town really drunk and then tell him when he sobers up that he promised to marry you and I'm going to hold him to it."

"Oh, that's an excellent plan. And as soon as I'm married, the first thing I'll do is make sure he *never* spends time with a horrible friend like you."

Still, for about a year the visitors to the camp were all there to meet Mother and be charmed by her and congratulate Father and Mother on the wedding. The only time Rebekah was noticed was when somebody had to ooh-and-ah over how much she looked like her mother. And since Mother spent so long every day tending to her hair and clothing, and because she moved so gracefully and spoke so charmingly, by contrast Rebekah no doubt looked like something dragged into camp by a dog. You look so much alike, and yet your daughter seems to have been living in a thicket, that's what they probably *meant*.

And that's why nobody wanted to marry her now. They all met Mother and realized that Rebekah had been raised, not by ladies, but by men. What good is beauty if the possessor of it doesn't know how to behave beautifully?

Rebekah tried, of course. It's not that she didn't know how to be courteous, and she was naturally shy with strangers, so it wasn't that she was too boisterous. She just . . . didn't know how to be charming. And even as she watched Mother do it, she didn't understand how it was that Mother made grown men get tongue-tied and stupid in her presence, and then laughed and made them feel as though she liked tongue-tied, stupid men.

Maybe it's a gift of Asherah.

A thought that Rebekah knew was absurd—how can something be a gift of Asherah if there *is* no Asherah?

But it looked like magic to Rebekah. And when she tried to imitate her mother, she only looked ridiculous. Not that anyone saw her. Whom would she practice on? Servant boys? Servant *men?* Oh, by all means, let's go down *that* road again and see if we can have another fellow thrown out of camp because he thought he had a chance with the master's daughter.

Rebekah's only practice was in her tent, alone with Deborah, and Deborah always burst out laughing before Rebekah was more than a few sentences into her Mother imitation. "You sound *just like her,*" Deborah always said. "It's so *funny.*" Which told Rebekah that she didn't sound just like Mother—she just sounded like somebody *trying* to sound just like her. Because if she *did* sound just like Mother, then Deborah would be charmed. Not amused.

That winter the rains were few and far between. It meant that all next year would be spent searching for pasture ever higher and farther abroad—and so would all the other herding families. "The desert grows," Bethuel said, "the grass doesn't. Wells go dry, and we'll be fighting more and more over those that remain."

It was just Father, Mother, Laban, Rebekah, and Pillel at this meeting in Father's tent. Only Mother looked unworried.

"We have two choices," Father said. "Because we always do, when times are hard. We can strike camp and go out wandering, negotiating with the locals at every well, fighting when we have to. Or we can sell some of the animals in the city and try to keep the balance between the land we traditionally use and the size of the herds that can live on them. The danger in that is that wandering families that make the other choice will be coming *here,* and we have to keep constant vigilance to protect our lands."

Father and Pillel went back and forth on this for a while, with Pillel warning that if they were to sell too many animals, too fast, the local price would drop, and Father countering that they could sell off small groups of animals in more distant cities. Until Mother finally sighed and entered the conversation. "Write for me, will you, Rebekah?"

Mother could write for herself now, but she was still slow and had to concentrate on it. So when she wanted to say something complicated, she still needed help, and Rebekah didn't mind.

"There's another choice," she said.

Rebekah wrote it.

Father rolled his eyes. Apparently this was an old argument.

"We've been camped here so long that it's only a small step to moving into town," said Mother.

"A small step," said Father. "Let's see. We free all the herdsmen, which reduces them to beggary and puts their families at the edge of starvation. Or we sell them to another household. And we move into the city where I do . . . what?"

Mother was not fazed. "We build a real house here, and we gradually train more and more of the herdsmen as farmers. We use land along the stream and channel the water onto the fields."

"When there's water," said Pillel.

"And when real drought comes," said Father, "instead of having herds we can move somewhere else in search of water and pasture, we have a farm that consists of dust and sand and starving farmers."

"And yet the villages thrive," said Mother.

"For a whole generation, Canaan has been virtually unin-habited," said Father. "The people had to move out of the villages during the great drought. Only instead of going wan-dering as grandfather did, as Uncle Abraham did, they had nowhere to go except to sell themselves into slavery as if they had been conquered. Half the families in our household entered into service at that time. That's what you want for us?"

Mother shrugged, but it was obvious to Rebekah that the argument wasn't over yet. For the first time Rebekah realized that Mother really wasn't born to the desert life and still, after all these years, didn't like it.

So during one of their chats, Rebekah tried to draw her out about it.

"Yes, I grew up in Ugarit," said Mother. "My grandfather was an Amorite prince who came out of the desert on a raid but realized that the city life was better and came back and bought his way into citizenship. He kept his herds, but grad-ually shifted to vineyards and olives. I never saw three sheep together until I married your father."

"So why didn't you marry someone from the city?"

"These desert people," she said. "They'll *live* in the city, but they won't marry there. Father wouldn't even consider any suitors from Ugarit. He wanted me to marry a man who worshiped the god with no name."

"He has a name," said Rebekah, almost by habit. "We just don't say it."

"No, you just don't *know* it," said Mother.

"Which is how we can be sure not to say it," said Rebekah.

"You can bet your father knows the name of God, and he'll tell Laban. Or write it down."

But Rebekah was thinking of something much more important. "So you grew up in a house that served the God of Abraham."

"I grew up in a house that served the god of getting rich," said Mother. "Which meant going to all the religious festivals in the city, no matter what the god was, so that everyone would accept my father as a true citizen instead of a foreigner who bought his way in."

"The way the Hittites do, worshiping whatever god the locals worship."

"Except my father would come home from the festival and laugh about the stupid beliefs of the local people. 'How ignorant they are, to think that their stone god can do anything other than bruise your head if you bump into it.'"

Rebekah laughed, but realized Mother wasn't much amused by it. "My father and I didn't get along," Mother said. "He was a hypocrite, pretending to serve one god while secretly serving another. Only it seemed to me that he served neither and denied both. That's why I say he worshiped wealth. He cared about nothing else. That's why I ended up married to your father. He had the biggest bride-gift."

"That's *all*?"

"Well, of course he was from a lofty family. Terah's boys made quite a name for themselves, and not just Abraham. So nobody could criticize Father for marrying me off to a man who had once been Abraham's heir."

"But you chose to worship Asherah," said Rebekah.

"I didn't choose Asherah," said Mother. "She chose me."

Rebekah waited for more explanation.

"I promised your father never to talk to you about Asherah."

"Why? Does he think you'll convert me?"

"Yes," said Mother. "For a man who doesn't think Asherah is really a god, he has a very healthy respect for her powers of influence."

"Or for yours," said Rebekah.

Mother made a display of exaggerated innocence. "Mine? Powers of influence? I couldn't influence a locust to eat a leaf."

Rebekah laughed. "All the same," she said, "you have to tell me."

"I was drawn to Asherah anyway," said Mother. "Because the only worshipers of your God that I knew were insincere, while the girls I grew up with in the city, all my friends, took Asherah very seriously and prayed to her fervently, to make them attractive to their husbands so they would put babies in them."

"That's a prayer that's sure to get granted," said Rebekah.

"Well, you'd think so," said Mother. "Only in Ugarit there were real problems for a time—few babies were conceived and fewer born alive. The people were sure that they had offended a god, of course, and Father sneered at them for that. But I suspect that's part of the reason he wanted to find a husband for me from outside the city."

"So you prayed to Asherah."

"It was a very hard thing for me to do. But my womanhood hadn't come upon me, and I was almost as old as you are now. I feared that I was going to be barren. I *looked* like a woman, but I was like a husk with no grain inside. I had prayed to your God many times but nothing happened. And then I went with some of my friends to Asherah and prayed."

"And it came."

"Not at once," said Mother. "Not until the third time I went to her, and made a covenant with Asherah that if she made me a woman, I would serve her every day of my life."

"And then."

"A month later," said Mother.

"But it might have come then whether you prayed to Asherah or not."

"Yes, of course," said Mother. "Just as it sometimes rains after your father prays to his God for rain, and sometimes it doesn't, and who knows whether it would have rained anyway? But I had made a covenant, and my womanhood came, and I keep my word."

"To Asherah."

Mother cocked an eyebrow. "Yes, well, I did disobey your father after promising not to present you to Asherah. But my covenant with Asherah came before any covenant I ever made to your father. And besides, if you have to choose between serving a god and serving a man, how hard is it to make *that* decision?"

"But if you serve a man who serves the same god as you," said Rebekah, "then there's never such a choice to make."

"Oh, my darling girl, I shudder to think of how many times in your life you're going to have to eat *those* words. Besides, my dear, didn't you just urge me to break my word to your father and tell you about how Asherah chose me?"

That was an embarrassing truth. "Well, you didn't convert me to Asherah, so we didn't violate Father's intention," said Rebekah.

"You *are* human, my dear," said Mother. "Just like

everybody else. And your faith in your God is no different from my faith in mine."

Rebekah didn't argue—what would be the point? But the truth was beyond anything Mother could have guessed. Because the God of Abraham didn't just answer prayers in ways that could easily be coincidence, the way Asherah did. Rebekah hadn't exactly heard the voice of God the way the stories said Uncle Abraham did, but she had been given words to say, had been given knowledge in her heart at key times in her life. Ideas had come into her mind that could only have been a gift of God.

She couldn't tell her mother about these things, though, because Mother was so sure of herself that she would dismiss Rebekah's experiences as being her own imaginings. You're a clever girl, that's what Mother would say, so you think up clever ideas and then give the credit to your God. Very modest of you, but what you really end up worshiping is yourself, don't you think? Oh, Rebekah knew exactly how Mother's mind worked, because didn't she think of these doubts herself, during dark moments when her life didn't seem to be going very well? Then she would think back and remember how it *felt*. How when these ideas from God entered her mind, they came with such surety that she simply knew them to be true and acted on them in the moment. While her own ideas came with doubt, and she had to wrestle with them before she could act. It was completely different—and impossible to explain. At least to someone like Mother, who could explain anything away with a flick of her wit.

Be honest, Rebekah told herself. I do the same thing. I did it just now, to her, explaining away the prayer that Asherah answered.

From the outside, my faith in God looks just like her faith in Asherah. But I know the difference. I have felt him touch my heart and mind, and there is no possibility of doubt for me.

When her prayer was "answered," Mother took it to mean that she was chosen by Asherah. Has God chosen me?

Immediately she rejected the vanity implied by the question. Chosen her? What would that mean? Abraham was chosen. He had the birthright. But Rebekah? There were no great promises to her. God had never actually spoken to her, not in words.

No, God has merely answered my prayers from time to time, as he might do for anyone who does her best to serve him.

Except that Father and Laban have never spoken of having that sudden breath of knowledge like those God gave me.

Again she tried to drive the thought from her mind. She was *not* chosen above her father and brother.

"It is really quite rude," Mother said, "to suddenly fall silent during what was supposed to be a conversation."

"I'm sorry," Rebekah apologized, and offered some excuse about going off into her own thoughts. When Mother asked what those thoughts might be, Rebekah evaded her and, with her newfound skills at conversation, turned the topic to something else. Mother knew what she was doing, of course, but how could she complain when she herself had taught Rebekah how to do this?

The next summer Rebekah got her first suitor in a year, and it wasn't a real one, just a visit from a traveling merchant who sat down with Father and told him that an up-and-coming young merchant in Byblos had asked him to find out, if he could, whether Rebekah was still unmarried and what it would take, as a bride-price, to win her hand. As Laban reported the scene to Rebekah later, Father was outraged, but he contained his anger and patiently explained that concubines might be bought that way, but his daughter was not for sale. "These merchants," Laban said, no doubt echoing Father's sentiments, "they live by buying and selling, so they think *everything* is for sale."

When Pillel heard the story, though, he got curious and had one of his men go to Byblos and find out about the young merchant on whose behalf the traveler had made his outrageous inquiry. It was months later that word came back, but Pillel made his report to Father and Father in turn told Laban and Rebekah about it as if it were a huge joke. "Do you know who it turned out to be?" he asked.

They had no idea, of course, since they didn't know anyone from Byblos.

"Belbai," said Father.

For a moment Laban's face was blank, though Rebekah remembered at once. Khaneah's son, who had been beaten and expelled along with his mother from the camp, because he had written ugly things about Rebekah.

Then it dawned on Laban, and his face filled with rage.

"No, don't be angry," Father soothed him. "It's nothing more than a testament to your sister's beauty. The boy is still entranced!"

Laban wrote in the dirt, "I should have killed him here."

Rebekah punched him in the arm, thinking he was merely exaggerating, but Father took him seriously. "Perhaps," he said. "Pillel even offered to have him killed for me."

"Father!" Rebekah cried, and even though he couldn't hear her, he certainly could read the expression on her face.

"He committed a crime worthy of death," said Father simply. "I could have killed him then in perfect justice. But now? No. I let him go, and that's that. You're not to do anything either, Laban. Do I have your word?"

Laban set his lips and hesitated.

"I want your oath before God," said Father. "You will cause no harm to Belbai, yourself or by anyone else's hand. Swear!"

Laban wrote the oath Father demanded.

"And don't think," said Father, "that God will not hold you to that oath just because you wrote it instead of saying it with your lips."

Laban rolled his eyes.

"The boy has done well for himself," Father said. "In fact, he's really quite clever. He took his knowledge of writing and started teaching it to other poor boys in the streets of Byblos. Now they call themselves scribes, and they write things for people. The regular scribes were outraged and tried to get it stopped, but since they weren't using cuneiform, they weren't actually doing the same thing, or so the judge ruled. And since our writing system is so much easier to learn—so few characters to memorize!—Belbai can train his boy-scribes in no time, and soon they were all over the city, offering their services for even the most casual messages, and at a half the normal price. Now he's rich. He owns a house. His mother has servants of her own."

"From something he stole from us," Laban wrote.

"I don't recall ever trying to keep this a secret," said Father. "It's a gift of God. And even though it was intended for writing the holy words, I don't think it offends God that we use these letters to help a deaf man hear—or to help a poor lad prosper in a faraway city."

Rebekah took Father's view of it—she didn't see what Laban was so angry about. It was a little mad of Belbai to think there might be a chance that Father would let him have Rebekah as a wife, but she certainly didn't begrudge him his ambition or the prosperity that came from it. Indeed, it was ambition that had gotten him in trouble in the first place, only now it was working for him instead of against him.

And it was flattering that the thing he wanted to do was marry the girl he had once longed for in camp.

When she told all this to Mother, she took a darker view. "Unless of course he was brooding and seeking vengeance and hoped to have you as his wife in order to mistreat you."

"Oh, Mother, how can you even think that?"

"There are many husbands who beat their wives for less reason than that," said Mother. "No, Pillel was right. He should have had the boy killed without consulting your father first. Bethuel is too merciful for his family's good. This boy is clearly obsessed with you. He'll cause you harm someday."

"Or he loves me," said Rebekah.

"You say that as if you think it's not the same thing," said Mother, amused.

"Love and obsession? Tenderness and harm?"

"The man who hurt me worst in my life," said Mother, "was the one who loved me most."

And, when she thought about it, Rebekah realized that she could say the same thing.

What was love, then? Something to be feared and shunned, because it caused so much pain?

That was a question that was useless to ask, she realized. Love was love. You didn't choose when it would enter your heart, any more than you chose what kind of people your own parents would be. You just loved whom you loved. And then hurt whom you hurt, and forgave whom you forgave, and lived your life day to day as best you could.

After Belbai, though, other suitors began to show up. Apparently whatever bad impression it gave when Ezbaal's suit was rejected had faded, and even unveiled, Rebekah was still considered a good match. And Rebekah was getting older. Sooner or later, Father would say yes to one of these men, and Rebekah would agree, because if you waited too long, they stopped coming.

Late one afternoon, in the quiet hour when supper was being prepared and she had a lull in her work, Rebekah rose from the bed where she had thought to nap, went to her tent door, and prayed. She made no demands; she was not impatient. Just offered the suggestion that if God had kept her from Ezbaal in order to find a better husband for her, it would be good if he sent that husband soon.

Of course, as soon as she was through with the prayer, she realized that it wasn't that different from her mother's prayer to Asherah. Now it would be easy to persuade herself that any husband she ended up with must have been the answer to this prayer. After all, she prayed and . . . he came. How soon was "soon"? For that matter, how much divine intervention did there have to be for a man to seem "sent"?

There sat Mother at the door of her tent, taking advantage of the last bright light of the afternoon to work on sewing nice tight stitches in the linen of Father's new undergarment. Feeling smug, no doubt, because she had achieved exactly what she wanted. Her story about Asherah choosing her wasn't designed to convert Rebekah to Asherah—it was designed to make her doubt that the God of Abraham answered prayers any better.

Rebekah wanted to go over to Mother and argue the point with her, explain why her experiences with God were completely different from Mother's with Asherah. But Mother would only look at her with that puzzled expression and say, "What did I say to bring *this* on?" and Rebekah would look like a fool even to herself. No, Mother had planted the seeds of disbelief, and it was Rebekah's business now to make sure they took no root.

Mother saw her and waved cheerfully.

Rebekah waved back, determined not to let Mother annoy her today—especially not for something she had done long before. She went to the main hearth and picked up one of the large water jugs. It was a chore she often did. So much water had to be hauled from the communal well for each day's cooking that it was like spinning thread—whoever had a free moment could always be of service by spending a few minutes doing it. Besides, for Rebekah it had the added benefit of giving her some time away from the annoyances of camp.

It wasn't far to the well, but it put her within sight of the village of Haran on its hill, and there were several girls from town about Rebekah's age at the well already. They had long since gotten used to seeing Rebekah without the veil, just as they had eventually gotten used to seeing her with it. Still, there was a little strangeness between the village women and the women of Father's camp, and after a cheerful greeting, the girls ended their gossip and headed back to the village, each with a jug on her shoulder.

Rebekah heard and saw enough as she approached, however, to know that their gossip was about the dusty traveler
who stood beside the well, murmuring to himself. He was an
older man, not ancient but with a beard thick-streaked with
grey. There were several heavily-loaded camels only a few
rods back from him, and a few men with them. He could be a
merchant, with that amount of cargo, but he wasn't dressed
like one. More like a servant, in fact. Like Pillel. Rebekah was
intrigued, but of course it would be immodest to speak to a
stranger, and instead she began lowering the pitcher into the
well and raising it to fill her water jar. Each time she did, of
course, she made the jar all the heavier, so that carrying it back
would be harder. But what was the point of making the trip to
the well, if you came back with the jar only half replenished?

"Girl, could I have a little water from your pitcher, so I can
drink?"

She looked up and saw that he was now speaking to her.
His request was so tentative sounding, so . . . *shy* . . . that she
had to smile at him, to reassure him. "Of course," she said.
Never mind that he had called her "girl" as if she were not a
daughter of one of the great wandering families. People were
not always what they seemed. He might be a servant who
took her for another, but then, he might be a man of such high
birth that he assumed he could speak familiarly to anyone he
met.

As she poured from the pitcher into his cup, she glanced
back at his men and camels. The animals looked tired. They
must have traveled all day in the heat, and they looked
exhausted.

He put the cup to his lips and drank.

"Bring your animals up to the trough, sir," she said, "and

I'll pour water for them as well." And then, without waiting for his answer, she picked up the water jug she had been filling and poured it all out into the trough.

The man looked at her oddly and said nothing, but returned to his men. Soon the animals were drinking lustily, the men quietly stroking them and murmuring to them. These fellows had an air about them, of easy confidence, that impressed Rebekah. Most travelers were suspicious of everyone and everything—after all, there were many dangers along the road. But these men seemed to fear nothing—they were alert, but not wary. And . . . they seemed to like each other. To get along, at least, and that was a good thing. It meant they were well led, because in any group there would be quarrels in the course of a journey. She had watched Father more than once as he worked to smooth differences, and quietly separated men who irritated each other. Her respect for the man who led them grew.

She worked to refill her water jar as the older man rummaged through one camel's load. Surely he didn't mean to insult her by trying to pay her for the water. She hurried in order to be gone before he could do something so patronizing, for she didn't want to embarrass him by explaining whose daughter she was, for then he would have to apologize for asking her to pour for him in the first place. It was a conversation she didn't want to have.

Sure enough, he hurried toward her as she shouldered the heavy jug. She was too late—so heavily loaded, she couldn't get away in time.

"Whose daughter are you?" asked the man.

Well, that wasn't what she expected to hear. In fact, it suggested that he *had* known that she was no servant.

She turned to face him.

"I ask," he said, "because I need to know, if you'd kindly tell me, whether there's room for us to lodge in your father's house tonight?"

"I'm the daughter of Bethuel, son of Nahor by his wife Milcah," she said—name enough that unless he was from some hopelessly remote place, he would recognize the stature of her family. As for lodging, Father never turned away a traveler who seemed honest, which this man certainly did, though he had not had the courtesy to give his own name. "We have plenty of food for you and for your animals," she said, "although a house with walls is not within our power to offer, since my father's household live in tents."

Still the man did not thank her. Instead he bowed his head and sank to his knees, saying, "Great is the Lord God of Abraham, who blesses my master and never leaves him wanting for mercy or for truth. For I had not finished my prayer before the Lord answered it. He has sent me to the house of my master's brother."

Master? So this man was someone's servant—but one with great trust, no doubt a steward, like Pillel. Which had been one of her first impressions of him. And his master was kin of theirs? But he hadn't used the general term for a relative. Rather he had spoken as if Father were his master's own brother. But she would have known the stewards of any of Father's brothers—messages were always passing back and forth among the families.

Unless he meant that his master was the brother of her grandfather, Nahor. But only one of Nahor's brothers was still alive.

Abraham.

This man was Abraham's steward.

She dared not ask him, though, for what if she was wrong? What if he was the steward of one of her father's brothers? Then she'd look like a fool, for who would look for Abraham's steward to be traveling this far north, and with such a small company? What possible business would Abraham have with Father, anyway?

And then the question was answered before she could begin to think through the possibilities, for what the man had looked for and found was a gold bracelet, which he was now offering to place upon her wrist. He had come as an emissary from one great house to another. He had come with gifts for a girl.

It was not just this man whose prayer was answered almost in the moment of asking. She, too, had prayed for the Lord to hasten her marriage. And in the moment she finished her prayer, she had thought to go for water to the very well where this man was waiting. The steward of Abraham, who had come here in search of his master's relatives. And his first act was to give her a gold bracelet—no, now there was another, and earrings as well. There could be no mistaking the meaning of such an act.

And no mistaking the meaning of her allowing him to place the goldware on her. She took off the tiny earrings she was wearing and replaced them with the far richer gold of the earrings he offered. From the color, this gold was almost pure; she handled it carefully, because such pure gold would be soft. It might bend or flake if she handled it roughly.

She found that she was trembling, and it was hard to get the earrings on. But when she was done, she looked the man in the eye and said, "It is truly an honor to receive a man who follows the God of Abraham."

"I have already said and done more than I should," said the man. "But it is plain that the Lord has prepared the way before me."

"Let me go to my father," she said, "and he'll send men to guide you to where your animals can be unloaded and penned, and where you and your fellowservants can lodge."

"We will be here, watering the camels, and awaiting the will of the Lord."

Rebekah turned to pick up her water jar, and then realized that there was no way she could bear to walk slowly carrying water, when the Lord had brought a suitor from the one house that would mean more than Ezbaal's. Leaving the jar behind, she walked, then trotted, then full-out ran up the path that wound around the hill toward the camp of Bethuel.

Before she could get to Father's tent, she found Laban and Mother conferring outside her tent, and before she could say anything to them, Mother said, "Where did you get those?"

Laban looked at her closely. "We don't have anything like that."

"Actually, I do," said Mother. "But they were a gift from my husband before we were married."

"A man gave them to me," said Rebekah.

"And you took them? You *wore* them? Do you have any idea what that implies?" said Mother, getting angrier by the moment.

"I know exactly what it means," said Rebekah. "The Lord God of Abraham has brought me my husband."

Which left Mother momentarily speechless.

Laban gave her a strange look and said, "Where is this man?"

"You'll find Abraham's steward waiting by the well, along with my water jar and pitcher. I offered him the hospitality of our camp and said that Father would send a man to lead him here."

"Abraham's steward?" asked Laban.

"*The* Abraham?" asked Mother.

"Perhaps," said Rebekah. For the man hadn't actually said so, had he? "He might be."

"He *might* be? And you took these gifts?"

"They can always be given back, Mother," said Rebekah.

But they wouldn't be. She knew it, with the certainty she always felt when the knowledge came from God.

CHAPTER 8

R ebekah was already giving instructions to the women to prepare food and ready the large extra tent for an honored guest and his six men when Laban came running to her, out of breath.

"You have to come," he said.

"Already?"

"He won't eat, he says, or even drink more than the water you served him at the well, until he states his errand."

"He's a driven man," said Rebekah.

"Well, he needs you there."

"I'm never there when Father talks with suitors," she said.

"Then you refuse to come?" asked Laban, amused.

"Of course I'm coming," she said. She took a moment to give the last few instructions to the women about how things should be arranged for the meal, and then hurried with Laban to Father's tent.

"Well?" asked Rebekah. "What do you think?"

"He's a servant who is used to commanding like a great lord," said Laban.

"He didn't seem bossy to me," said Rebekah.

"Great lords aren't bossy. They just say what they want and expect it to happen. They just say, 'I think it might be nice if Rebekah were here,' and off goes the son of the house to obey the guest."

"So why did you go?"

"Because Mother agreed with him and sent me to fetch you."

"So she's writing for Father."

"And sizing up the fellow with her own eyes."

"His animals were taken care of?"

"Trust me a *little*, Rebekah. The animals have been unloaded and they're eating their fill. We also brought up the water you dipped, so he and his men could wash their feet from their travels. Anything else you want to check on?"

"I just asked."

"You were checking," said Laban. "You always check on everybody else. But who checks up on you?"

"No one ever has to," said Rebekah.

Laban laughed. "Well, I suppose that's true. Since you check everything three times, how could you possibly leave anything undone?"

"But I always worry that I might have," said Rebekah.

They were at Father's tent now. Laban led the way inside. The front door stood open for light, as did the two side doors that were usually kept closed. To Rebekah's surprise, everyone was standing.

"Are we awaiting someone else?" asked Rebekah.

"He won't sit," said Mother dryly, "until he has delivered his message."

That was pointless, Rebekah thought, and she turned to Abraham's steward. "Sir, this is a courteous house. No one can sit until you are seated. You would do us all a great kindness if you sat down. Your message can be spoken seated as easily as standing, I think."

The man blinked, then raised his eyebrows. "The damsel speaks wisely," he said. "I feel the eyes of God upon me, and so I'm afraid my urgency ran stronger than my common sense." He seated himself. "Thank you for the generous way you have received me and my master's other servants. You have treated us as if we were all lords."

"The servants of a great lord receive some of the honor due to their master," said Mother.

Laban was writing furiously. The servant saw this, and waited to begin until Laban had finished writing.

Father spoke. "Please tell us your errand."

"I am Eliezer, steward of the household of Abraham, husband of Sarah, and son of Terah, your grandfather."

When Father read the words and nodded, he went on.

"The Lord has blessed my master with flocks and herds, silver and gold, menservants and maidservants, camels and donkeys. But this was nothing to him compared to the greatest gift of God: His wife, Sarah, gave birth in her old age to a boy-child named Isaac."

Isaac. Rebekah well knew the name and the story of the birth. But today Eliezer was telling this story because it was part of his errand. It was, she felt sure, the name of her husband. The miracle baby, grown to be a man, and now in need of a wife to bear children, so Abraham's line could continue and the birthright could pass to another generation. A woman who will partake of the blessings of Sarah, to be the mother of nations in some future time.

Me.

"Abraham has begotten other sons to concubines, but Isaac is sole heir to all that Abraham has, including the birthright."

When Father read this, he nodded. "We know of the birthright. For a while I was in line for it myself, till God chose otherwise."

"A short while ago, my master called me to him and made me swear the most holy oath, that I would find a wife for Isaac, but not from among the daughters of the Canaanites in whose land Abraham dwells. Rather he sent me north to the land of Haran, to Abraham's father's house, to his kindred, to find a wife for his son."

Rebekah saw how intently Father and Mother and Laban all listened to the man. She realized that she was the calmest person in the tent. But then, it was her prayer that was being answered here.

"But how would I, no more than a steward, and a man of Damascus by birth, hope to choose the woman who should be Isaac's bride? The choice could not be mine. It had to be the Lord's. So this evening, as I stood by the well of Haran, knowing that the women of this place would come there for water, I prayed that God would show me the woman he chose. I asked for this sign, that when I asked a woman for a drink of water, she would not only give it to me, but would also offer water for my animals."

Mother raised an eyebrow at this. Rebekah suspected what she was thinking: Eliezer had not chosen an easy sign for God to fulfill. The kind of woman who would, of herself, talk freely to a stranger at the well, and pour water for him, was not the kind of woman that he could bring home as bride for his master's son. So he made the sign even more outrageous—that she must offer to water his animals as well, even though he had servants with him who were perfectly capable of doing it. What woman, of low or high station, would go so far?

And when Father read Eliezer's words, he looked sharply at Rebekah, for of course he knew that they would not be having this conversation if Rebekah had not fulfilled the sign in every particular, which meant that she had behaved in an outrageously immodest manner.

Rebekah merely bowed her head demurely. Let Father think what he would. She was led by God today. What seemed brazen to her parents had felt like ordinary generosity to her at the time. Or not even that. It had simply felt right.

Eliezer went on. "Your daughter, with astonishing kindness, put my request and the needs of my animals above her own modesty. I received my sign from the Lord in every particular. Then, to learn that she is in fact the daughter of Bethuel, a young woman whom any great man would desire for the bride of his heir—and, of course, my own eyes told me of her beauty, which will greatly please my master's son."

Rebekah saw Laban smirking, and imagined what he'd say to her later about what he'd do if Father ever suggested that Pillel should go choose a wife for him.

"And now, if you will treat my master with kindness and faithfulness, tell me. And if not, tell me there is no hope for my master's suit, so I can know which way to turn."

Father began nodding as he read this, though Rebekah

well knew that the demand for an immediate answer was very abrupt. No, it was rude.

So Rebekah wrote her own words in the dirt, the letters facing Father, even as Laban was still writing Eliezer's words.

"I will obey God's will," wrote Rebekah.

The words were simple enough, but Rebekah knew that Father would understand all that they meant. That she believed this man's sign was indeed from God, that she would marry Isaac, and there was no reason to pretend to negotiate. This was the wedding she had waited for.

"My master is old," said Eliezer. "He cannot travel. Nor will he allow Isaac to leave his side, for there are enemies of God who would seek out the young man to kill him in order to try to thwart the will of the Lord."

Rebekah wondered if those enemies included Ishmael, Abraham's firstborn, the son of a concubine, who had been expelled from Abraham's camp as a boy nearly at the age of manhood because of the threat he posed to the baby Isaac. But surely one brother would not threaten another, no matter how angry or jealous he might be.

Father looked intently at Rebekah, and then at Laban and Mother. He had nods from all of them before he answered. "This comes from God. What does it matter what we think, good or bad?" Father shook his head, but then he gestured toward Rebekah. "Look, there she is before you, my daughter Rebekah. Take her, go, let her be the wife of your master's son. The Lord has made his choice. Her son will have the birthright."

Rebekah felt a thrill go through her. The thing was done. So quickly, so simply, after all these months—no, years since the suitors had started coming. This was the reason she could not say yes to Ezbaal. Even that proud desert lord would understand a woman's refusing him in order to marry the heir of Abraham.

Eliezer knelt up and then bowed himself down to the earth, right across the place where they had been writing. His right hand stretched across the place where Laban had written Eliezer's words, and his left hand touched Rebekah's own writing, though whether he planned it or it was simple chance, she did not know.

"O God, Master of my master, Father of all fathers, Lord of all lords, for thy sake this great family offers up their brightest jewel to adorn thee in thy glory, and thou hast chosen to bind this gift into a setting of the purest gold of my master's house."

It was a very poetic thing to say, and the words might have thrilled her if Rebekah was to be won with words. But since she was already won by her faith in God, she only admired the words and then wondered idly if Eliezer had thought them up in advance, composing them during the journey north from Canaan, or if the words simply fell unplanned from his lips.

Eliezer knelt back up and opened the bag at his waist. He brought forth more jewelry and laid it upon the rug before him. The pieces were of the purest gold Rebekah had ever seen, their luster deep and rich in the evening light that slanted into the tent, or of a silver that showed no sign of tarnish. The gems set in the rings and necklaces were polished perfectly and seemed to glow with inner light. All the workmanship was extraordinarily delicate and even. Rebekah had never imagined that such things could exist, let alone be offered as a gift for her. And not the bride-gift, either, for these were clearly intended to adorn her body, not remain behind with Father and Mother when she left.

Eliezer dipped again into his bag, taking out yet another necklace, which seemed every bit as fine as the gifts he brought for her, and laid it before Mother. Then a cup covered with hammered gold, crazed with an intricate pattern of inlaid silver, and inset with precious stones, which he set before Laban, who picked it up with awe.

Nothing for Father, of course. The bride-gift, when it was offered, would be for him.

Then Eliezer reached out his hand toward Rebekah. "It is not my hand that I offer you, mistress, but the hand of my master's son Isaac. Will you take it?"

"Even if he had come without gold and jewels," said Rebekah, "but adorned only with the simple faith in God that you have shown today, I would take the hand that is offered to me." And she reached out and took his hand in both of hers, and bent over it, and kissed it. "It is not your hand I kiss," she said, "but the hand of your master's son Isaac, who will be my husband, and I will be his wife."

Eliezer looked her in the eyes, and she could see how he focused on first her left, then her right eye, back and forth, as if he were searching for something in her face. Whether he found it or not she could not tell, but after a long while, he took back his hand and rose to his feet. "I have done the errand my master sent me on. Now, I will accept your generous offer of food and drink for me and my men."

There was a feast that night, with singing and celebrating. Rebekah knew it was all in her honor, but it began to seem to her that the women were far too happy for her comfort. Were they celebrating the happiness of her wedding, or the fact that they would no longer be taking instructions from this child?

She knew that this was an absurd idea, but somewhere in the evening's festivities she wanted someone to say some small thing about how much Rebekah would be missed.

Actually, she wanted people to weep and tear their clothes because she wouldn't be with them anymore, but she knew that was out of the question. I'm being a selfish, petty child, she told herself. What is there to be sad about? I'm not dying, I'm going to be married, as noble a marriage as there can be, and I was chosen as Isaac's bride, not by the calculations of men, but by the will of God. It's what I was praying for only this evening. Everything is *perfect*.

She was able to keep a good face on things until she saw two of the women burst into tears and throw their arms around Deborah. "Oh, you darling, how we'll miss you!" "Nothing will be the same with you gone!" On and on.

In all her life, Rebekah had never been jealous of Deborah. And she did *not* begrudge her sweet nurse the generous affection of the women of the camp. It was simply . . . it was just that . . .

She murmured something to her mother about needing to see to something in her tent, and fled.

Not to her tent. If someone came looking for her, she did not want to be found. Instead she went by a roundabout way to the pen where Eliezer's camels were resting. The faintest light of day was still in the sky. There would be moonlight tonight, so the celebration could go on for a while longer; but the cool breeze from the desert promised a chilly night.

The camels noticed her coming, but cared little. Tears may have flowed down her cheeks as she walked here, but now, looking at the lumpen faces of these beasts, she had to laugh. All it took, she realized, was thinking of something other than myself.

"Are you that eager to go?" asked Eliezer.

Only then did she see that Abraham's steward was inside the pen, using a wooden comb to work something out of the hair on a camel's flank.

"In fact I am," said Rebekah. "But no, I didn't think of leaving tonight."

"They let you leave the feast? It's your farewell, isn't it?"

"I thought it was your welcome."

Eliezer laughed.

The silence between them soon weighed too much to bear.

"I hope you know that I didn't accept your proposal because of the jewelry."

"There'd be nothing shameful if you had," said Eliezer. "My master's wealth and reputation will mean your children will grow up with every protection, every opportunity."

Rebekah understood this. "I just wanted you to know my eyes were not dazzled."

"So if it wasn't the jewelry, what was it? I wasn't a bad-looking man in my youth, but age has done its work on my face, so I know it wasn't *my* beauty."

"Just as I know it wasn't mine."

Eliezer laughed again. "I hope that doesn't bother you. That you weren't chosen for your beauty. You could have been, of course."

"I wasn't asking for flattery."

"You weren't getting any. The choice was God's to make, unless he left it to me."

"And if he had left it to you?" So much for not asking for flattery, she thought.

But he caught the playful spirit of her words. "I don't know. I haven't seen your cousins."

"All the unmarried girls have pimples and goiters, except for the one-legged one and the leper twins."

"Then Isaac is thrice-blessed, to have you be the choice."

"I can read, you know," she said.

Why did I say that? she wondered immediately. But at the moment it seemed very important to her that he know.

"I was a little surprised to see the holy writing being scratched in dirt, saying the most casual things. It . . . it's foolish, I know, but seeing every word I said getting written down made me turn everything into a speech. Something fit to be written. Only I'm not much of a speaker."

"It all sounded very elegant to me."

"Everyone can hear in Abraham's household. So I'm afraid your reading days are over."

Hearing that filled her with dismay. Because she would miss Father? Yes, of course she'd miss him, but that wasn't why she hated hearing that she would not read anymore. "I hoped I could read from the holy books."

"That's the birthright," said Eliezer.

"I didn't want to own them," said Rebekah. "Just read."

"Nobody reads them but my master and his son."

"The words of God? Are kept secret?"

"They read aloud," said Eliezer. "We hear the words."

"Oh," said Rebekah.

He got a contemplative look on his face. "Of course, the lady Sarah read them."

"But I'm not the lady Sarah?"

"You're the lady Rebekah," said Eliezer.

"Not the daughter of a king."

"I've said too much," said Eliezer. "I've told you that you may not do something, when it may be that you can do it. I have no authority."

It was Rebekah's turn to laugh.

"You find that amusing?" Oh, he was quick to take umbrage—he could laugh at her, but didn't like being laughed at.

"You have your master's trust," said Rebekah. "That looks like authority to me."

"I meant authority over the birthright," he said. "But you knew that."

"Yes."

Silence again. Except for the normal noises of camels getting settled in a strange place at night. And the distant sound of singing from the people gathered around the fire.

"So," said Eliezer at last. "If it wasn't the jewelry that made you accept, what was it?"

"Your eloquence?" she answered playfully.

"You accepted the jewelry without question, and wore it at once. I don't know why I dared to offer it, but you wore it. You decided then. At the well. Before you knew my name or the name of my master."

"I knew who you were."

This made him stand upright and look at her in real surprise.

"No, no, I simply figured it out. From what you said after I told you who I was. That you had been led by God to the house of your master's brother. I know the stewards of all my father's brothers. If a new one had been chosen, I would have known. So it had to be my grandfather, Nahor, and his only living brother is Abraham. I doubted he was looking for a bride for himself, but even if he had been, I knew I would say yes."

Eliezer looked at her with puzzlement. "You could have anyone, I would think."

"I said no to Ezbaal," she said. She was a little ashamed of bragging about it, but she didn't want him to think she hadn't had suitors.

He looked suitably impressed. "I'm not surprised that he asked. I'm quite surprised your father said no."

"My father said yes. Or would have. But I said no. It's a long story. I'll tell you on the journey, if you want to hear it. I guess stories of the doings at Bethuel's camp don't get told far and wide like the stories of Abraham."

"My master is very old. Few people come to tell him stories now. He falls asleep often, so it's hard for him to follow a tale."

Silence again.

"Are you going to tell me, or not?" asked Eliezer.

"Tell you what?"

"Why you said yes so quickly. Why you wore the jewelry without waiting to see what your father would say."

"Oh, didn't I tell you already? Because I was also guided by the Lord."

"You took no journey."

"Didn't I? I passed through the trackless wilderness of a proposal from a great man who happens to worship Ba'al, but whose offer was not to be refused. How do you think I emerged on the other side, unless God helped me? And then, for the past year, I have waited for God to show me why he spared me from an idolatrous house. Finally, this afternoon, I prayed to the Lord that it was time to bring me a true husband. If I was going to get one. The moment I finished praying, the thought came into my mind that I should go fetch water."

"But you fetch water often."

"Usually I take a turn every day or so."

"So it wasn't unusual for you to think of that."

"Eliezer, I might pour water for any stranger who asked me, too, but that doesn't mean that it wasn't a sign from God when I did it for you."

He smiled and nodded. "True enough. But I had already been on the road for a week before you prayed."

"And when you said your prayer, I had already been walking toward the well for several minutes."

He laughed out loud. "You're a sharp one," he said. "Ah, yes. You don't talk like a girl your age."

"I'm older than I look."

"What, thirty? Forty?"

"That would be telling."

"You speak with . . . authority."

"Do I? My father entrusted me to watch over the work of the women of the camp for many years."

"Instead of your mother?"

"Another long story," she said.

"Then it will be an entertaining journey back to Kirjath-arba."

At that moment Rebekah became aware of approaching footsteps. She turned to see Mother only a few paces away.

"So you find the camels better company than your family?" asked Mother, only halfway joking.

"I got lost on the way back to the fire," Rebekah answered. "I was making sure the beasts were ready to resume their journey tomorrow."

"Tomorrow!" said Mother, and she gave one barking laugh. "My, but you *are* peremptory. Did you think this was all the farewell we'd give our daughter? This is your welcoming feast, Eliezer, and a celebration of the betrothal. It will take at least a month to prepare a proper sendoff for our daughter. There are clothes to make, good-byes to be said. Of course, you're welcome to go home to your master and return in a month to bring her back. As for now, Rebekah, you've been missed at the fire, and if the party is ever to end, you have to be there to receive everyone's congratulations."

"Forgive me for delaying everyone's sleep," said Rebekah, trying hard to keep any sarcasm from entering her voice. "I've never been betrothed before, so I didn't know my duties."

"Don't get snippy with me, young lady," said Mother— again with that joking-but-still-serious tone. "Or we *will* let you go off tomorrow with this . . . this kidnapper." Mother shot him a smile of dazzling intensity. Rebekah had never seen a man who was able to resist that particular smile. And, sure enough, Eliezer was no exception. Whatever he might have been thinking and feeling, he immediately broke out into a smile of his own.

It would be so useful to have that smile, thought Rebekah. But whenever *she* wanted to get someone to do what she wanted, she always got too serious for smiling, and launched into explanations designed to persuade them. Which some- times worked but often didn't, and life would certainly be simpler if you could make other people turn into grinning dolts by flashing them a particular smile.

Soon they were back at the fire, and now Rebekah found herself the center of everything. Nobody was talking about missing her yet, but now she understood why. Like Mother, they assumed that there would be at least a month, probably more, before Rebekah left. In fact, that was probably the normal thing, and it was only Rebekah's ignorance of weddings that kept her from realizing that this feast tonight could not possibly be a farewell for her.

Except that Eliezer had assumed what Rebekah assumed—that God had not wasted any time about granting their prayers, and they would not waste any time about getting on with fulfilling his will.

Rebekah felt just a little foolish about having had Deborah spend an hour with her this evening, helping her choose which of her clothing would be useful in her new role as a wife, and which would be left behind because it was too girlish. The truth was, there wasn't all that much that was worth taking along. Abraham's household was bound to have plenty of fine seamstresses who could fashion new clothing for her. She really needed only enough for the journey and her first weeks as a bride.

Now, of course, she realized that for the next month all the seamstresses in camp would be taken from their other duties and devote themselves to sewing the clothing Rebekah would need. Mother would know exactly what to do.

The feasting wound down soon after Rebekah returned to the fire—as Mother had said it would. And that night, Rebekah slept easily, knowing that this was not her last night in Father's household after all.

In the morning, she woke early, as always, but felt a little sleepy and a little lazy, as well. The household really wasn't her concern anymore. For good or ill, it was Mother's to rule, and Rebekah could spend a little more time than usual on herself.

Deborah was delighted, of course, because she loved to play with Rebekah's hair. But they were not half done when there was a loud clapping outside her tent, followed at once by Laban's voice.

"Rebekah, are you in there?" He sounded urgent.

"Can't somebody else take care of whatever it is?" she asked.

"They want you," he said, and now she realized he was upset. "Father and Mother. And that *steward.*"

"My hair's only half done."

"You're going to make them wait for you to do your *hair?*" asked Laban.

"That question from the boy who used to tease me when my hair *wasn't* nicely done?"

"Rebekah, he thinks he's going to take you away this morning. Now. And for some reason Father is leaving it up to you!"

That was enough to get Rebekah on her feet, quickly brushing out her hair so it hung thick and wavy and unadorned, as if she were a little girl. In a moment she was outside the tent with Laban, hurrying to Father's tent.

"Laban, this makes no sense. Mother already decided I was staying, and when it comes to that sort of thing, she doesn't change her mind."

"You think she didn't argue? I tell you, she tried everything. Her laugh. Her smile. Her famous frown. That sarcastic snippy sound that unrams a man in six words. The whole arsenal. And he only smiled and said, 'My master is old. He hopes to see his son married before he dies.' He had Mother bargaining with him. If not a month, then ten days. Then a week. How can we make dresses for her—and he says, don't you think my master has dressmakers as fine as any in Haran? An answer for everything. And I was arguing too, you can be sure of that, but he says to me, 'Please don't hinder me, seeing how the Lord has blessed my errand and made it prosper. Send me away so I may go to my master.' The same thing, over and over, as if we hadn't spoken, and I guess we got so excited we stopped writing things for Father, until he finally roars for everybody to be still, and he says, 'We'll call Rebekah and see what *she* says,' and Mother is just speechless that Father would even suggest leaving it up to you—"

"Speechless? Mother?"

"Well, for a moment, but when she starts to write some kind of argument, Father takes the stick out of her hand—you know how he does that, to make us stop talking—"

"Oh, yes. I've had welts on my palms, he rips the stick away so fast sometimes."

"And so there I went to fetch you, and now here we are, and isn't this completely mad? Of course you'll—"

But she didn't wait for him to finish his sentence. Instead she walked into the tent and found the same group that had been there for the betrothal yesterday, except that this time Pillel was with them.

Mother was the first to speak. "This . . . man . . . thinks that his master is at the point of death and expects you to go, today, with no chance for farewells, no clothing, no parting gifts, no chance for me to say good-bye to the daughter I have only had for the past year—"

And with those words Mother burst into tears.

Another weapon in her arsenal?

Rebekah doubted it. Mother did not use tears the way some women did—tears weaken a woman and make her a supplicant, and Mother's other charms worked so well that Rebekah had never seen her resort to crying. Besides, it didn't sound like the demure weeping of someone doing it for effect. These were deep, heartfelt sobs. Rebekah found it strangely pleasant, to think that her mother would weep like this for her. Pleasant—not distressing. As if she were seeing it from a distance. Something happening to strangers.

These aren't strangers, these are the people I love most in all the world.

And yet, in her heart, she was already gone. All that foolishness of waiting around for clothing to be made—what was the point? She had already felt it this morning. The sense of detachment. Of having no duties here. Of already being gone.

A month of that? I'd lose my mind, she thought.

Father, seeing that no one was saying anything and that Mother was not likely to be easily comforted, turned to Rebekah and asked, simply, "Will you go with this man?"

"I'll go," said Rebekah.

Mother's weeping stopped almost at once. Proof that it had been a device after all? No—it was a sign of a deeper shock. Mother looked up at her with the face of tragedy. The face that she might have worn when her husband sent her away from her family all those years ago.

Rebekah immediately fell to her knees and embraced her mother, held her tight and close, and whispered in her ear, "I love you, Mother, but this is what I was born for, and it's my time. We had a year. Thank God for that year."

"Or curse him," Mother said—not quietly, "because a year was all we had."

"It was not the God of Abraham," said Rebekah, "who cost us the first fifteen years of my life." Then she kissed her mother to take away the sting of those words . . . though later she would realize that Mother probably assumed she meant that it was Father's fault, while Rebekah meant to blame it on Asherah.

Rebekah rose from before her mother and embraced Laban. "I hope I have sons as fine and good as the son my parents had," she said. "I hope they're as good to each other as you have been to me." He hugged her back, but said nothing, and when they parted she saw why. He was weeping—silently, but too intensely for him to speak.

Father rose to embrace her. For a moment she almost cried herself, wishing with all her heart that she could speak to him as she had spoken to the others, that just this once God would give him the gift of hearing. But as she embraced him, she spoke anyway, loudly enough that Mother and Laban and Pillel could hear her, so one of them could tell him later what she said. "You raised me to be the true servant of the God of Bethuel. Now see how he blesses me because I had you for my father." She kissed him and embraced him and now she did weep into his shoulder, not really for parting from him now, but rather for the memory of all the hours she had spent at that shoulder when she was a toddler and he carried her everywhere. It was her childhood, and the father of her childhood, that she mourned for. It was the songs she sang for him, and even if she stayed now, he would hear no singing from her.

Finally she pulled away from her weeping father and

turned to Pillel. She offered him her hand, but when he reached to take it, she pulled him, too, into an embrace. "You are a man of honor," she said, "and you have deserved the perfect trust we all have had in you."

She did not look to see whether there were any tears in his eyes. She wasn't sure which would be worse—to see that there weren't any, or that there were.

Now she was face to face with Eliezer. "I packed last night," she said. "So did my nurse, Deborah. I'll show your men which sacks and boxes to take."

Eliezer nodded gravely, his eyes never leaving hers.

"What?" she asked him.

"You," he said. "I don't know if Isaac is ready for you."

"Do you think the Lord chose the wrong bride after all?" she asked.

"Of course he doesn't think that," said Mother, her voice husky. "He thinks you're a marvel. Because you are. And I can tell you right now, no man on earth is ready for this girl, but he'll never realize it because she'll never let him see it, because that's the kind of perfect wife she'll be, and don't you forget it."

The words seemed aimed at Eliezer, but it was Father and Laban and Pillel she looked at when she spoke.

"I don't know if I'll ever forgive any of you," said Father, "that I haven't been told a word of this since she said, 'I'll go.'"

In the end, she took more than Deborah with her. Mother insisted on it—it would shame Bethuel's house if she came with only one servant. Besides, as Mother pointed out, Rebekah needed to have servants in her new home who were loyal only to her. "Any women already there will be loyal to whoever has been ruling there, and they'll be quick to find fault with you and slow to obey. You need women who need you as much as you need them. The women you take with you from this household will get enormous prestige from being closest to you. Eventually they'll marry within your husband's household, and everyone will live together in perfect harmony."

This last was said with just enough irony for Rebekah to know Mother didn't think she was fool enough to believe it. Rebekah chose five girls that she liked and who looked eager to be chosen, and as they hurried to say their good-byes and pack their few belongings, Rebekah saw to the loading of the camels. She had chosen five because the women would have to ride, and with three camels fully loaded with their possessions and supplies, there were only seven that would have room for passengers.

Rebekah gave gifts to the mothers of the girls who were coming with her, which did little to make them feel better but at least showed that Rebekah understood that they were making a sacrifice. The girls themselves varied from excitement to be seeing the world to abject homesickness, but Rebekah knew that if any of them was too unhappy she'd find a way to get her home as quickly as possible. Though it wouldn't be wise to let them know that right now.

Deborah was the only one who really worried Rebekah. The girls would be resilient, and no doubt would enjoy playing the role of confidantes of the lady of the household. They would probably shed their tears of homesickness, but they would also adapt quickly to their new home. Deborah, however, had no concept of taking pride in her closeness to Rebekah. It would be strange to her, and Rebekah did not know what she would do if Deborah were desperately unhappy.

It was Deborah herself who put her at ease. When Rebekah said something about hoping she'd soon get used to her new home, Deborah only laughed. "Silly, I've done this before. When I came here. And I'll be happy for the same reason I was happy here."

"What reason is that?" asked Rebekah.

"You, silly," said Deborah. "I have my darling girl." And with that Deborah walked away in order to submit to the indignities of being put on top of a long-suffering camel.

Soon they were all mounted and the camels were on their feet, so that Rebekah looked down on Father's camp from a point higher than the tops of many of the tents. It looked so different from here. The tents were all so small, and filled such a small space. The green-and-gold hills around the camp were so much larger. And Rebekah knew from all her previous trips from one pasture to another that these hills were not even particularly large ones, and that they went on row after row, from here to the great river Euphrates, or if you went the other way, through great mountains and then down to the sea. And even that was only a small portion of the world. Yet this camp had been her world, really, despite visits elsewhere. It had held all the people that she loved. And she would always love them, even though she did not know whether she would ever see them again. Because she would carry them with her in her memory. She would see everything with eyes they had taught to understand what they saw, and she would hear everything with ears that had learned language from their voices.

How could she ever love a husband as much as she loved her father, her brother, her newfound mother? How could she ever understand a new household the way she knew every soul in this camp? How could she ever feel that she truly belonged somewhere, the way she belonged here?

Today, there was no shortage of weeping servants, and what Rebekah had wished for last night, she had in plenty: They grieved to lose her. They had not resented her leadership. They loved her, and were sorry to see her go.

Then all the good-byes had been said, and though the sun was already warm and they were only a few hours from noon, Eliezer began to tug the lead camel, starting the procession moving forward. Rebekah understood: Hot as this day's travel would be, it was necessary to go as far as they could the first day, to put distance between them and their past.

As her own camel lurched forward—the second in the caravan, and the first with a rider—she heard Laban call out to her. She turned as best she could, in her awkward perch on the camel's hump, and saw him running toward her.

"Rebekah!" he cried out. "You are my sister, but now you'll be the mother of thousands of millions! Let your seed possess the gates of all those who hate them!"

Laban's blessing rang in her ears as they moved away into the hills. The mother of nations—is that what she would be? But that was the promise of Sarah, wasn't it?

Mine now. Because I am marrying the heir of the covenant between God and Abraham.

Possess the gates of all those who hate them. That sent a chill through her, when she thought about it. Yes, her children would become a great nation—but great nations have enemies who hate them and want to destroy them.

In our little encampment in the hills just outside Haran, who hated us? Our name is known, but no one resented us here. We were never important enough. But my children will be the chosen of God, and all those who hate the Lord will hate them.

O God of my father, she prayed, watch over my family. The family I leave behind, and the family my new husband and I will create. Let them have as much joy in their lives as I have had. And let them have no more sorrow than I have suffered. For surely none of thy daughters has ever been more blessed than I.

It seemed to her that she wept halfway to Damascus, but Deborah assured her later that she was smiling and happy during the whole trip.

CHAPTER 9

R ebekah was surprised at how new the land seemed as their caravan made its way through the hills of Canaan. Everywhere, it seemed, people were tending to new olive trees and grape stalks, or building new houses. And the coastal cities that they could glimpse, now and then, when through a break in the hills the plain along the shore of the Great Sea came into view, seemed to gleam bright and new in the sun.

Eliezer seemed to have seen everything. The hill country had been so desiccated during the great drought of the past few generations that the villages were empty ruins, and only a few villages managed to hold on to life. The rest of the land belonged to the great nomad princes in those days. But now, with the rains more dependable again—though nothing like it had been before the drought, Eliezer assured her—the people could come back. "And where water is, people follow," he said.

"You could not possibly be old enough to remember how things were before the drought."

"Even my master isn't that old," said Eliezer. "But it was written down in the scrolls. The great plain between the rivers was all grass as high as your head, with clumps of trees everywhere. Elephants roamed free then, before the great hunters like Nimrod killed them all. These hills were heavily forested—all of them, not just the great cypress forests of Lebanon. But during the drought, trees did not grow back when the old ones were cut down, and the soil turned to dust and blew away. Great clouds of it, so it was dark for days at a time, the sun just a faint yellow disk in the dirty sky."

It was hard to imagine such a cataclysm. But Eliezer assured her that the drought was nothing compared to Noah's flood.

"It wasn't just the rains or the rivers rising, the way that we see every year with the Nile or the Euphrates."

Rebekah almost laughed at that—as if she had ever seen the Nile, or lived close enough to the Euphrates to know the seasons of the river.

"The great ocean was broken up and leapt over its shores."

"How could that be?" she asked him. "The waters pouring upward?"

"All things are possible with God," said Eliezer.

"But there has to be more to the story than that."

"Isaac will read it to you sometime, I'm sure of it. There are two different versions of the story, but one of them was written in Noah's own hand, and he saw it, so it must be true."

He also explained that the cities of the coast were new. "There used to be nothing but fishing villages along the Canaan shore. But then traders came from islands out in the Great Sea, and merchants began to prosper from the trade. Abraham understood at once. These foreign merchants were tired of having to deal with the seafaring traders of Sidon and Tyre. They're hoping to establish these cities of the Canaanite coast as rivals to the Phoenician cities. But it will never work, not the way they're doing it."

"Why not?"

"Because there has to be someone to trade with," said Eliezer. "Sidon and Tyre, Byblos, Ugarit—all the great cities of the north—they're in the perfect position, between the sea and the great kingdoms of the plain-between-the-rivers. Huge caravans go from the coast toward Babylon, Sumer, Ur-of-the-South, and even beyond, to the Medes, the Elamites, the Persians, and kingdoms so far we've never heard of them. But here, what lies behind the coast? Great kingdoms? That's laughable. You can see these hill villages that are being reestablished, and beyond these hills is the valley of the Jordan, which is prosperous enough these days. But then comes nothing but savanna and desert, a land for wandering herders like us, but there aren't enough of us. We buy what we buy, but you can't build a city from the profits of trading with us."

Rebekah had never heard anyone speak like this, viewing the world as a great whole, not just individual cities and their hinterlands.

"My master sees more than that," said Eliezer, chuckling. "He knows the names of the stars, including the one closest to where God dwells."

"God lives on a star?"

"Near a star. The stars are suns, like the great fire in our sky, only very far away. And they have worlds around them also. God made them all."

Rebekah looked up at the stars for several nights after that, wondering at the thought that the world she knew was only one of many hundreds, even thousands, each possessed of its own star. Do they see our sun shining in their sky? Do they know we live?

God knew, whether anyone else did or not. God saw her world, God saw *her*, and cared enough about her to choose her to be the mother of the next generation of the birthright. There was nothing so large that God could not see it all, and nothing so small that God would not notice it. For the first time she began to realize why people clung to their idols. A god you could touch, one you made with your own hands, was somehow safer, closer. You could talk to a god that you had right in your house, or in the temple or the grove, and hope that it might hear you.

Yet it did not matter whether *you* could see your god, if your god could not see you. And those real, tangible, safe, close gods were as blind and deaf and dead as the stones or stumps they were carved from. While the living God, faraway as he was, could reach into the heart of anyone who prayed to him and listened for his answers and obeyed him when the answers came.

They wound their way farther south into rougher country, and here there were no villages being built or cities visible in the distance. The closest sea was not the Great Sea to the west, but rather the Sea of Salt to the east, and instead of the great wheeling fisherbirds, the most common flying things were

locusts skimming over the ground from bush to bush. The
men also grew more vigilant than ever, keeping watch all
night. They lit no fires now, but lived on unleavened bread,
cheese, and the wine they carried with them. "This won't go
on for long," said Eliezer to the girls when they complained.
"We're nearly there."

"But why does Abraham choose to live in such a forbid-
ding land?"

"It's not quite as bad at Kirjath-arba, where my master
keeps his camp. And among these hills there are springs and
wells, and plenty of grass. Still, you're right, it seems a miracle
that a great herding family could become wealthy in this
land—but then, it *is* a miracle, for God blesses my master to
prosper in a place where anyone else would starve. Here he is
left alone—he doesn't have to send his men out to war the
way Ezbaal and Ishmael and others who live in more desir-
able lands have to do. My master has had his times of war, but
now is a time of peace, for him and his son."

"And Isaac—is he also a man of peace?"

"Yes," said Eliezer. "He's even more devoted to the holy
writings than my master is. I think that if he didn't have duties
that forced him out into the fields and pastures, he'd spend all
day reading. It's the great joy of his life." Then Eliezer smiled.
"Or was, until now."

"What's different now?" And then she realized how stupid she was—of course he was referring to her arrival. "Oh.
We'll see how long it takes before I drive him even deeper into
the writings."

Eliezer just laughed. "No one is *that* attuned to God."

They came out of a particularly rough passage on paths
that seemed invisible, they were so stony, though Eliezer and

his men gave no sign of having to search for the way through—they walked it as surely as she walked the path from Father's camp to the well of Haran. Before them was an oasis, a green place with orchards and bean fields and vineyards, as well as pens for animals and several tents. Still, the tents seemed few for the camp of a great lord, and so she asked doubtfully, "Is *this* the camp of Abraham?"

"Oh, no," said Eliezer with a laugh. "You'll know my master's camp when you see it. This is the well of Lahai-roi. These fields belong to my master, of course. But any land given over to tents is land you can't farm, and so we keep this place empty of people except for those actually working the soil and tending the trees and vines."

"Who is that man walking through the fields? He seems to be coming to greet us."

Eliezer looked where she was pointing, and then gave a grunt of surprise. "It is the son of my master."

"My husband?" she asked, suddenly breathless.

"I didn't know he'd be at Lahai-roi." Eliezer looked at her as she tried to arrange her hair. "It's no use," he said. "No matter what you do, you still look beautiful."

"I do not," said Rebekah. "His first sight of me should not be like this, filthy from traveling."

"Too late, don't you think?" said Eliezer.

"Make my camel kneel, please," said Rebekah.

At Eliezer's command the caravan came to a halt and Rebekah's camel went to its knees. Eliezer reached to help her down, but she had done this often enough to know how to alight from a camel on her own. Lightly she sprang to the ground, and, keeping the camel between her and Isaac, she quickly found what she needed. She pulled the veil from the sack where she had packed it, and put it over her head.

"What are you doing?" asked Eliezer.

"My husband's first sight of me is not going to be looking like this."

"So it's better he sees you with a sack over your head?"

"A veil."

"I know it's a veil, you wore it during the windstorm on the third day of our journey."

Deborah was also off her camel, and she helped Rebekah tie the veil in place.

"He'll think I found him a woman so ugly she has to be hidden from view," said Eliezer.

"He'll think what he thinks," said Rebekah.

"Then again," said Eliezer, "if he saw you looking as lovely as you did atop that dromedary, he might think that I chose you for beauty alone. This way, he'll know you couldn't possibly have been chosen by anyone but God."

Rebekah knew he was gibing with her, but she could not banter in reply. She was too frightened. This was not how it was supposed to be. She was supposed to come into camp and have a day in her tent before she had to emerge to meet anyone. It was not supposed to be in a field, with him covered with the sweat and dirt of the day's work, and her grimy with travel, her hair windblown, the inextinguishable stink of camel permeating her clothes.

And yet . . . this had not been an ordinary courtship by any standard. She had accepted him without seeing him, without even hearing his name mentioned, because she knew that it was God's will. Would he not be just as obedient to the Lord?

I don't want him to marry me because of obedience, she realized. I want him to marry me for love.

But that was absurd. What was prettiness? Hadn't she hidden her face for years because she did *not* want to be loved for a face that happened to have no oversized or misplaced features?

She didn't know what was right. She only knew that she was afraid, and in the veil she felt safer.

She stood beside Eliezer as Isaac passed among the bean plants. He was a tall man, and slender, though he had the arms of a shepherd—arms that could carry a goat or restrain a sheep for shearing. He was not as young as Ezbaal, but there was no white in his beard or his hair, and he moved with the vigor of youth, leaping over as many rows as he stepped through. But despite his smile, she saw something sad in his eyes. Why should that be? What sorrow had he known, this man who was born as a miracle?

"Why is he so sorrowful?" she whispered to Eliezer.

"Sorrowful?" he answered. So apparently he didn't see what she saw in her husband.

"Eliezer," called Isaac. His voice was deep and rich, his word clear.

"Master!" answered Eliezer. "As you can see, I succeeded in the errand your father sent me on!"

Isaac finally reached them and greeted his steward with an embrace. Rebekah was glad to see that—he was a man who could show affection to a servant, who could value a man as a man. Then, as he and Eliezer exchanged pleasantries about the work in the fields and whether the journey had been hard or easy, he cast his gaze among the girls still perched on their camels, finally alighting on Deborah and then on Rebekah in her veil.

"I saw no one wearing a veil when I first caught sight of you," said Isaac to Eliezer.

"The lady was afraid she might blind you with her beauty," said Eliezer.

Isaac was obviously not sure how to take this. Nor did Rebekah much appreciate his little joke. "Eliezer thinks I was foolish to cover myself," she said, "but I am pretending that this meeting is not happening, so that you can see me for the first time clean and rested, not weary and filthy and stinking from the road."

Isaac smiled at her. "So we are not really talking."

"This is all illusion," she said. "A dream."

"And yet everything else about the day is real." He touched his chest. "*I* am real."

"They told me nothing about you, sir," said Rebekah, "except that you serve the God of Abraham, as I do."

Deborah piped up from behind her. "He's tall. And he has a pretty face."

Isaac grinned at Deborah. "I know flattery when I hear it. I'm Isaac, son of Abraham. If this weren't a dream, I'd ask you your name, my lady."

"I'm not a lady," said Deborah, blushing. "I'm only Deborah."

"My nurse," said Rebekah. "I grew up without a mother. It's Deborah who filled that place in my childhood, and even now in my heart."

"I am honored to meet the mother-in-her-heart of my bride." He turned to Eliezer. "Am I to be told her name, or is this one of those frustrating dreams where you find out every-thing except what you most need to know?"

"Sir," said Rebekah, "Eliezer has quite a story, and I'm sure my name will come up in the telling of it. Meanwhile I am eager to reach our destination, so I can prepare myself to meet the man I have promised to marry. So why don't you two talk while the camels keep moving?"

Isaac raised an eyebrow and smiled at Eliezer. "Shy enough to wear a veil to meet me, but not at all shy about letting her wishes be known."

Rebekah blushed under the veil. So she shouldn't have made the request. But it would have been intolerable to have everyone stand there in the hot sun, making no forward progress, while Eliezer told him all that had happened. And despite his jesting comment, he apparently agreed with the wisdom of her plan, for he came to her and offered his hand. "May this man in your dream offer you his insubstantial hand to help you rise onto your imaginary camel?"

"The camel, sir, is real," said Rebekah. "Because I never have such pungent stinks in my dreams."

She put her hand in his and leaned on him lightly as she leapt up onto the camel's rigging. In a moment she had her-self arranged, and it was Isaac who gave the command for her camel to rise, and he took her camel's reins and walked beside her. Eliezer had no choice but to come back and walk beside him. So she was within earshot as Eliezer told the story of his prayer at the well, and the sign God gave him.

Isaac heard of the signs and wonders without comment. Only at the end, when Eliezer had told him how it was Rebekah's own choice that made it possible for them to begin the return on the very next morning, did Isaac speak. And that was only to say, "And when she came to the well, Eliezer, was she wearing the veil? Or did she have a face then?"

"She had," said Eliezer, "the loveliest face I have ever seen."

"Ah," said Isaac.

"But that was not why I chose her," said Eliezer.

"No, of course not," said Isaac. "God chose her."

They walked in silence for a little while.

"But I have one question," said Isaac.

"Yes?" answered Eliezer.

"If she had been ugly, would you have asked her for a drink?"

Rebekah laughed. "Now *there* we come to the boundaries of faith," she said. "Eliezer chose a sign that allowed him to pick which girls to ask for water."

"It's a good steward who takes every precaution," said Isaac.

Eliezer shook his head. "You can joke about a sign from God."

"I'm teasing *you*, Eliezer," said Isaac. "Not the Lord God." He looked up at Rebekah. "One thing that isn't clear to me," he said. "Am I dreaming you, or are you dreaming me?"

"Both," she said.

"Then I hope you'll forgive me if I say that, pleasant as this dream is so far, I can't wait for it to end, so I can meet the woman whom, with Eliezer's prior approval, God has chosen for me."

"I am also eager for the dream to end," said Rebekah.

"Because it's hot under that veil?"

"Because I left my family to become your wife, not to ride a camel. Because now it feels as though everything up to now has been a dream, and I'm ready to awaken and begin my real life now."

Isaac nodded and said nothing, then turned again and smiled up at her. "You could not have said anything that would have made me happier."

Were his eyes glistening as he said it? Had she touched his heart? That wretched veil, it kept her from being sure what she had seen.

They talked on as they journeyed. Isaac answered her questions about the fields and orchards that they passed, and she answered his questions about her family and her uncles and their families. And more than once, as she saw his bantering wit, his kind way of speaking to and about the men and women they passed in the fields, and the keen understanding he brought to every subject he discussed, she silently spoke her thanks to God for letting her husband be such a man as this. There was none of Ezbaal's arrogance. Isaac wasn't trying to impress her with his authority or strength. He was simply being himself. Or if this was a pose, at least he had the wisdom to know that posing as a simple, good man would impress her far more than posing as a great lord. And if he weren't a simple, good man, how would he know how a simple, good man would act? No, this was no pretense. He was the kind of man she could love. The kind of man whose love she wanted to earn.

Everything was perfect, except for the veil on her face, which began to seem completely unnecessary, something meant to help her cope with a fear she no longer felt. She almost took it off, except that the moment the thought formed and her hands began to move, she was filled with dread. What if he didn't like her? Right now he was talking with a stranger behind a curtain. When the veil came down, when she passed through that curtain, would he greet her with a smile and say, Ah, it's you, I've been waiting for you. Or recoil and say, I don't know you.

"There is one thing," said Isaac, "that you ought to know before you reach the camp."

"Only one?"

"One that Eliezer didn't know," said Isaac.

Eliezer visibly perked up.

"Father has taken a woman."

"What?" said Eliezer.

"A concubine, not a wife. Keturah."

"How interesting," said Eliezer.

To Rebekah, it sounded as if he were saying, "What a disaster."

"He assures me that none of her children will be in line to inherit, and he said it in front of her, so there'd be no misunderstanding." Isaac chuckled. "Then he told me that beyond that, it was none of my business."

"Keturah," said Eliezer, "will have a hard time taking the lady Sarah's place."

"Mother's place," said Isaac, "has not been taken. I didn't come out here to Lahai-roi merely to watch for your coming, though I confess I spent more time watching the canyon mouth than working. I also brought something else."

He indicated a direction with his head, and Eliezer looked and laughed.

Isaac explained to Rebekah. "My mother's tent. Keturah may warm my father's bed in his old age, but she isn't the lady of the camp, and she won't have anything that belonged to my mother."

"I take it Keturah is not your . . . friend."

"Oh, she's a very dear friend. In fact, she offered herself to me several times. A couple of the offers came from her father, a Canaanite merchant with an enormous fortune, and a couple came from her. The first two had a dowry attached, quite a nice one. The second two offers came with . . . no complications other than the loss of my soul because of sin."

"Ah," said Rebekah. A woman who was determined to be part of Abraham's family, one way or another, front door, back door, or under the side of the tent if need be. "So it's true love."

"I think she's sincere enough. She believes in God, but takes rather a personal view of him. Thinks the only way to worship him is to be married to the birthright, one way or another. It was partly because Father was afraid I might marry her that he determined that I could not delay my marriage any longer."

"Was there any danger of succumbing to her charms?" asked Rebekah.

Isaac looked at Eliezer, who looked back at him with a smirk. "She's a charming girl," Isaac said. "Very ambitious. Very possessive. Very . . . *organized.* While she's there with Father, I don't plan to spend much time in Kirjath-arba. Lahai-roi is a good place. And besides, my mother's tent is here."

"I appreciate your giving me this information. It will be useful, I think," said Eliezer.

"Father's a little prickly about this, because he thinks I'll be jealous that Keturah is so in love with him."

"And you're not."

"I'm annoyed," said Isaac, "but not for any reason he thinks. The problem is that if I make any complaint about her, he won't see it as a legitimate problem, he'll see it as my finding fault because I'm jealous."

"But Abraham is a just man."

"If it came to an all-out conflict between me and Keturah, I would prevail, for many reasons. Father's loyalty to his son. His memory of my mother. And the fact that in any quarrel between me and Keturah, I would be completely in the right." He grinned at Rebekah. "But I foresaw that the bride my friend Eliezer would bring home for me would immediately seem to Keturah to be a dire threat to her place as queen of the camp."

"Queen?"

"In all but name, and I suspect she whispers it when she thinks Father is asleep and no one else can hear. My concern was that you should not begin your married life having someone criticizing you and complaining about you constantly. Even though I would support you completely, why should Father's old age be filled with conflict between his bride and his son? So we will set up our home here in Lahai-roi, and visit Father when we are invited, or when we choose. I thought you could bear Keturah's charms more easily knowing each time that you would soon go home to a place where she has no authority."

"That was very kind of you."

"Not that I want to bias you against Keturah," said Isaac. "Please form your own opinion of her."

Eliezer glanced at Isaac with a sly smile.

Then, to Rebekah's surprise, Isaac turned her camel's head to the left and led the caravan off the main path toward the camp at Lahai-roi. A few minutes later, the camels were all kneeling, and servants were helping the girls down from their mounts. Rebekah was pleased that Isaac delegated Eliezer to help her down from her camel, and went himself to help Deborah. It was the perfect gesture of respect, exactly what would have been owed to Rebekah's mother, had she been there, and Deborah was flattered and delighted by it.

Isaac had already determined which tent would be for Rebekah's women, and either he had supposed she might have a chief servant or he was improvising, but either way he had a tent which he designated as belonging to Deborah alone. "I fear you will be lonely," he said, "never sharing a tent with Rebekah again, so if you wish any of the other girls to sleep in your tent, you have only to tell me and it will be a great honor to the ones you choose. And when you wish to sleep alone, that will also be done."

What Rebekah heard was that Isaac had very firmly informed Deborah that there was no possibility of her sharing Rebekah's tent now.

"My betrothed is noble of heart as well as birth," said Rebekah.

"And for the woman whom God has brought to me, I have no fine new tent to offer. Only this old one, much used." And he gestured toward Sarah's tent.

Tears came to Rebekah's eyes. "I thought you brought it here to keep it from Keturah."

"I brought it here," he said, "so it could be the home of the woman most precious to me, as it has been all my life."

"I hope," said Rebekah. "With all my heart I hope. That I will be precious to you."

"You already are," said Isaac. "God has gone to great pains to choose a wife for me. I'd have to be a fool not to love the gift as well as the giver."

Rebekah reached up, untied the neck-binding of the veil, and pulled it off over her head. If her face had been grimy before she put it on, it was now streaked with sweat, and hair that had been windblown before was now matted and wet. "You see me at my worst, sir," she said. "But how could a stranger enter your mother's tent?"

"I promise you, she cleans up nicely," said Eliezer.

Isaac reached out and took a bead of sweat from her cheek with the back of one finger. His touch was gentle, yet her skin tingled where he touched her. "My wife will see me sweaty with work or filthy from travel, and I will see her that way many times as well. And we'll see each other at our best, too. But never will she be more beautiful to me than she is this moment. I see nothing but goodness in your face. That is your beauty, Rebekah."

Quite before she realized it, tears streamed down her face. Of relief. Of . . . no, it was too soon for love. But of gratitude, yes, and admiration for the perfect kindness of his words, of the gesture of letting her dwell in his mother's tent. And also because she thrilled at the way her name sounded when it came from his lips. "Oh, Isaac," she said. "Did those words . . . did the Lord give them to you?"

"No, sorry," said Isaac.

"Don't be sorry," said Rebekah. "I hoped they were your own."

He took her by the hand and led her to a small altar built of fitted stones. No bullocks could have been sacrificed here, it was too small, and besides, the stones looked new-cut, and there was no staining of ashes. Still holding her hand, Isaac knelt across the altar from her, and with very simple words promised her she would be his wife forever. Then he told her the words she was to say to him, and she said them. With only Deborah and Eliezer as their witnesses, while the rest of the camp was busy installing Rebekah's maids in their tent and unloading and caring for the camels, Isaac said the words that bound them together in a marriage with no end. Her sons, he added, would be his only heirs, as he was the only heir of his father.

Then he leaned across the altar and kissed her.

"Now," he said, "the woman who enters my mother's tent will be my wife, and from that moment it will no longer be known as Sarah's tent, but as the tent of Rebekah. Now, dear girl, you're filthy and you smell like a camel. Go in and clean yourself up and change clothes, and then come out of the tent of Rebekah to be presented to my household as my wife."

"I thought . . ."

"Is something wrong?" asked Isaac.

"I just thought . . . that your father would have to give his permission first, or at least meet me."

"My father gave permission when he sent Eliezer on his errand. And he *will* meet you, but not as a girl waiting to be married. He'll meet you as my wife."

Rebekah imagined how it might be, Isaac presenting her to his father and his father's concubine . . . and realized something. "You are protecting me," she said. "When I first meet Keturah, I'll already outrank her."

"My dear wife," said Isaac, "you outranked her the day you were born. I married you here because who are we to delay what the Lord has ordained? All that kept us apart was distance, and when that was gone, there was no reason to delay." He leaned down and kissed her again. His lips were gentle, too, and yet the kiss was firm, and his hands on her shoulders were strong yet not forceful.

"A boy will be waiting outside your tent," said Isaac as he led her to Sarah's tent. "When you're ready for Deborah or any of your other handmaidens, you have only to speak loudly and he'll go fetch whomever you want. He'll make no mistakes. He's a clever boy, and I asked him to know the names of all your servants within the first few moments they were here."

"No one has ever . . . no one has ever watched over me so carefully," she said. Though in a sense she had been carefully sheltered all her life, what she meant was that no one had watched out for her *feelings* or tried to anticipate what would make her more comfortable.

"Well, soon we'll become completely used to each other and you'll be watching out for me as much as I watch over you," said Isaac. "Now go inside. My people are eager to meet you."

Inside the tent, Rebekah took a few minutes to look at what was there. The furnishings were simple yet of the finest quality. If these were indeed Sarah's rugs and Sarah's bed, Sarah's boxes and jars and table, then her taste was exquisite, that of a queen who had nothing to prove to anyone, and so made no gaudy display; but neither was she ashamed to own things of the highest quality.

But if these are Sarah's possessions, what will it be like for him to come to me here, and love me in the way a man loves a woman? Won't his mother's shadow loom over us? Every-thing he sees here will remind him of his childhood at her knee.

Without offering the slightest disrespect to the memory of

Sarah—indeed, Rebekah was fascinated by the great lady, and longed to know everything about her—she nevertheless had to make sure that from now on, when Isaac thought of this tent, when he saw the inside of it, he would not immediately remember his mother, but would remember Rebekah instead.

She called for Deborah, and in only a short time she was there. Within an hour, Rebekah had been thoroughly washed and her hair plaited like a bride's. Then she sent Deborah from the tent with instructions to go tell Isaac that Rebekah was ready.

Deborah looked at her with concern. "But—"

"Go," said Rebekah.

Deborah went.

Soon she heard a soft clapping outside her tent.

"Isaac?" she asked.

"I'm here," he said.

"I'm afraid to go out and meet your people," said Rebekah. "Could you come inside for a moment to encourage me?"

The tent door opened and Isaac stepped inside. It took a moment for his eyes to adjust to the darker interior.

"Who is encouraging whom here?" asked Isaac.

"You are," she said. "Before you present me to your people, shouldn't I present myself to you?"

"Eliezer has no idea how nicely you clean up."

"Isaac, God brought me here to conceive a child," she said. "Not to meet your household." She took the two steps that closed the distance between them. "Let's put first things first."

He seemed to think it was a good idea. And here inside the tent, he was the same man she had seen outside it—a man with strength who chose to be gentle, a man with authority who chose to be kind. She had always thought it would be frightening to know a man this intimately, but with Isaac her fear was gone almost before she had a chance to notice it.

It was Isaac, not Deborah, who helped her dress and assured her that her hair looked perfectly arranged. And if his judgment was not perfect on that matter—Deborah did a quick fix as soon as Rebekah emerged from the tent—she was perfectly content that he thought she looked perfect despite her imperfection. It was a promising beginning to a marriage that would shape the future of the covenant between God and Abraham. Because, as Rebekah well knew, a man could serve God with all his heart and still rend his family apart, misshaping the lives of his children in the process. It was not possible that a man like Isaac could make any such mistakes.

PART IV

THE SEED
OF
ABRAHAM

CHAPTER 10

Contrary to what Rebekah had been led to expect, Keturah was flawlessly gracious. She embraced Rebekah at once and seemed genuinely dismayed that the wedding had already taken place, and insisted that there would still be a feast as if the wedding still lay in the future.

"Isaac was beginning to be like an aging uncle," said Keturah. "He was just pottering about mumbling things from the holy books and looking confused when anybody talked to him. But now—it's as if you took twenty years off his age!"

"I hope he doesn't do the same to me," said Rebekah.

Keturah looked puzzled for a moment, and then laughed. "Of course! You're not twenty years old yourself, are you! I am, though. Barely!"

"Still, that's not such a great difference in our ages."

"It's our husbands who are old men!" Keturah laughed aloud at her own joke. Then she leaned close to Rebekah. "I notice you had the self-control *not* to look around and see whether Isaac heard me. That's good—some women think their husbands are *babies* and have to be protected from everything."

Rebekah wanted to say, Even a grown man might wish to be safe from insult in his father's house, but in truth Keturah had said nothing wrong, and perhaps the only reason Rebekah felt snippy about it was because of what Isaac and Eliezer had said just before they arrived at Isaac's camp. All Keturah was doing was trying to make friends with her.

Or . . . perhaps she was asserting seniority because of her age, so Rebekah would not challenge her leadership of the women.

"I think," said Rebekah, "that Isaac is planning for us to live at Lahai-roi. I hope we visit here often enough for us to become friends."

Keturah's expression changed to one of mock dismay. "Oh no, it's going to be awkward for a few days."

"Why would it be?" said Rebekah.

"Because Abraham is absolutely determined that his grandchild—the birthright grandson, to be exact—is going to grow up right here where he can keep an eye on him."

"Well, perhaps that's a decision that can be made when I've actually given birth to such a child," said Rebekah.

"I don't know. When Abraham gets an idea in his head . . ." She leaned close to Rebekah, as if confiding a secret. "He's a very old man, you know, and he gets impatient when people don't see things his way immediately."

"I'm sure everything will work out," said Rebekah. "No need to think about that now."

"I hope you *do* end up living here," said Keturah. "Even though it does mean you'll be ruler of the women."

Rebekah at once protested, though in fact she was relieved that Keturah had brought up the subject and declared her own disadvantage so cheerfully.

Keturah dismissed her objections. "Don't be absurd, Rebekah. I may be a wife here, of sorts, but I'm not *the* wife."

Rebekah did not say that technically a concubine was more servant than wife. "I'm not *the* wife either," said Rebekah. "I'm the son's wife."

"But he's *the* son, and that makes you *the* wife. The one who will bear the birthright boy."

"May God grant that prayer," said Rebekah.

"If he hasn't already," said Keturah.

Did she really say what Rebekah thought she said?

"Oh, don't blush and look shy. Isaac has been shockingly chaste. I assumed the reason he married you so quickly was because he couldn't wait a moment longer!"

Rebekah looked away, not wishing to continue that line of discussion. "I wonder what I should call him."

"Your baby?"

"Your husband." She had always thought of him as Uncle Abraham, but now he was her father-in-law.

Keturah laughed loudly. "Oh, everybody calls him Father Abraham except me, I just call him Abraham. In public. What I call him in private is *private*."

She grinned as if she was dying to tell. But Rebekah continued to look off into the distance and said nothing to encourage *that* topic, either.

So Keturah went on. "And Isaac, of course, he just calls him Father." And then, as if it were a secret: "One thing you have to know—in this camp, what Father Abraham decides is what *will* happen. He talks to God, you know."

"So I heard," said Rebekah dryly. "But that's how it is with every herding family. The patriarch is the judge and lawgiver. He's what a king would be, in a city."

"Only the kingdom is very small," said Keturah, laughing.

"In this case," said Rebekah, "the kingdom is very large."

"Well, for a *camp* I suppose it is, but I've seen the cities of the coast."

"Really? All of them?"

"I've actually *been* in Gerar."

"It must have been impressive," said Rebekah. "I hear it's almost a tenth of the size of Byblos, and Byblos is large enough to be considered a good-sized town in Egypt." Rebekah felt just a little bad about letting herself get caught up in a contest of words with Keturah, but there was something about her that just made Rebekah want to argue.

"Oh, I know, all those magnificent places, so far away. Abraham's been to Egypt, you know."

"I've heard stories," said Rebekah.

"But still, how can you call Abraham's camp a *large* kingdom, if you're going to go comparing Gerar to the cities of Egypt!"

"Because Uncle Abraham's kingdom is the whole world, Keturah," said Rebekah.

Keturah looked at her as though she were out of her mind. "Well, I think King Abimelech of Gerar would have a different opinion."

"The name Abimelech suggests that he's a worshiper of Molech," said Rebekah. "And if that's the case, then he believes, at least in principle, that it's a good thing to burn children alive to please his god."

"What does *that* have to do with the size of kingdoms?"

"It means that in the eyes of the only true and living God, Abimelech is a petty king serving the most vile of false gods. While Uncle Abraham has the birthright of God, which lifts him above all kings of all lands."

Keturah got a strange look on her face. "You don't really believe he's above all kings."

"You're his wife, and you *don't?*"

"I just . . . no one ever said it quite that way. But now I think about it, I suppose it's true. What an odd thought. That here in this camp, the shepherds take their instructions from . . . the king of the world."

"Let's just call him the steward of the kingdom of God."

"Now you *are* joking, to call Abraham a steward! That's making him like Eliezer!"

"To God," said Rebekah, "Abraham *is* like Eliezer."

"My husband is no servant," said Keturah, getting a little upset.

"All human beings are either servants of God, or servants of his enemies," said Rebekah. "So I think your husband would prefer you to think of him as the servant of God."

"Now I know why Abraham won't let women even look at the holy writings," said Keturah, and she turned her face a little, putting an end to that line of conversation.

Which was fine with Rebekah, because Keturah's last remark stabbed her to the heart, though Keturah could not have known that it would. Uncle Abraham wouldn't let women so much as *see* the holy writings? Keturah must have misunderstood. Or maybe *she* had been forbidden to see them because she was so flighty that . . . no, there was no use in speculating. She would simply ask him. He couldn't refuse her. She could *read*, after all. And if she was trustworthy enough to be wife to one heir of the birthright and mother of the next, surely she could be trusted to *look* at the writings that were part of the birthright.

Deborah rescued her from the stalled conversation with Keturah by coming to whisper to her about how one of the handmaidens was being very forward with some of Abraham's shepherds. Keturah overheard and started to say, "Oh, let girls be girls," but Rebekah was already on the way. Let girls be girls? Well, why not let lambs be lambs and wolves be wolves? What would happen to the flocks then? Deborah knew better than Keturah the consequences of letting young people go wherever their desires might lead them. The whole idea of caring for children was to keep them from doing stupid, dangerous, wicked things that could not be undone, until they learned enough self-control and good judgment that they could be expected to make their own decisions. Not one of these girls was at such a point—least of all the one who was flirting, since the very act of enticing a shepherd who had been alone in the hills for weeks or months was proof enough of idiocy.

Naturally, the flirt—Miriel, a girl who was certainly of marriageable age—was pouty and resentful when Rebekah called her away and warned her against giving some shepherd the wrong idea about her availability. But it was one of the other girls who, overhearing it all, made the obvious retort: "It's easy for you, *you're* married!"

"For a day," said Rebekah. "And what kind of marriage do

you think I would have had if I had been the kind of girl who went about flirting with shepherds?"

Miriel gave one sharp bark of a laugh.

"What was funny about that?" asked Rebekah, trying to keep anger out of her voice.

"You were never going to marry a shepherd," said Miriel. "But that's who we *are* going to marry. Like our mothers did."

It was a telling point. Rebekah started to answer with some kind of explanation about how *these* shepherds weren't looking for more than a momentary wife, when she heard Isaac's voice from behind her. "You're mistaken, girl," he said. "That's exactly what Rebekah *did* marry."

Of course all the girls blushed and hid their faces and the sillier ones giggled, but Rebekah realized that of course he was right. She wished she had thought of saying it herself. Except that it was better coming from him; if she had said it, it might have sounded as though she were denigrating her own husband, who was, after all, heir to the birthright, and not just a shepherd at all.

When she pointed this out to him as they walked toward Abraham's tent, Isaac only laughed. "Still a matter of shepherding. People don't understand what it means to be a shepherd. You aren't master of the sheep. They're too stupid to have a master because they don't understand obedience— only imitation of the other sheep, and fear of predators. No, a shepherd is *servant* of the sheep, protecting them, bringing them to food. And that's what we are to all our people— weren't you shepherding those girls? And with the holy writings, well, they have a life of their own, much greater and longer than my own life could possibly be, and I will only serve them for a time."

"And part of that," said Rebekah, "is keeping them from danger."

"There are predators," said Isaac. "Sometimes I wish no one knew about the birthright. There are those who think that if they could get their hands on the holy writings, it would make them prophets, like Father."

"Has anyone tried to steal them?"

"Father is a great man, and people fear his wrath. It may be a different story when a weaker man has the birthright."

It took Rebekah a moment to realize that Isaac meant himself. "You're not weak," she said, wrapping her arms around his waist.

"I was pleased to see how strong *you* are," said Isaac, deflecting her reassurance. "There you were, speaking like a stern mother to a girl who has to be older than you."

"Oh," said Rebekah. "Well, yes, I am, but I . . ."

"But you have been mistress of your camp. Eliezer told me something of your life. To believe your mother was dead when she was not—I don't know if I could ever . . ."

Forgive. She knew what word was next. She looked up, expecting to see anger. Instead, she saw that his eyes were full of tears.

"Isaac," she said. "What's wrong?"

"Just . . . my mother," said Isaac. "Thinking of my mother." He brushed away a tear. "As I said . . . a weaker man."

"I hope," said Rebekah, "that someday I have sons who love me so much they would shed a tear for me a year after I died."

"I have no doubt that you will be such a mother," said Isaac.

"And you will be a father like Abraham," said Rebekah.

But to that, Isaac said nothing, and she wondered why not.

Uncle Abraham's tent stood in splendid isolation, on the top of a knoll, and there were men whose sole duty, apparently, was to keep people from approaching, for unlike the tents of most great patriarchs, there was no busy coming-and-going. Yet the work of a patriarch was to deal with the needs of his people; how could Abraham rule if he saw no one?

She understood, however, when she saw him, for he was older than any man she had ever seen. He sat in the door of his tent, on a low stool with a back to it, so he did not have to keep himself upright, and he seemed to be asleep, though his left hand trembled slightly even in slumber. His face was gaunt, hollow under the cheekbones, as if each year had eaten away a little at his cheeks until he had only a parchment's thickness of skin hiding his teeth and jawbones from view. Indeed, his face seemed little more than a skull with skin and wisps of hair and beard reaching out in every direction as if they grew with no goal but to escape by whatever route they could find.

If Isaac had said, "Oh, look, Father seems to have died," Rebekah would not have been surprised. But then, as they approached, the old man's eyes fluttered open and he slowly turned his head to regard them. He moved no other part of his body and said nothing until at last they were standing before him.

"Sit down," he said. "Don't make me lift this old head."

His voice was thin and reedy and full of air, like a whisper with only a hint of melody in it. It was hard to hear him.

They sat on a rug that had been laid out for visitors. There was a patch of bare earth between their rug and his, and for a moment Rebekah found herself reaching for a stick so she could write, as she had for so many years written every word she said to Father. But if Abraham was deaf, no one had mentioned it. She held the small stick she had picked up and played with it in her fingers, feeling a little foolish.

"She's a beauty," said Abraham.

Rebekah bowed her head.

"The Lord has been kind to me," said Isaac.

"Couldn't wait for me to perform the marriage," said Abraham.

Isaac said nothing.

Abraham said nothing. Waiting for an answer?

Finally Rebekah spoke. "The Lord seemed to be acting in haste, and so we hurried," she said. "I hope we did right."

"*You* did what your husband said," Abraham answered. "No one can fault *you*."

Still Isaac said nothing.

"Talk to me, Isaac," said Abraham. Then, to Rebekah, "He's stubborn when he's pouting."

Was Abraham trying to tease Isaac out of his silence? If he was, it didn't work. Rebekah did not look at Isaac, though, for that would seem a tacit admission that she, too, thought he needed to speak.

"What am I to call you?" asked Rebekah. "All my life I've spoken of you as Uncle Abraham."

"Call me Grandfather," said Abraham, "so your children will learn to call me that."

Rebekah realized at once that this was the good choice, for no one else in camp would be bearing him grandchildren—it was a name for her alone to use, at least until she had children who could speak.

"Grandfather," she said, "I hope you'll pray that I conceive a son very quickly."

"I pray for that every day," said Abraham. "I don't know how long I have to live, and I want my grandson close to me." He coughed—a weak, empty cough that seemed to shake his whole body to produce only the slightest of sounds. "I don't mind this nonsense of camping out at Lahai-roi for now, but when that first son is born, you two will come home."

Finally Isaac spoke. "Thank you for the invitation, Father," he said. "I'll consider it."

"Why do you defy me?" asked Abraham.

Isaac said nothing.

Abraham spoke to Rebekah. "I won't have this boy growing up soft. Too close to his mother. Women can't help it, they treat their boys as babies far too long, and it breaks their spirit. I indulged Sarah because she treasured Isaac, but at what cost to him?"

She could hardly believe he was criticizing Isaac this way in front of her. The tension between father and son was so thick that Rebekah felt as though she could hardly breathe. But then, as she thought about it, Isaac wasn't the only target of Abraham's soft, sharp words. How dare he assume that just because she's a woman, she would be too indulgent with her son?

Maybe nobody else stood up to Abraham in this camp, but Rebekah had no intention of turning over her firstborn son to this old man to raise. "You aren't suggesting that you intend to take our son away from us and raise him yourself?" asked Rebekah.

Abraham coughed again, then laughed dryly. "Oh, that would be sad, wouldn't it. A baby raised by an old man who

REBEKAH

has to sit in the sun just to keep his body from getting as cold as death in the middle of the day."

"We'll do all things according to the will of the Lord," said Isaac softly.

Abraham spoke to Rebekah instead of Isaac. "He sounds obedient, doesn't he? But I know defiance when I hear it." He turned to Isaac. "And I've done nothing to deserve that attitude from you, my son. Nothing but give you all that I have."

Rebekah could not keep still. "He wasn't defying you, Grandfather, he—"

"'According to the will of the Lord,' he said," Abraham echoed. "Meaning that unless I'm prepared to say the Lord told me they must live with me, he's not going to do it."

"That's not at all what he meant. That's—"

"That's exactly what I meant," said Isaac.

The words hung in the air like the aftermath of a thunderclap.

Abraham finally broke the silence. "You see the dangers of interpreting for your husband."

"She's loyal," said Isaac. "To her family. And to God."

"Eliezer told me the story of her refusal of Ezbaal," said Abraham. And he began to laugh. It sounded like reeds brushing against each other in a breeze.

Isaac also laughed, a deep, throaty sound that was rich with life.

There they were, laughing together, and Rebekah was baffled. Until this moment it had felt like a war between them—the last thing she had ever expected—and yet now they were laughing like old friends. What was going on between them?

"Poor Ezbaal," said Isaac.

"The Lord chooses strong women for us, my son," said Abraham.

"She's already standing up to *you*," Isaac pointed out.

Rebekah wanted to protest, but of course he was right, so what was the point of arguing?

"I've never had a shortage of people who stand up to me," said Abraham. "In my old age, I wasn't wishing for yet another."

"The Lord sends us what we need, not what we want," said Isaac with a smile.

"I hate it when you quote me to myself." Abraham turned to Rebekah. "Let me tell you right now, so you know: I like you. I like everything I've heard about you and I like what I've seen. But if the Lord wants somebody else to make the decisions here, all he needs to do is take me home. I'm ready whenever he wants me back. Until then, I'll listen to what you have to say, but I hope you'll do me the same courtesy. At least try doing it my way before you decide I'm wrong."

"Grandfather," said Rebekah, "in all matters pertaining to your household, you'll have my perfect obedience. But I, not you, am the one the Lord chose to be the mother of my children. And if he wants someone else to do that job, all he needs to do is have me die in childbirth. It happens all the time. But if I'm still here after our first son is born, then I *will* be his mother."

Abraham studied her for a moment, smiled broadly, then turned to Isaac. "Mark my words, she'll spoil the boy."

Did that mean he was giving in? Rebekah thought not. He was merely choosing not to press the issue further right now.

"I'll make sure she doesn't," said Isaac. "But for the moment, I'll be content if the Lord gives us a boy in the first place. And just so you know, Father, Mother never spoiled me. She was harder on me than you ever were. Perhaps you've forgotten how rigorous she was."

"I miss your mother too, you know," said Abraham. "Every hour of every day, I have things I want to tell her. And ask her. And show her. It's as if I lost half myself."

Once again Isaac said nothing, and this time Rebekah knew enough to keep silent herself.

Abraham, therefore, was the one who broke the silence, explaining to Rebekah, "Isaac doesn't like it that I took Keturah as a wife."

"I'm perfectly happy for you," said Isaac. "I appreciate your waiting until Mother was buried."

His voice was completely level, not a hint of sarcasm, but Abraham recoiled as if someone had thrown something at his eyes.

"Your mother is my wife forever," said Abraham. "Worlds without end, she's half my self."

Isaac said nothing.

Again, Abraham directed himself to Rebekah. "He was always with his mother like a moth around a flame, darting everywhere but never very far."

Abraham seemed to expect some kind of answer from her, but as long as Isaac wasn't answering, Rebekah did not want to say anything more. She had already gotten herself into enough difficulty.

But no one was speaking, and Abraham was looking at her with such intensity that she could no longer keep still. "I wish I could have known him as a child," said Rebekah. "But I grew up hearing legends about his birth."

"Ah, the legends, the stories," said Abraham. "The myths, the outright lies. Gossip. Slander. Scandal."

"Miracles, that's all I heard," said Rebekah.

"Truly?" asked Isaac.

"In my father's house," said Rebekah. "I once heard something else from visitors, but in my father's house, there were no stories but of God's goodness to Abraham and Sarah."

"Then you heard the truth," said Abraham. "God has blessed us beyond all measure."

Again a silence fell, but at least this time it didn't follow some jab from one of the men, or some foolish statement of Rebekah's. It seemed contemplative.

"I wish I had known her," said Rebekah.

They both knew she meant Sarah. "She was born to be a queen," said Abraham.

"I thought it was her older sister who—"

Abraham interrupted her with a sharp dry laugh. "Qira. If she was a queen, so is every ewe in the flock. So much strength, but all of it devoted to getting her own way, and none of it to serving her husband or her children."

"Father likes to tell about Qira," said Isaac, "because it always amazes him how different two children of the same father can be."

Again a silence fell, and for some reason Rebekah thought that this was the awkward silence following a thrust in their duel. But who did the stabbing this time? And who was stabbed?

Then she put it together. Abraham's remarks about how soft Isaac was because Sarah was too protective of him. And now Isaac talking about how different two children of the same father could be. It was about Ishmael. Isaac was making a jab at himself. And Abraham was letting it stand.

But why? Ishmael was a great lord of the desert, everyone knew it—he was feared by anyone who might be his enemy and shunned by his rivals, who dared not face him. He went where he wanted, from well to well, and took what he needed. He was also known as a generous man, but when you can take anything you want, simply leaving people with what they already had can seem like generosity. He was ostensibly a worshiper of the God of Abraham—at least it was said that he bowed down to no other god. But he was certainly not what anyone could call a holy man, not in any of the stories Rebekah had heard.

If Abraham thought her husband was weak, surely it did not imply that he thought Ishmael was strong!

Whatever was going on here was too deep for her. If it wasn't a war, it was some kind of struggle between father and son. Yet when they laughed together—she had never seen Father and Laban seem so close, so at one with each other.

One thing was certain. She did not dare bring up what Keturah had said, about women being forbidden to see the holy writings. If he was already talking about needing to oversee the rearing of a grandson that hadn't even been conceived yet, the last thing she needed to do was to give him grounds for thinking of her as even less trustworthy than he already did.

So she asked for the one thing she had wished for in her and Isaac's hurried wedding. "Grandfather," she said, "will you bless our marriage?"

Isaac moved next to her, and she looked up to see him gazing at her. Had she said something wrong?

"My wife is wiser than I am," said Isaac. He turned to Abraham. "Will you, Father?"

Tears came to Abraham's eyes. "The old man still has a few blessings in him," he said. "Come here, children. Kneel before me. Hold hands, yes, like that." And there on the spot he gave them a blessing such as she had never heard Father give in all the marriages he had blessed. Abraham promised them great blessings in life and after they died as well, and he placed them under the covenant that he himself had made with God, that as long as they obeyed the Lord they would be blessed with progeny as numerous as the sands of the sea or the stars in the sky.

At the end of it, Abraham put a hand on her shoulder and said, "I love most in all the world the kind of people who put themselves in the Lord's hands with perfect trust. Eliezer told me that you were that kind of person. As long as you bend to the Lord's will, I can put up with a little defiance of mine. Not a lot, but a little." He smiled. "My son deserves to be happy. I think, with you, he will be."

Rebekah found herself weeping. This was the Abraham she had longed to meet, not the old man gibing at his grown son, but the voice that pierced her to the heart with the words of God. She could feel the power of what he was saying; it was the way she felt when God had filled her with the knowledge of what she was to do. Peace and perfect trust, that's what it was, knowing that God held her in his gaze for this moment, and knew her, and loved her, and wanted her to be happy.

That night there was feasting, and all the next day Rebekah was introduced to Abraham's servants, and to friends and visitors who had come from nearby to meet the wife of Abraham's heir. There was singing and dancing. The food was magnificent, the stories enthralling. They could not have shown her more honor.

But none of it could still the fire that burned in her from having Abraham rest his hand upon hers and Isaac's and blessing their marriage to last forever, like his own marriage with Sarah, even beyond the gateway of the grave.

She did not even mind so much the disappointment of not having seen the holy writings.

After all, someday they would be Isaac's, and he would make his own rules about who could and could not see them.

CHAPTER 11

A t the time, her life seemed full of worries and little disasters—a quarrel with Keturah that led to a spiteful silence that lasted nearly a month before Abraham finally intervened; Miriel running off with a boy from a nearby village, only to come back two months later, tearful and pregnant; Isaac's refusal to ask his father to let Rebekah look at the holy writings, or even to explain to her why he wouldn't. Years later, however, looking back at these first years of her marriage, Rebekah would think of them as an idyllic time and yearn for the simplicity of her life then.

After all, these problems were solved easily enough. Keturah's constant efforts to provoke a quarrel and get Abraham to side with her against Rebekah ended soon after the birth of Keturah's second son, when Rebekah had not yet conceived any child at all. That was victory enough, and when after only five years she was nursing Medan and Midian while Zimran and Jokshan played at her feet, she could finally afford to be magnanimous to her poor barren stepdaughter-in-law. What threat could a childless Rebekah possibly be to Keturah? Instead of finding reasons to prevent Rebekah from visiting Abraham's camp, Keturah issued an endless stream of invitations, to Isaac's and Rebekah's amusement. They might even have been irritated at how Keturah loved to play the matriarch and display her children, but it was so much more pleasant now that the one-sided war between her and Rebekah was over that neither of them could complain.

As for Miriel, Rebekah and Isaac together approached a worthy man among the farmers of Lahai-roi and offered him his freedom, and Miriel's too, if he would marry her and raise her child as his own. Eliezer had a few caustic words to say about how, with rewards like that, they'd soon find all the girls in the camp pregnant, but Rebekah pointed out that none of the girls envied Miriel or wanted to emulate her. And Rebekah's other handmaids served much more happily now that Miriel was not among them, constantly complaining and goading them to be resentful of everything along with her.

In a way, the person most affected by the whole incident with Miriel was Deborah. When the girl came back pregnant, this of course stirred Deborah's memories of the young man who had seduced her in her youth, and her first reaction was to announce cheerfully to Rebekah, "Now Miriel can be nurse to *your* baby!"

"Deborah," Rebekah said, "even if I *had* a baby, which I don't, Miriel would be my last choice to nurse her."

This disturbed Deborah to the point of tears, and it took hours of tender questioning before Rebekah could finally help Deborah figure out why this had made her so sad. Finally the words came, as much a surprise to Deborah as to Rebekah: "You hate Miriel because she's just like me!"

Rebekah was so surprised that she laughed, which sent Deborah into a new fit of crying until Rebekah could explain to her that Miriel was nothing at all like Deborah. "Miriel's careless and complaining and lazy and irresponsible, while you're the opposite—careful and patient and hard-working and dependable all the time."

"But she was bad and had a baby when she wasn't married, and so was I."

"You were both young at the time, but you were an innocent child who was deceived by a man, while Miriel was definitely *not* innocent and asked for what she got."

"Eliezer said that she should be stoned to death," said Deborah.

"That's the law, but nobody uses it against young unmarried girls like Miriel. That's for married women who betray their husbands."

"I would never do that," said Deborah.

"I'm glad they made you my nurse," said Rebekah, "and if there were a girl here just like you were in those days, then if I *had* a baby she could be the nurse. Because I couldn't imagine a better gift for my children than to have a nurse like you as they grow up."

Yet Deborah burst into tears again, and this time they were deep, wracking sobs. It was not hard to find out why she was crying this time, though. "I miss my baby so much," she said. "Why didn't they find me a husband like Isaac's going to find for Miriel?"

"*Try* to find," said Rebekah. How could she explain to Deborah that she had been doubly unmarriageable because of the simpleness of her mind? "And maybe they would have, only that was when *I* needed you, and they gave me to you instead. I'm sorry you only had me when you would rather have had a husband."

It was a shameless manipulation, but it had the desired effect, as Deborah hastened to reassure Rebekah that she'd rather have been her nurse than have a hundred husbands.

Later, though, when the whole Miriel affair was settled, Rebekah talked to Isaac about Deborah's reaction and said, "The thing that surprised me most was that she could shed tears for her baby as if she had only lost the child yesterday."

"To her that's how it seems," said Isaac.

"I suppose it's part of her simplemindedness, that the passage of time doesn't make the sorrow fade," said Rebekah.

Isaac laughed ruefully. "No, I don't think so, or all parents are simpleminded."

"Do you mean that with all the babies that die young, their parents still mourn for them nearly twenty years later, as if they had only just died?" She thought of her mother. She must never have stopped grieving over losing her children.

"Maybe those who have other children to comfort them are better able to keep the grief at bay," said Isaac, "but they never forget, and the memory of the child they lost is always like a knife in their heart."

She had never felt so young and unobservant. "How are you so wise about it?" she asked.

"Because my father never got over losing Ishmael," said Isaac.

That baffled Rebekah. "He didn't lose Ishmael. Ishmael is very much alive and has twelve sons and is one of the great lords of the desert."

"My mother made him send Ishmael away to keep me safe," said Isaac, "and so Father lost him when Ishmael was twelve, and never had that boy in his life again. Only the grown man—grown and raised by his mother. Hagar was one to hold a grudge forever, I can tell you, and when he returned here as a grown man to make peace with Father, he wouldn't speak to Mother and Mother wouldn't let him come close to me, which made Ishmael storm off in a rage. It broke Father's heart, to lose Ishmael. And he still mourns for the happy child Ishmael once was."

"You can't know what Ishmael was like. You were just a baby when it all happened."

"I heard the story of how Ishmael was sent away. And all the rest of it I either saw for myself or heard from Father."

"Ishmael couldn't hate you for something that happened when you were an infant."

"As if hate went by logic or justice," said Isaac. "Very well, perhaps he doesn't hate me. Perhaps when Father dies he won't come down here with all his men and burn the tent down over our heads and kill me and you and any children we might have."

Isaac said this very mildly, but Rebekah was shocked. "Is that something you think is possible? That he would do that?"

"That's what Mother feared. No, expected. She was the one who insisted that all our shepherds be trained for war, even though Father was at peace with everyone."

"But you," said Rebekah. "What do *you* think?"

"I think the Lord will fulfill his promises to Father, and I think it will be our children through whom those promises are fulfilled."

"But that doesn't mean Ishmael won't try it, is that what you're saying?"

"Even Father only knows as much of the future as the Lord shows him."

"Why doesn't Ishmael hate your father then? He's the one who sent Hagar away."

"A man hate his own father? Make war on his father? Ishmael may have been raised on hate and vengeance, but to strike a blow against your own father would make him a monster in everyone's eyes. He'd have no friends in the world, and only the worst of his men would continue to follow him."

"But he might kill a brother."

"Half-brother. Who stole his inheritance simply by being born. Rebekah, you only had the one brother; you don't know what it's like. There's no one you love like a brother, and no one you hate like a brother, too."

Which opened her eyes to an aspect of her husband that Rebekah had not thought of before that day. Just as Ishmael had been raised in hatred and vengeance, so Isaac had been raised in fear of what Ishmael would one day do to him. Both mothers had poisoned their children in the effort to protect them and teach them their place in the world. And yet Isaac could still say, There's no one you love like a brother.

Isaac loved Ishmael. Who could have guessed it? The great desert lord, the raider and wanderer, whose herds were rumored to cover the grassland from horizon to horizon when he was on the move, whose twelve sons were said to be so mighty with the sword that each one could lead an army, so that if a nation made war against Ishmael he could conquer twelve of their cities in a single day. And Isaac, the quiet herdsman and farmer, the man whose anger showed only in his silences, who led his people with wisdom and a willingness to listen to all—Isaac loved Ishmael.

As for the holy writings, Rebekah had few chances even to ask about them. She knew that Isaac went to Kirjath-arba often in order to study with his father the writings of the birthright, and when he returned he often told her stories from the records, or recounted revelations received by prophets in times past. He told her of the great flood in the days of Noah—a story she had heard since her childhood, but without ever knowing why the Lord caused the flood to destroy Noah's people. He told her of the great prophet Enoch, who built the city of Zion and by the power of God hid it from his enemies. He told her of Adam and Eve, of Shem, Ham, and Japheth; of the great tower built by Nimrod in the middle of the plain-between-rivers, to imitate the mountains the prophets climbed to speak to God; of the way the Lord humbled Nimrod by confusing the languages of the people he had gathered to build Babel. And there were more recent stories, of Melchizedek the king of Salem, of Abraham himself and his trials and visions, of the first Pharaoh and his false claim to have the birthright, of the way every form of writing in the world was an attempt, like Pharaoh's, to create holy writing in imitation of that which had been kept by the servants of God since Adam's time.

Rebekah listened to everything, fascinated yet frustrated, for always Isaac told the stories in his own language, plain and simple, and Rebekah was sure that he was leaving things out in order to keep his wife from being confused. She wanted to shake him sometimes and say, Haven't you known me long enough to realize that I'm not Keturah? That I don't need everything simplified in order to comprehend it?

She tried to prove her worthiness to have the full account by asking questions of such detail that he would eventually give up and say, Read it yourself! But all he said was, "Please don't frustrate yourself trying to understand what's out of reach. When God wants his children to know more, he tells them; but until he tells us, we have to be content with what we have."

Then she decided to show him that she could read and write. Of course, there was a danger in it, too—after all, many years had passed between the time Father learned to write and the time he taught the letters to Laban and Rebekah, and he admitted at the time that he wasn't sure he had all the marks correct. Nor could she remember which marks were the ones Father had doubted. So she might show nothing more than her ignorance. Still, if she could show that her writing was mostly correct, wouldn't that convince Isaac to show her the mistakes and prepare her to read the holy writings?

She left him notes scratched in the dirt near his tent door, where he would have to see them. Later, the notes would be swept away, and he would know the information she told him, but he said nothing about the fact that she could write until finally she could stand his reticence no longer and asked him outright whether her writing was correct.

Being Isaac, he said nothing.

"You must tell me," she said. "You seem to understand my writing. But Father was never sure he had all the letters right."

"They're good enough," said Isaac, "for writing to a deaf man. But I'm not deaf."

"I know you're not deaf, Isaac, I just wanted you to help me learn to do it correctly."

"You want me to make Father furious when he finds out I've been preparing *you* to receive the birthright."

Rebekah was appalled. "I don't want the birthright, I just want to read the writings myself!"

Isaac looked at her as if she had just mooed like a cow. "What do you think the birthright *is?*" he asked.

"To *have* the writings, not just to read them!"

"How do you think we protect them, except by keeping them out of other people's hands?"

"I don't want them in my hands," she said. "I want them in my head."

"And I've been putting them there," said Isaac. "Story by story. I know you hunger for the words of God, and I honor you for it. I think that's why God chose you to be the mother of my heir. But don't reach for things that haven't been given to you by God."

"And how do you know the ability to read and write wasn't given to me by God?"

"Because it was given to you by your father."

"As yours was given to you."

He went silent on her then, which meant he was very angry.

She hated it when he was angry. "I'm sorry," she said. "But I hungered for this all my life."

"Adulterers hunger for adultery, too, but it doesn't mean God wants them to have it."

That was such an outrageously unfair, inapt comparison that she wanted to scream at him that she was not so stupid as to think those two hungers were even remotely alike, and that she hoped *he* was not that stupid, either.

Instead, she merely asked one more question. "And how

do you know Father's deafness was not caused by God precisely so that I would be able to read and write?"

Isaac said nothing, but for once that was just fine with Rebekah. It let her leave the tent with her last words hanging in the silence. Let him think about *that*.

Well, if he thought about it, it made no difference, because nothing happened, nothing changed.

Such things nibbled at her during those years, making her fretful and frustrated, so that she forgot to notice that she was almost completely happy. She had a loving husband who, except for a couple of minor disagreements, gave her complete trust and freedom to rule the women of his camp. She had quickly won the respect and then the affection of the women, and the girls she brought with her, once the Miriel situation was cleared up, fit in with the household as smoothly as she could have hoped. She was free to worship without any nonsense about images to help the servants keep their minds on God. And even when she did have conflict, as with Keturah for the first few years, she was able to sidestep any kind of confrontation and live in peace.

There was only one problem she faced that was real, and that was the fact that she had no child. Yet this real problem was the one that troubled her least, for she knew that the Lord had chosen her to be mother of Isaac's heir, and she remembered the story of Sarah, so she had no reason at all to doubt that, when the Lord was ready, she would have at least the one son required in order to preserve the birthright. So when Keturah and others offered their kind remarks meant to encourage her that she, too, would have babies, even if she never had as many as Keturah, who now was up to six sons and four daughters, Rebekah accepted their encouragement with a smile and went about her business untroubled. She did not even pester the Lord about it very often, though now and then she offered a prayer like the one she had said the evening that Eliezer came to the well at Haran: "I know you're going to give me a son, Lord, and it occurs to me that now is as good a time as any."

Then a month would pass without a child in her womb, and she would sigh and think about something else. And even though she sometimes felt a bit of impatience, she never doubted that eventually she would have a son.

When she wasn't distracted by these concerns, she spent her days doing the kind of work she had done in her father's household—but the burden was lighter. The camp at Lahai-roi was only one part of Abraham's vast holdings, and Rebekah sometimes suspected that Abraham had made sure that the less reliable servants were assigned somewhere else. At other times, though, she thought that the reason Lahai-roi was always peaceful and harmonious was because of Isaac's way with people. He listened to everyone and was always calm. No one could tell him a tale of some outrage committed against them and get him furious before he heard the other side—a trap that Father had sometimes fallen into. Everyone knew that with Isaac, judgment would be just. There were no favorites. And since Rebekah herself had always tried to be just as even-handed—though she was never able to keep her silence the way Isaac could—the women lived together as harmoniously as the men.

She remembered how Father's camp had been at Haran, during the year after Mother came home, and how Mother had, without really meaning to, stirred up almost constant turmoil, and she was grateful that she and Isaac worked together so well. And it wasn't just that they didn't interfere with each other. She respected his judgment; she asked his advice. If he didn't ask for hers, that was no surprise—after all, he had been doing this work as an adult before she was born. But when she made suggestions to him, he listened, and when he agreed with her, he used her advice and told the people that it was her idea. That had to be part of the reason the women had so readily accepted her—they knew she had Isaac's respect because he showed it.

She came to believe that besides being husband and wife, they were friends, the way it was said that Abraham and Sarah had been friends, treating each other as equals.

It was as perfect as life ever gets, except that they had no son.

They were in Abraham's camp to celebrate the circumcision of Keturah's sixth baby boy, Shuach, when the peaceful course of her life as Isaac's wife began to turn. She and Isaac were used to these events—it was Keturah's sixth son, after all, and they left for Kirjath-arba expecting the usual festivities. But to their surprise, a large group of tents and several holding pens for camels and other animals had been erected in a place of honor, so near to Abraham's tent that it was obvious many servants' tents had had to be moved to make room. Isaac, Rebekah, and their party stopped on the first high ground that gave them a view of the changes. Deborah and two handmaids—new girls, the original ones all having married or returned to Haran—and the few men needed to bring the lambs that would be Isaac's share of the sacrifice, his gift to the baby, and his contribution to the feast, all waited patiently while Rebekah waited for Isaac to say something.

Which, of course, he did not do for the longest time.

Finally, as she so often did, Rebekah offered her best thought. "Is it Ishmael?"

"He's never come to a circumcision of one of Father's sons since . . ."

He let the sentence dangle unfinished.

"Since your own," Rebekah said.

Isaac's silence was his yes.

So she would meet the famous Ishmael and see the brothers together with their father. She knew at once, though, that nothing about this would go well for Isaac. Ishmael had come with style—his tents were new and clean and bright-colored, and from the number of animals he had brought, his gifts would make Isaac's look paltry.

Rebekah tried to put a good face on it. "If he came with so many in his group, I'm glad he brought enough animals to help feed them!"

"Ishmael would never want to use up any animals that are part of my inheritance," said Isaac.

There was no obvious tone of sarcasm, but Rebekah had not lived with this man all these years without knowing that this was about as openly nasty as he usually got. And if he was this snide—for Isaac—upon first seeing that Ishmael had come for the circumcision, what would happen through the rest of the day?

"I wonder if he brought his wife, or any of his sons."

"I'm sure he did," said Isaac, "since I don't have any."

It was the first time Isaac had ever reproached her for her barrenness, and it stung. "You have a wife," said Rebekah, a little acidly.

"That's where I'll have the victory," said Isaac, and he turned to her and smiled. It was a warm smile, but there was sadness in his eyes. Then he walked on down the path, and Rebekah followed him.

Thank you for trying to make me feel better, she said to him silently. But today I would rather have a face like a locust if it would put one child in my arms.

Once they got to camp, things were worse than Rebekah had anticipated. What was roasting over the fires was not kid or lamb or calf, but deer—Ishmael had gone hunting and brought venison for the feast. She would have known it by the smell even if she hadn't seen the spitted carcasses, and she thought of offering to cook the lambs they brought for the feast in the way she had learned as a child, so that it would smell and taste like venison. But she thought better of it at once. It was not Isaac's way to try to match his brother; rather he would declare himself the loser immediately and praise Ishmael's gifts without giving a sign that it even troubled him that his own were small by comparison. And the worst thing would be to make it look as though Isaac were trying to imitate Ishmael.

Besides, Isaac would immediately tell everyone that the reason his lambs tasted like venison was because Rebekah was so clever, deflecting all praise to her. There was nothing she could do to help. This would play out however it played out, with Ishmael doing whatever he came to do, and then they would go home to Lahai-roi and forget about it.

It didn't take long, once they got to the camp, to meet Ishmael. He was a bold, loud man—much more like Father, Rebekah thought, than like Ezbaal—and nothing like Isaac or Abraham. He hailed Isaac from several rods off and strode briskly toward them, calling out Isaac's name and opening his arms for a hearty embrace. Isaac greeted him with seeming cheerfulness and matched his energy in the hug. Of the two of them, Isaac was the taller, so it shouldn't have seemed that Isaac was getting swallowed up by Ishmael, but that was how it looked. There was something large about Ishmael, something in the way he carried himself, as if all the air for six spans around him turned when he turned, and moved with him when he walked.

Then it was time for introductions, and Ishmael did indeed have three of his sons with him—the second oldest, Nebajoth, who was a grown man, and the two youngest, Naphish and Kedemah, who looked to be in their middle teens, with only boys' beards. "I didn't really plan to bring them, but then I didn't plan to come, either," said Ishmael, his voice carrying, Rebekah was sure, into every corner of the camp and probably throughout the surrounding hills. "But these lads were with me across Jordan visiting with cousin Moab when the runner came with word that Father had yet another son, and all of a sudden I realized—here's Father having more sons, when Malchuth and I have had all that we're going to have and feeling content with them. And I said, 'Let's go visit Father and beg him to stop before he passes me up and I have to take another wife just to stay ahead!'"

Oh, how he laughed at his own joke—and so contagious was his laughter that so did everyone else, including Isaac. Including Rebekah, though she stopped at once when she realized what she was laughing at. For Ishmael had, indeed, managed to make the first thing he said to Isaac a barely-disguised sneer at the man who was not even in this supposed competition to see who could have the most sons.

Rebekah wanted to say, We'll have a son in the Lord's good time, and unlike your sons, our son will have the birthright and the covenant of Abraham. But that, of course, would be a vile thing to say, so she kept it to herself, trusting that anyone with any sense would think it anyway.

Apparently Ishmael had not brought his wife or any of his daughters, or if he had, they were not out and about. And Keturah was still in confinement, so that Rebekah was spared the personal humiliation of having to be compared to women who had borne children—for she knew Ishmael would not shrink from using her barrenness as another reproach to his brother.

"I wish I had known you were coming, Brother," said Isaac. "All I have are the small gifts I brought to honor the baby. My hands are empty when I greet my elder brother."

Those were loaded words. It might even be taken as an affront, calling Ishmael the elder brother when it was Isaac who had the legal status of firstborn son. But after only the barest moment of hesitation, Ishmael beamed and hugged Isaac again. "I need no other gift than to see my brother and know that he's glad to see me."

Then Ishmael turned to Rebekah. "By Ba'al's left nostril, is this what you married?"

It was an appalling statement that left Rebekah completely confused. Here in Abraham's own camp, he swore by Ba'al. But then, he did it in a way that was more mocking than real. And how was she to take his impersonal reference to her?

"This is my wife, who was given to me by God," said Isaac, putting his arm across Rebekah's shoulders.

"God has a good eye for women," said Ishmael.

Did he mean it as flattery, and was simply inept at it? Or was it a calculated blasphemous insult? Rebekah had no idea what was intended, and so had no idea how to respond.

Except, as Mother had shown her, it was never wrong to be courteous. Affixing Ishmael with her best imitation of Mother's killer smile, Rebekah approached him and raised a hand in greeting. "I grew up hearing the name of Ishmael in my father's house. I'm honored at last to meet a legendary man."

"Gossips, that's all they are, the people who spread those tales. Do you know that I've already heard tales about *you?*"

Here it comes, thought Rebekah. "I hope some of them, at least, are kind."

"Oh, they all are. The stories I've heard compare you with Sarah—Isaac's mother, you know, the runaway priestess and all that."

There it was, the comparison with a woman who, for many years, was thought to be as barren as sand.

"I'm honored that anyone might think I resemble Abraham's wife." There, let him chew on that for a moment— a public reminder that Sarah was Abraham's wife, and Ishmael's mother was never more than a concubine. Not even that much, really. Sarah's servant, and no more.

"I hear Sarah was beautiful when she was young," said Ishmael, seemingly undaunted. "There's even a story that you're *so* beautiful that when Isaac took you to Gerar and he did that same business that Father did with Sarah in Egypt— you know, saying you're his sister, and then all of Gerar is cursed until King Abimelech finds out that you're married and so on and so on."

"I've never been to Gerar," said Rebekah.

"Oh, I didn't say I believed the stories. Though now that I see you, the part about your being beautiful enough that someone might kill for you—I believe *that.*"

This was going too far. Whether he meant it that way or not, his last statement could be taken as a threat against Isaac, and Rebekah wouldn't have it. She turned to her husband. "Shouldn't we go to your father, Isaac, and let him know that we're here?"

Ishmael would not be so easily deterred. "Look how she deflects praise—beautiful *and* modest."

For once Isaac answered for her. "She's a virtuous woman."

Ishmael turned and muttered something to his sons, who tried to contain their laughter. Though few heard the words he said, it was obvious that whatever joke he made had been in response to Isaac's calling her virtuous. There was no way not to be insulted.

Except that Rebekah had heard his joke. She had spent years learning to hear even muttered remarks, so she could write them down for Father. If she were to keep this from becoming a quarrel—or a sign of cowardice when Isaac did not turn it into a quarrel—she would have to respond to the insult directly.

So she faced the onlooking crowd and said, loudly, "I think you might not have heard my brother-in-law say, 'That explains why she's barren.'"

The shocked silence grew, if possible, even deeper. Ishmael blushed to have his words openly repeated—it was, truly, a churlish thing to say—and the smiles disappeared from his sons' faces.

Until Rebekah laughed. "You silly man," she said, as if he had only said something playful, rather than an insult designed to diminish her and her husband in everyone's eyes. "Don't you know that the Lord takes his time when he's about the business of creating the next generation to have the birthright? It does no good to try to hasten the Lord. I'm sure there's a story about that floating around somewhere."

She knew perfectly well there was—the story of how Sarah, despairing of ever having a child, gave her handmaid Hagar to Abraham to have a child on her behalf. The son born from that union was Ishmael. His existence was owed entirely to Sarah's trying to "hasten the Lord."

He understood her perfectly, of course, and nodded at her for having landed a blow in their little war of words.

"Well, I can see I'm going to enjoy visiting here a lot more often than before," said Ishmael. "Finally there's someone I can joke with who answers me gibe for gibe."

Rebekah could not resist deflating his patronizing attitude. "What gibe?" she asked innocently—so innocently that everyone laughed.

Apparently, that exchange had been enough to satisfy Ishmael's need to shame Isaac—or perhaps Rebekah's retorts had been bold enough to make him think twice before insulting her again. Whatever the cause, Ishmael became affable and stopped making barbed remarks. But the damage had been done. Isaac was enveloped in a cloud of deadly silence, and everyone knew he had been shamed, even if most of them weren't quite sure how it had been done.

And there was more to come, though this time not directly from Ishmael's mouth. With all of Keturah's other sons, Isaac had performed the actual circumcision under Abraham's direction, since the old man's hand wasn't steady enough to perform such a delicate operation safely. This time, however, Ishmael asked—publicly—for the privilege of circumcising his youngest half-brother. "It was at my birth," said Ishmael, "that circumcision was first commanded as a mark of the covenant. And I've circumcised all my own sons, and all my servants, too—I'd like to think I have a deft hand with the sacred blade."

Rebekah murmured to Isaac, "And to think that all these years *you've* been doing it with an ax."

She didn't know whether Ishmael heard her or not, but he turned to her and flashed her a huge grin. She regretted at once that she had not kept her sarcasm to herself. It only made Isaac look bad, to have someone murmuring snide remarks into his ear.

Worse, though, was the fact that Uncle Abraham had noticed her whispering, even though there was no possibility that he had heard her. "What did you say?" he demanded. "I didn't hear you, Rebekah. What did you say?"

"I simply didn't know," said Rebekah, "that it was anything more complicated than a straight cut. Does Ishmael scallop the edges?"

Ishmael laughed heartily. "It's not really the cutting," he said. "It's taking off as much as you can without removing anything that should be left attached."

"It's not a matter of skill," said Abraham impatiently. "Isaac has circumcised five of my sons. Why not let Ishmael circumcise this one?"

Once Abraham had spoken, no one was interested in arguing the point. So it was Ishmael who stood before Abraham and made the baby give that little screech at the sudden discovery that really painful things could happen now that he was out of the womb—even with adults standing around watching.

Ishmael could not resist showing off a little. As Shuach

cried lustily, Ishmael turned around, brandishing the knife, and asked innocently, "Anyone else?"

Rebekah laughed because it was genuinely funny, and yet was angry because this was a solemn occasion and not a time for jokes.

Then Abraham stood up slowly from the ground, Eliezer and Isaac helping him to rise, and reached out to take the baby. "Serve God all the days of your life!" he said to the baby.

Then he turned to Rebekah and said, irritably, "And how long am I supposed to wait for my grandson?"

She couldn't believe he had asked her such a thing in front of everyone.

"That's a question better asked of God," said Rebekah, "than of me."

"I'm old, and I want to see my grandson before I die!" Abraham turned to Isaac. "Why haven't your prayers been granted, that's what I want to know. What sin stands between you two and the favor of the Lord? Is it yours, or hers?"

Was Abraham joking? Rebekah had no way to tell—the remark was so outrageous that it had to have been meant ironically. But even if it was intended as a jest, it wasn't funny.

Isaac said nothing, of course.

Except that this time he should have spoken, Rebekah thought. It was wrong of him to leave her undefended. "I have repented of every sin I've known of as soon as I recognized it," said Rebekah, "and prayed for God's forgiveness. But if you know of any other sins I have committed, I'd be grateful if you would take me aside privately and tell me about them."

If Abraham noticed the implied complaint that he was accusing her so publicly, he gave no sign of it, except to turn from her to Isaac. "You're a high priest, aren't you? Ordained with the power of God? Well, use it!"

Ishmael was enjoying all this enormously, Rebekah could see, even though he kept his head down and seemed to be concentrating on cleaning his knife.

Isaac finally answered. "I don't trouble the Lord, asking for blessings he's already promised to give."

"What does that mean? Aren't you even praying for a baby? Is that it?"

"We pray," said Rebekah.

At the same moment, Isaac answered, "Of course not."

Oh, thought Rebekah. He *isn't* praying for a baby?

"You taught me," said Isaac, "that it's foolish to pray for the sun to rise, when the Lord has ordered the universe in such a way that it always rises."

"Yes, well, are you always having babies?" asked Abraham.

"The Lord has said that I will," said Isaac.

Ishmael spoke up. "I think the Lord promised Father that his descendants would be as numerous as the sands of the sea, but I've never heard that the promise was limited to his descendants through you." Ishmael was smiling, but to Rebekah his envy and bitterness seemed painfully plain. "I've given him twelve grandsons, which isn't a bad start."

Isaac looked at his older brother mildly and said, "I can wait for the Lord."

"Well, you might think of *me* in all this extravagant patience and meekness of yours," said Abraham. "I'm not going to live forever, much as it might seem that way." Abraham smiled at both his sons, and Rebekah saw how deftly he and Isaac had kept Ishmael's envy from provoking any kind of confrontation.

Then Abraham turned to Rebekah. "You asked me to name the sin that's keeping you from having a baby. Well, now I know what it is. Pride! You two are so proud of having perfect faith that you haven't even bothered to humble yourselves and *ask* the Lord for a son!"

Rebekah longed to make some sharp retort—something about how much good it did for him and Sarah, given how long the two of *them* prayed for a baby. But one does not affront the patriarch in front of company. Especially when arguing with him would involve insisting that yes she *was* humble.

"Father," said Isaac, "as always, I am taught by you. Rebekah and I will return to our tent at once and pray for the Lord to grant us a son. I will pray that the next circumcision in this household will be that of our boy."

He took Rebekah's hand and led her through the crowd of family and servants, which parted for them.

In the tent, Rebekah stopped by the door and, with a suppressed cry of rage, she waved her arms around like a madwoman. "I could scream," she said when her momentary childish display was over.

"I appreciate your controlling that impulse," said Isaac. "I appreciate even more the fact that you did not argue with Father. He never used to be this way, when he was younger. He just . . . says what's on his mind. He didn't mean to shame us."

"But he *did* shame us all the same," said Rebekah. "We've done no wrong."

"I'm not sure about that," said Isaac. "Maybe it *was* a kind of pride, for me not to pray for a son."

"It was faith, not pride," said Rebekah. "And one thing's certain. I will never raise our children under their grand-father's control. The last thing children need is someone who always says whatever's on his mind. They're too fragile for that."

Isaac looked at her with deep sadness in his eyes. "But what if it would be better for our son to be raised under the influence of a stronger man than me?"

"There is no stronger man than you," said Rebekah.

To which Isaac answered not a word.

He stood in the middle of their tent—not the largest guest tent, either, since Ishmael had that—and raised his arms toward heaven and began to speak to God. Rebekah loved to hear Isaac pray, because he did not speak in a public voice meant to be heard by others, and there were no fine phrases. Rather he prayed as if he were talking to a dear friend or lov-ing father, his voice full of love and trust as he poured out his heart in simple language. .

He asked the Lord to forgive him for not praying before. "I don't know why I didn't, but it's an evil spirit that counsels a man not to pray, and I'm glad you inspired Father to wake me up to my error." He explained how much he and Rebekah longed for a child. One of the things he said touched her espe-cially. "Rebekah is the greatest blessing a man could have in his life. She has brought me nothing but happiness, and gives the same gift to all the people around her." Rebekah was pretty sure this wasn't actually true, but she was glad her husband thought so.

"She deserves to have this reproach taken away from her,"

Isaac went on. "Fill her arms with sons, Father. Whether her husband is worthy or not, *she* is worthy."

He went on, talking through all his feelings, all his hopes and dreams for his sons, along with all of Rebekah's yearnings that she had shared with him over the years—and some that she had not. As he talked, tears came to her eyes and finally streamed down her cheeks, for she could tell that his words were not coming only from him, but God was in them; God was teaching her husband the words he should say to God in prayer.

Isaac, too, wept in the midst of his entreaties.

But when he was done with the prayer and sank to his knees and bowed his head, as worn out as she had ever seen him, even after a day's work, she realized there was one thing he had not said. In all his reasoning with the Lord, he had never mentioned Abraham's desire to have Isaac's heir born while he was still alive to see it.

Well, that's right, thought Rebekah. Let Abraham put that in his own prayers and see what the Lord wants to do about it.

The silence lingered for a while. Then Isaac sighed and buried his face in his hands. "Those were hard words to say," he said.

"I'm glad you said them," she answered.

"And do you know why they were so hard?" asked Isaac.

"No."

"Because Father told me to say them."

"Not those exact words."

"It made me feel like a little child, to have my father tell me to go say my prayers." Isaac gave a quiet little laugh. "But the fault is mine, because apparently I *did* need my father to tell me."

"And you were humble enough to do it when he told you to," said Rebekah. "I'm afraid I'm so stubborn and rebellious that it would have taken me days to cool off enough to realize that he was only commanding me to do what I wanted to do already."

"Well," said Isaac. "Now it's done."

"Not quite," said Rebekah.

"What else?" he asked. "I'm all talked out."

"Good," she said. "Because the next part doesn't have much talking in it."

CHAPTER 12

The rest of the festivities passed peacefully enough. Abraham didn't single them out for any more humiliation, and Ishmael made no more gibes. As for Isaac, he acted as if nothing had happened, talking cheerfully with everyone as he always did. Nor did he give any sign that he noticed how there was always a crowd gathered around Ishmael; he was often in that crowd himself, and now that Ishmael wasn't jabbing at him, they even seemed to enjoy each other's company. It occurred to Rebekah that if they hadn't been brothers, they might have been friends, in the weird way that people of almost opposite personalities often become close, admiring in the other the traits they lacked in themselves. For once the rivalry had receded into the background—for the moment—Ishmael seemed genuinely interested in the things Isaac talked about.

In particular, Ishmael listened closely to Isaac's explanation of something he had been piecing together from the various records. "To put it plainly," said Isaac, "the world is drying out, at least this part of it. Until grandfather Terah's time, droughts were rare and brief. The problem was far more likely to be flooding. And the land we move through used to be very different. Tall grasses and trees—everywhere, groves and stands and single trees. And seasonal streams in areas where there's nothing but dust or sand today. I think it's safe to say the world has changed. The drought never ended. We just got used to it. We found ways to work around it. To live in spite of it."

Ishmael got caught up in the details of the evidence, how Isaac had discovered this in the casual mentions of animals that used to be hunted in regions where no one could remember ever seeing them—and some animals that seemed to be of great size but whose names now meant nothing at all to Isaac. "What's a curelom?" he asked. "Does anyone know?" Of course no one did. "Well, it was big, and now it's gone. Hunted or driven or droughted into oblivion."

"Or it got a new name," said Ishmael.

"Quite possible," said Isaac. "That's the problem with not having the original writers here to talk to."

Rebekah was glad to see them being excited together about the holy writings. But of course the information Isaac had been working on was not particularly holy. It made her all the hungrier to have a look at them, and a little bit more irritated that she could not.

On the way home, after a week in Kirjath-arba, Rebekah found herself getting nauseated from the swaying of the camel. After throwing up twice, she had to get off and walk.

When she was still nauseated the next two evenings, without coming anywhere near a camel, she began to suspect that it might be with her the way it was with some women, who threw up frequently during the early stages of pregnancy. She said nothing about it to anyone, but of course word got around that she was sick most days, and that led to the inevitable gossip, so that only two weeks later Isaac came to her and said, "Am I going to be the last to know?"

"Last to know what?"

"That you're expecting a baby."

"No, you're apparently second from last, since *I* don't know."

"You don't? Then why are all the men talking about how all the women are talking about how you're throwing up all the time because you're pregnant?"

"Because I've been throwing up a lot, and whether I'm pregnant is always one of the most thrilling topics of speculation in this household."

"So . . . you're not pregnant."

"I didn't say that."

"Then you *are* pregnant."

"I don't know."

"What are you doing to me? Either you are or you aren't."

"That's true. Either I am or I'm not. But it's too soon for me to be sure. I might just have some disease. Or there might be some food my body suddenly doesn't like."

"Or you might be pregnant."

"I might be."

"When were you going to tell me?"

"When I *know!*"

"Don't you think I want to know that you *might* be?"

"Well, my vomiting hasn't exactly been a secret."

"Apparently it was to me."

"Oh, should I have thrown up at your tent door every night before supper?"

He burst out laughing. "Don't get so upset at me."

"You were getting upset at me."

"I was teasing you."

"Who can tell?"

"Usually, you can."

"Well, excuse me for being on edge, but what do you expect? After all, I might be pregnant!"

A few weeks later, she was certain enough to tell Isaac he could send word to his father if he wanted to.

"I don't know if I want to," said Isaac. "The first thing he'll do is insist we move to Kirjath-arba."

"No, no, no, no, no," moaned Rebekah. "Isn't it bad enough that I already lose my supper most nights? Do I have to have Keturah hovering over me being endlessly wise and helpful about pregnancy, this being my first time and her being so experienced . . . honestly, Isaac, I think it will be better for our child if his mother doesn't commit murder while he's in the womb."

"So let's not tell Father until the time is right."

"And when will that be?"

"When the boy is thirteen?" Isaac suggested.

"That would be cruel."

"That's why it was a joke."

"A joke, yes. Cruel, yes. But also a very attractive idea."

"If we wait to tell Father until you're farther along, we can refuse to leave Lahai-roi because it's not safe to move you."

"It's already not safe," said Rebekah. "I certainly can't ride there, and I don't think the woman with Abraham's and your heir in her womb should be walking all that way."

THE SEED OF ABRAHAM

Isaac nodded and twiddled his beard. "I suppose that means we can break the news to Father any time, since you already can't go there."

"I also don't want to move to Kirjath-arba after the child is born."

"If it's a girl, you won't have to."

"I especially don't want to move there if it's a boy."

"I've been thinking about this ever since Father first brought it up," said Isaac. "My father may not have long to live. Hasn't he earned the right to have as much time as possible with my son before he dies?"

"Please don't think I'm being disrespectful, Isaac, but your father's imminent death was Eliezer's excuse for hurrying me here to marry you without allowing my family a chance to give me a proper send-off. That was many years ago. I'm beginning to think, with the evidence I've had so far, that your father is going to live forever. Or at least longer than me, which amounts to the same thing as far as I'm concerned."

"And this makes you sorry?" asked Isaac, only half teasing.

"No, I'm delighted, I hope he does live forever. But it does make me less inclined to try to raise my son under his constant supervision, just because he might die."

"He *will* die sometime, you know."

"And then he'll be caught up into heaven and he'll be with God, who'll probably let him see the whole future of all our children and their children till the end of the world."

Isaac studied her face. "You're not joking."

"No, I'm not. Well, about your father being immortal, yes, of course that's a joke. But I don't want to try to raise our

275

children under your father's watchful gaze. Everything I do is going to be wrong."

"I thought it was Keturah's hovering that had you worried."

"Maybe you've forgotten, but I haven't. Your father thinks he's going to take charge of the rearing of our son."

"He's a very wise old man. And a good one."

"But he has his children, and we have ours. I didn't notice him handing you over to old Terah to raise."

"Because Terah was an idolater who once colluded with men who were plotting to kill my father."

"So if he hadn't done those things, Abraham would have been right up there in Haran to hand over the baby."

Isaac laughed. "All right, of course he wouldn't. But it's different in our case."

"Isaac, it's *not* different. I can't believe you don't see it. The reason your father wants to supervise the raising of this baby is because he doesn't think either of us can do it right. Especially not me. He thinks I'm going to treat the baby like . . . like a baby. Which is precisely what I'm going to do, when you stop and think about it, and it's none of his business. I'll bet somebody treated *him* like a baby, too."

Isaac grew very still, and when he spoke he was almost inaudibly quiet. "Well, you see, he's afraid that if he doesn't intervene, our son will turn out to be *just* like me."

Rebekah was relieved that Isaac understood the situation without having to have it spelled out for him. "Yes! And that's just . . . unbelievably stupid! I want our boy to be as much like you as possible. I would be thrilled if he was just like you."

Isaac looked at her as if she were an idiot. "Why?"

"Because—because you're a wonderful man. A man of God. A good ruler of a household, a *perfect* husband, a . . ."

The look on his face turned sadder and sadder with everything she said.

"What?" she demanded. "What's wrong with having a son who's like you? I *love* you!"

"Only because you're a woman," said Isaac.

"Well excuse me, Isaac, but I think having me be a woman was one of the primary instructions your father gave Eliezer when he sent him off to find me."

"Yes, that was pretty much the minimum. Whomever he brought back, she definitely had to be a woman."

"And our son will probably marry a woman, too, don't you think?"

"That would be my choice for him, yes," said Isaac. "It's been a long tradition in our family, extending all the way back to Adam, I believe."

"So maybe *that* woman will think he's just as wonderful as I think *you* are."

Isaac turned away from her then. "Pleasing women," he said, "is not how a man is measured."

"It's how *women* measure men!"

"No it's not," said Isaac.

"Now you're the expert on how women think about men?"

"You're the expert on how *you* think about men," said Isaac. "But tell me honestly, having listened to the gossip of women for all the years of your life, how often do the women say, 'Oh, and he's so nice and thoughtful and kind.'"

"They say that a lot."

"They say that when they can't come up with any *real*

praise for a man. When they don't think much of him and they have to say something nice."

"Maybe stupid women think that way—"

"Why do you think Father sent Eliezer instead of letting me find a wife for myself? I'm a grown man, you know."

"I thought . . . because your father didn't want you leaving his camp . . ."

"Oh, and that's *better*? My father doesn't even trust me out of his sight?"

"Well, of course he does. But I thought maybe it was because of Ishmael—you know, how his first wife, that Egyptian woman, whatever her name was, I never met her—"

"Meribah."

"He divorced her and sent her away because she was wrong for him somehow."

"She had a penchant for frenzied worship of Asherah in the company of men she wasn't married to."

Rebekah had never heard that. "Really?" Mother certainly hadn't indulged in that kind of "worship" of the goddess.

"It doesn't matter," said Isaac. "Father sent Eliezer because he didn't think the right kind of woman would find me attractive. He didn't want me to take the leavings of men like Ezbaal. Or Ishmael."

"I turned Ezbaal down," said Rebekah, "and Ishmael never asked."

"Right. Yes. But if I had been there, quiet Isaac, studious Isaac, Isaac who never gets angry and doesn't like to go out hunting and has only killed animals for sacrifice, Isaac who looks like he should be a strong man but he just couldn't get interested in handling a sword or practicing battle so he never became very skilled at it, Isaac who—"

"It sounds like you want our son to grow up to be Ishmael!"

Isaac cocked his head and thought about that. "Well, yes, except for the part about breaking most of the commandments whenever he feels like it."

"And the part about being a show-off and a braggart."

"He's not just bragging," said Isaac. "He really is what he seems."

"A bully?"

"A great man."

Rebekah finally understood. "You're telling me that you reject *yourself* as the father of our child."

"No, no, that's not it at all."

"Yes it is," said Rebekah. "That's exactly what you're saying. But I'll have you remember something, my beloved husband. The Lord could have had the birthright go to Ishmael if he wanted to. But he didn't. You're the one who was chosen."

"I just happened to be born to my mother instead of a concubine."

"No, you didn't just 'happen' to be born. The Lord chose what spirit to put into each little baby and he chose *you* to be born as the boy who would grow up to have the birthright."

Isaac leapt to his feet and began to pace. He never did that. When he was upset he always became physically still. Yet here he was, walking around slapping the walls of the tent in a haphazard way as he moved, as if he wanted to brush everything out of his way, make everything around him disappear. He was truly upset, and she didn't understand why.

"Rebekah," he said, "I don't know why we're even having this discussion, it's probably a girl."

"Probably," said Rebekah, more because he seemed to

need agreement than because she thought God would give them a daughter first.

"But we've *got* to have this discussion because the baby's the answer to prayer. How could the Lord answer that prayer and not give us a boy? Can you tell me that?"

"So it's a boy," said Rebekah.

"My mother *was* too possessive of me," said Isaac. "She really did watch over me too much. Kept me from getting into fights with other children."

"Oh, she should have been *stoned* for that."

"It made a coward of me."

"You're the bravest man I know."

"I avoid every fight I can avoid. I back down immediately."

"Any fool can bluster his way into a fight. It takes courage to make peace."

"Oh, right, well, if that's how you define courage, then I really am the bravest man around, because I can't stand to quarrel. It makes me ill. It makes me . . . stand up and walk around hitting the walls of the tent."

"Are you saying that we're quarreling?"

"Yes."

"Well, maybe you are, but I'm not."

"Now you're being silly, Rebekah. Nobody can quarrel alone."

"Apparently it's another of the skills you deny that you have," she retorted. "The ability to quarrel without the other person realizing it. *I* thought we were discussing."

"You're a strong woman, Rebekah, and I'm a weak man. My son is not going to be weak like me, and that's what your strength and my weakness will combine to make of him."

"So you really are going to turn him over to your father to raise?"

"I want us to move close to Father so he can influence our son, yes."

"That's not where it will stop," said Rebekah. "Your father doesn't stop until he gets his way. If you take him there, you might as well leave me here for all the influence I'll have over my own son."

"Even Father isn't strong enough to erase your influence."

"But he'll try. And I can see now that you'll let him. Well, that experiment's already been tried. My father divorced my mother and sent her away, so my brother and I were raised entirely by our father. Why don't you do likewise? Divorce me, and then your father won't have to worry about my evil influence at all. In fact, it's something of a family tradition. My father did it, Ishmael did it, and Abraham did it with Ishmael's mother. It's really just a matter of time till you send me away."

"Never," said Isaac. "That will never happen."

"Well let me tell you a little secret," said Rebekah. "You'd better do it, either that or kill me, because I'll have to be either dead or gone before I'll let Abraham or anybody else take a son of mine and turn him into . . . into . . . *Ishmael.* I want *you* to be the father of our son, I want him to grow up wanting to be just like you. And I'm going to do everything I can to make sure that's exactly what happens."

Isaac stopped pacing and looked at her for the longest time.

"I should be proud," he said. "That you feel that way about me."

"Yes, you should," said Rebekah. "Because I love you to

281

the point of worship, don't you understand that? And you *earn* that love, you deserve it, not just from me but from everybody. Everything I see you do is good. You are exactly what a man of God ought to be. Until now! Until this! And this is complete madness!"

"If you knew my father better, you'd know a *real* man of God, and you'd be grateful that he wanted to help raise our son."

"When he's present, you step back and say little, and I don't want our son to grow up with his papa hidden in Grandfather's shadow."

"Father talks to God all the time, and this is what Father believes is right," said Isaac.

"Are you telling me that God has said Abraham should raise our son?"

"Father hasn't actually said so, no."

"And he's never going to, because God did not bring you and me together so that someone *else* could raise our child. That's your father's own idea."

"An idea he got from his disappointment in me."

"He's not disappointed in you."

"He had Ishmael," said Isaac, "and he had to send that beloved son away to make room for . . . me."

"He sent Ishmael away because he was a spiteful boy and there was a real danger that if he were close at hand you would be much more likely to meet with accidents as a child, one of which would eventually be fatal."

Isaac knelt down in front of her. "Don't you see that every word you say convinces me that I'm right and you're wrong?"

"What? What did I say?"

"You said the very thing my mother always said. You sound like her."

"No, I sound like *every* mother sounds, when there's somebody close at hand who hates her child, and when that hateful somebody is also violent and slack of conscience."

"And whom will you teach our son to be afraid of?"

"Of his own father's ludicrous self-doubt."

"Enough," said Isaac. "You're making this harder. Every word makes it harder."

"Only until you realize I'm right. Then it becomes easy."

He realized she was trying to soften their argument with humor, and so he smiled, though she did not think he really was amused.

"I loved my mother," said Isaac. "I spent my childhood trying not to disappoint her or worry her. And as a result, I ended up disappointing my father and, yes, myself. People come here to see the great Abraham, and they all come away thinking, What a marvelous man, a true prophet of God, but isn't it a shame about his son?"

"They never think that."

"I want my son to be a great man. A prophet like my father."

"Why can't our son be a prophet like *his* father?"

Suddenly tears appeared in Isaac's eyes. "Because I'm not like my father. Great visions of the stars, the creation of the world. The inspiration I get is more along the lines of where to camp, and which of two quarreling shepherds is lying to me."

"But, Isaac," she said, "God speaks to all of us in different voices and tells us what he needs us to know. He doesn't have to show you what your father saw, because Abraham wrote it down and so you have it. And when God speaks to *me* it isn't with a voice or a vision, it's with a sudden strong desire to do a righteous thing. Or sometimes when I already have the strong desire to do right, I don't know what the right thing *is* until God puts the certainty in my heart."

Isaac sank down onto the rug beside her. "God speaks to you?"

"Not for a long time," said Rebekah. "In fact, it was mostly when I needed God's help in ruling the women of my father's house and I had no idea how to do it. And then again when Ezbaal came and the Lord showed me how to get out of marrying him."

"Showed you?"

"The idea came into my head and I knew that it was right."

"So God talks more even to you than to me. And you wonder why I know people are disappointed to meet Abraham's son."

This idea was so absurd that Rebekah laughed—and regretted it instantly, for the look on Isaac's face, the way he turned away from her . . . he had meant it. "Isaac," she said, "I'm not a prophet at all. I have no authority, I have no birthright. I've just . . . sometimes I've been led, I've been helped. To bring me to *you.* So I could be part of *your* life, *your* work."

"I know." He sighed. "I know it. As Father says—or said, back when he was still a patient man and taught *me* to be patient—the Lord doesn't have to push you when you're already moving forward on the right path."

"That's right."

"The trouble is, that means that people who are on the

right path have exactly the same relationship with God as people who are so far off the path that they couldn't hear the voice of God if he shouted in their ears."

"I don't think so."

"Oh, I know that's not so. I mean—my life is happy. Mostly. A good life. The life you get when you obey the Lord's commandments and serve him as best you can. I have the knowledge that comes from studying the holy writings. I have the wife God chose for me. Maybe now I'm even going to have a son. I've been blessed, and it's unrighteous of me to covet more."

"I wish I could give you whatever it is you yearn for."

"What I yearn for," said Isaac, "isn't yours to give."

"So who has it, so I can make them give it to you?"

Isaac laughed. "You would, wouldn't you. And I might even tell you. If I knew what it was."

"Maybe I have what you need right here," she said, patting her stomach.

"With all the fathers and mothers I've known over the years, including my own," said Isaac, "I've never yet heard of any of them who said that having children was the *end* of their problems."

"But it might have been the end of their yearnings," said Rebekah. "At least of their yearning for children!"

Isaac sat down beside her, calm again. "Not even that," said Isaac. "Look at Father if you doubt me."

"I don't even try to understand your father."

"I wish you had known him years ago when Mother was alive. He complains about her now, how she raised me, but while she was alive, she was . . . he never . . . I don't know how to say it. He saw people more kindly. And not because

Mother was always compassionate—that's not so. She could be quite sharp in her judgment, and she didn't tolerate fools. It's as if he lived his life to try to make her proud of him, and she *was* proud of him and so he had nothing to prove. But with her gone, he's never content. Restless all the time. Nothing is good enough. And what you don't realize is, he's harder on himself than he is on anyone else."

"I wonder how that could be possible."

"Don't be snippy," said Isaac. "It's so incongruous with the sweetness of your face."

"Isaac, he's so hard on you it hurts."

"If I were a better man, he wouldn't need to be." Isaac got up. "And before you can argue with me and start this conversation all over again, I've got work to do."

"So do I."

"Don't you think you should rest?"

"Plenty of time to rest when I turn into a pregnant cow."

"A pregnant goat, maybe. Too small for cowhood."

"You just watch. I intend to be huge."

She was joking—or, perhaps, giving voice to her dread—but as the days went on she did get larger than she had expected. Not fatter—it was all in her belly.

They finally told people she was pregnant when the baby quickened and started moving inside her, though of course by then everyone already knew. The rumors had been flying so long, and the growth of Rebekah's belly was so rapid and noticeable, that it was almost an afterthought the day Isaac said, "You know, everyone's still pretending not to notice, and it's getting harder and harder for them, so we ought to admit the obvious and get the celebrations over with."

As they had anticipated, once the rumors became official

286

Abraham at once insisted that they come to Kirjath-arba. "When I told him you were too fragile to move, he said, 'And you think this is going to improve? Do it now.'"

"I won't," said Rebekah. "I'm not going to have this baby in Kirjath-arba."

"It would help me make him feel better about it if you weren't so robust."

"I still throw up every few days."

"And in between, you work as hard as ever. And walk as far, I might add. Don't you think word of that gets back to Father?"

"What I think is that it's not unreasonable for a woman to want to have her baby in her own home, among her own people."

"All of Father's people are your people," said Isaac.

"Someday, but not yet. These are the people I know, here in Lahai-roi."

"We've had good years. Enough rain. During the drier years, the well here gets brackish and there's not enough to grow crops."

"Isaac, do *you* want me to go to Kirjath-arba?"

"I was just saying, don't get too attached to this place, or these people. When Father dies, it will be *my* responsibility to keep the more difficult servants near me."

"I've dealt with difficult people all my life."

"In Father's eyes, I imagine you're one of the most difficult," said Isaac.

"I never meant to be." Rebekah sighed. "All my life I dreamed of what it might be like to live close to Uncle Abraham. To sit at his feet and hear the words of God. It never occurred to me that his wife would be . . ."

"An ambitious, annoying conniver?"

"Isaac, that didn't sound like *you*."

"I was helping you find *your* words."

"And I never thought that he would be so demanding."

"Well, if you want him to love you, maybe refusing to go to Kirjath-arba isn't the way."

"On the contrary, if I go to Kirjath-arba, he'll find new reasons to dislike me every single day."

Isaac laughed and let the issue drop, but it worried Rebekah that maybe Isaac was bearing all the criticism that she was trying to avoid. How did it make Isaac look, that he couldn't get his wife to obey her father-in-law, who was, after all, the ruler of this household? Poor Isaac, can't even control that wife of his. He really *is* a weakling.

The thought made her shudder. What kind of wife was she, to cause her husband shame and expose him to criticism?

But just as she was beginning to believe she ought to give in and go, the movement of the baby within her became much more frequent and violent. The baby never seemed to rest. Whenever she lay down to sleep, the baby began kicking and pushing until she could hardly stand it. And even as she moved around during the day, the baby would suddenly start lurching violently, first on this side, then on that, first at the top of her belly, than down at the root. The worst was when the baby placed a kick or a lunge firmly on her bladder—it was just too embarrassing to have to flee dripping to her tent, and she began to stay inside more and more, where Deborah could attend her.

"I've never been pregnant before," she asked the older servant women. "Is this the way it is for all of you?" At first they said yes, of course, but as she began to grow haggard from lack of sleep, some of them openly wondered if something was wrong.

"It's an angry baby," one of them said.

"It only means he'll be strong," said another.

"He's fighting the devil," one suggested.

"He dances with angels," countered another.

Finally, in desperation, Rebekah prayed fervently for the Lord to tell her what this meant, that the child was so busy. It would do the baby no good if Rebekah became ill from lack of sleep, and she was afraid that something was very wrong, that the child was struggling for life and there was nothing she could do to help him.

Then she tried to sleep, but again, as usual, the baby lurched and heaved and kicked and pushed and she kept waking in the middle of a dream, or dreaming that she was awake.

One of the times she thought she was awake, she saw some of her great ancestors—men she had never seen, whose names she only knew from family stories—Shem, the son of Noah, and Eber, the first to live as a wandering household, along with a few others about whom she knew less—Arphaxad, Serug, Peleg. "How is it with you, daughter?" asked Shem.

"I can't sleep," she said.

"You're asleep now," he answered.

"I'm not, I'm talking to you. The baby won't let me sleep."

"Which baby?" asked Peleg.

"The baby in my belly, of course," she said. "What other baby do I have?"

"But there are two of them," said Eber.

"Two?" asked Rebekah.

"Two nations are in your womb," said Shem.

"Are they at war with each other?" she asked.

"This isn't a joke," Arphaxad said sternly.

"I wasn't joking," said Rebekah.

And then, suddenly, she knew that she *had* been asleep, that these men had not come to her at all, because she was lying in her tent looking up into the darkness and no one was with her except Deborah, whose soft snoring wove through the pulsing rhythm of the locusts' night music.

Too bad it was only a dream, she thought. Too bad the ancient ones couldn't come and tell women about the children who would be born to them.

"What do we have to do," said Shem, "give a blast from a trumpet or send an army of angels before you'll believe us?"

"We should have gone to Abraham, and let *him* tell her," said Serug. "*He* knows when he's being given a true vision."

Again she awoke, and now the walls of the tent were becoming visible in the first light of dawn. Was it a dream? Had they really come to her?

"Both," said Shem impatiently. "We came to you *in* a dream. Now listen this time. You have two great men inside you, two mighty nations, two ways of life, and the one will be stronger than the other, and the elder will serve the younger."

The elder will serve the younger? "What does that mean?" she asked.

"What?" said Deborah. "Is it morning? It's too dark to be morning."

"Go back to sleep," said Rebekah. "I was talking in my dream."

But this dream did not fade as others did. It remained clear in her mind, every word they had said to her, especially what they had prophesied about her children—her twin sons, the two nations inside her.

Two of them. That explained everything. Why hadn't she already thought of the possibility? No wonder the baby never slept—it was two babies, and when one quieted down the other awoke.

But what could it mean, saying that the elder would serve the younger? This wasn't a case like that of Ishmael and Isaac, where the younger was born to the true wife, and the elder to a mere concubine. She was mother of both of them, and so the birthright would go to the firstborn, without question.

She told Isaac about the dream, and he was also puzzled. "Maybe it was nothing more than a dream," he said. "Then it wouldn't have to make sense."

"But I've never dreamed such a dream before. I didn't even know what these men looked like."

Isaac laughed. "If it was just a dream, you *still* don't know."

"They were so real. They got so *annoyed* with me."

"Ah, then it was definitely a true vision."

"Isaac, I think the Lord answered my prayer. He told me why the baby—the babies—were keeping me awake."

"Told you more than that, if it was from God."

"Does he mean our sons won't get along with each other?"

"From what you've been going through, I'd say they're already at war."

"But surely it was a prophecy about how things would be when their descendants have become mighty nations."

"Brothers born the same day, from the same womb," said Isaac. "Of course they'll quarrel."

"Why shouldn't they be close friends, sharing every-thing?"

"Maybe they will," said Isaac. "It's not likely, but I sup-pose it's possible. No two of Keturah's children get along for more than ten minutes at a time, but maybe *our* children will be completely generous of spirit and never resentful of anything."

"That's right, they'll be just like us, and never criticize any-one, and be pleasant to everyone and never think a harsh thought."

"Well, *you* don't have harsh thoughts, anyway."

"I have thoughts so harsh they could straighten a lamb's hair," said Rebekah. "*You're* the one who's always thinking the best of everyone."

"Am I? Well, let's try this one. When you told me your vision, do you know what I thought of first? That when the Lord finally gave someone besides Father a truly spectacular vision—"

"It wasn't spectacular, it was—"

"It seems spectacular enough to me," said Isaac, "because I didn't see it. So which of us is the one with thoughts so pure God can pour out his Spirit into a holy vessel?"

"Holy vessel? Me?" said Rebekah. "I'm much more critical and mean-spirited than you even know how to be, so if it depended on purity of thoughts—"

"My point was how unrighteous it was for me to envy your vision," said Isaac. "I was praying every day for you to be comforted, and you *were* comforted. And instead of being grateful, I'm selfish. Sometimes I despair of ever being a truly good man."

"Isaac, you're the best man I know," said Rebekah.

"Only because you don't really—"

She knew how the sentence would end, and she refused to let him say it. "I know your heart better than you do, because I can see what you *do*, how your life blesses everyone you touch."

"But *I* see how I envy my father and now my wife."

"Maybe your heart is already so full of love for others that you already know how to bless them without having any visions at all, do you think of that? Maybe you're so at one with the Lord that your whole life is one long continuous vision of a sort that people like me can only dream of!"

"Maybe you're a wonderful sweet loyal wife who thinks better of her husband than he deserves. The Lord truly blessed me when he gave you to me."

"He gave you to me as much as he gave me to you!"

Isaac smiled and kissed her and left her with the last word—and with no hope that he would ever believe what a good man she knew him to be.

For hours that morning, after her vision—or her dream, whichever it was—Rebekah was able to sleep undisturbed. She learned later that Deborah guarded her tent fiercely, making sure that no one bothered her, despite the chaos that soon erupted in the camp.

For soon after Isaac left her tent, five riders on camels appeared at the crest of the hill where the path to Kirjath-arba left the valley, and the runner soon returned with word that it was the master himself coming to Lahai-roi. Abraham, who hadn't left Kirjath-arba since he buried Sarah's body at Machpelah.

Everyone rushed around madly like birds before a storm,

pitching a new tent for Isaac as his own tent was prepared for Abraham to take possession of it. A fine young kid was butchered and spitted over the fire for the feast tonight, and all the women found opportunities to return to their tents and change into their finest clothing, or at least add a bit of decoration to their attire.

Finally, when Abraham was installed at the door of Isaac's tent, there could be no more delay. Isaac himself went to Rebekah's tent, thanked Deborah for letting her mistress sleep, and then passed through the door.

"Father is here," he said to her when she finally murmured a greeting to him.

"Father?" she asked, trying to imagine why Bethuel should come all the way to Lahai-roi. Then she came fully awake and realized what was happening. "How close is he? How long do we have to get ready?"

"All is in readiness. He's in my tent, and he wants to see you."

"But why didn't you wake me? I should have been helping. I had work to do, I—"

"Rebekah, I think it's *good* for my father to see you sleeping through the work of the camp. After all, you're the woman who can't travel to Kirjath-arba because she's so delicate."

"Oh," said Rebekah. "Yes, I suppose so."

"And don't make yourself beautiful," said Isaac. "Don't dress your hair."

"No, Isaac, there are limits!"

"Which is more important? To be pretty, or to stay in Lahai-roi?"

"Did he come alone?"

"He didn't bring Keturah, if that's what you mean."

"I am truly favored of the Lord."

A few minutes later, hastily dressed and with her hair at least a little smoother than it had been after her night of tossing and turning, Rebekah crossed the space between her tent and Isaac's, to take her place on a pile of three thick rugs before Abraham.

"It's going to be a big one," said Abraham, sizing her up.

"Two," said Rebekah.

"Two?"

"Rebekah had a dream last night," said Isaac.

"My husband's prayer was answered," said Rebekah.

Abraham looked at Rebekah thoughtfully. "Tell me the dream."

So Rebekah recounted her dream, as best she could remember it. She made it a point to include their rebukes of her, so it would be plain that she was not pretending to be particularly righteous or deserving and that the dead did not regard her with much respect.

Abraham listened to it all, then bowed his head. "It's from the Lord," he said.

Just like that? "How do you know?" asked Rebekah.

"I know," said Abraham.

She understood what he meant, and nodded.

"And I'm glad that the mother of my grandsons has a heart open to the spirit of God." He turned to Isaac. "The Lord gave you one of the best of his daughters."

Rebekah blushed and her eyes filled with tears. The man of legend whom she had admired throughout her childhood, whose name was linked with the name of God—after all these months of thinking that he didn't trust her to raise her own child, it was such a relief to know that he did not despise her after all. That he did not reject the vision she had, just because it came from her.

"Two nations," Abraham said. "Is every child born in our family going to found his own nation?"

"I don't know what it all means," said Rebekah.

"The Lord tells us what he tells us," said Abraham. "And then we do our best to understand it." He leaned forward and looked searchingly in her face. "Is it God who tells you to defy me and refuse to come live with me?"

And just like that, the glow of his praise faded, and she once again faced the stubborn old man who wanted to take her sons from her.

"Is it God who tells you to demand that Isaac and I not be allowed to raise our sons ourselves?"

His expression darkened. "I'm not asking you to *send* your sons, I'm asking my son to move home."

"Father," said Isaac, "her question is a fair one. Do you command her to come to Kirjath-arba as the head of the household, or as prophet of God?"

"Maybe I *invite* her merely as the child's—the children's—grandfather."

"I misunderstood," said Rebekah. "If it's the children's beloved grandfather who invites us, then my answer is, 'What a wonderful invitation! I wish I could accept it. But you can be sure I'll bring the children to visit as soon as I can after they're born.'"

Abraham turned away from her then and stared off into the distance.

"I'm going to die soon," he said.

"Forgive me, Grandfather," she said, "but you'll die when

the Lord takes you, and God's work in the world won't suddenly come to a halt."

She felt Isaac stiffen beside her, and Abraham slowly turned to affix his gaze on her. "I don't deserve that."

"Nor do Isaac and I deserve to have you doubt our ability to raise godly children," said Rebekah. "A man and woman are masters of their own children, and as long as they fulfill that responsibility honorably, no one has a right that supercedes theirs."

"Parents don't know everything," said Abraham. "Parents make mistakes."

"They do, sir," said Rebekah. "But the Lord who sends children to them knows the mistakes they'll make, and the things they'll do well, too. If he chooses to give these children to Isaac and me, who would dare to tell him he was wrong?"

"I'm saying that *I've* made mistakes, and I want to help you learn from them."

"It's one thing to learn from them, and something else to watch you make a whole new set of mistakes with our children."

Abraham turned to Isaac. "Why is she at war with me?"

Isaac answered quietly, but without hesitation. "Her mother had her children taken away from her, Father. She fears the same thing happening to her."

"I'm not taking them away from you," said Abraham to Rebekah. "I'm giving them to God!"

Suddenly Isaac leaned forward so far that his backside rose up from the ground and he had to support himself on the knuckles of his hands; he looked for all the world like a hyena or baboon challenging an intruder. "A man gives *himself* to God," said Isaac, "because he belongs only to himself. If my sons are given to God, it will be because Rebekah and I taught them well enough that they chose to give their lives in his service."

"So there's no reason for me to be alive at all," said Abraham. "I have nothing to offer, nothing that anyone wants. How tedious the burden must be, to have me still alive."

Isaac slumped and rocked back onto his seat on the rugs. "If you don't already know that I love you, there's nothing I can do now to prove it."

"Love me? When did you ever show you loved me?"

This was too outrageous for Rebekah to bear. "Every day of his life he shows you! He follows all your teachings, he serves God as you did, he shows nothing but respect for you!"

But Isaac brushed away her defense with a gesture of his hand. "I'll tell you when I showed you I loved you, Father. When I lay there under the knife, knowing I had the strength to take it away from you and walk away free—but I loved you more than I loved my own life."

"That was God's command, not mine," said Abraham.

"You were obeying God, but I was obeying you."

Abraham's breath became rapid and shallow. "After all these years, you rebuke me as if it were my idea. I thought you understood."

"I did understand," said Isaac. "To you, it was God taking your son. But to me, it was my father giving me up."

Now, finally, Rebekah understood. The story she had heard from Ezbaal's grandmother, who had learned it from Ishmael—it was true. There had been a time when Abraham stood ready with a knife to sacrifice Isaac. To sacrifice him to *God*, even though Abraham's whole life had been a struggle against the sacrificing of human beings to slake the imagined bloodthirst of nonexistent gods.

"I hated it," said Abraham. "It was the most terrible command the Lord ever gave me."

"And yet . . . you said yes."

"So did you," said Abraham.

Isaac looked down. "I'm not sure," said Isaac.

"I was an old man. You were young and strong. You let me bind you."

"I'm not sure whether I said yes to God, or to you."

"God was testing our faith," said Abraham.

"How do you know he wasn't testing our love?"

"By that standard," said Abraham, "your love for me was perfect, and mine for you . . . failed."

"If a man does not love God more than he loves his own sons, then he does not truly love his sons, either," said Isaac. "I know that."

"So why do you reproach me?"

"Because I'm human," said Isaac. "I know I consented, but my heart has its own memory. As I lay there, I couldn't help but think, Now I'll be dead and he can have Ishmael back."

"Is that why you won't let your sons be born in Kirjath-arba?" said Abraham. "Because I didn't choose you over God?"

Rebekah had had enough, and now she could speak her mind in a way that did not sound like an attack on Abraham alone. "Shame on all of us," she said. "Listen to what you've been saying."

"Now your wife judges her husband *and* her father-in-law," said Abraham, not without amusement.

"Our babies aren't born in order to fulfill *our* lives," said

Rebekah, "or to quell old fears or heal old injuries. They'll have their own lives, and their own relationship with God, and they'll make their own choices and create their own future. Their lives will not be about Abraham, or Isaac, or Rebekah. Their lives will be about themselves and their God. No one else stands between them. So whatever old pain you're trying to heal, work it out between each other, but let's keep our sons out of it."

She rested a hand on Isaac's head, hoping he would understands that she was sorry that she seemed to judge him. And he reached up and touched her fingers and took them gently between his own, as if to say, I love you anyway.

"I'm going to go rest now," she said to Isaac. And to Abraham: "Your journey has worn me out."

She waddled away toward her tent, with Deborah holding her arm.

"You were very bad to talk that way to your father-in-law," said Deborah into her ear as they walked. "You should be more respectful." She sounded more worried than reproachful.

Rebekah knew that she had behaved badly. That all she had really done was prove to Abraham that even if she had received a vision, she really wasn't the sort of woman who could raise the birthright son. And yet . . . what else could she have done? He did not take polite, respectful answers as if they mattered. "He's not the man I thought he was," Rebekah said quietly. "He's not the Abraham of the stories."

"Oh, he is," said Deborah, very seriously. "I asked long ago, when we first came here, and everybody said yes, he *is* the very same Abraham."

Rebekah lay down on the bed from which she had arisen

only a few minutes before. "I shouldn't meet with people I disagree with when I'm tired," she said. "I simply utter whatever comes to mind. I was awful."

And the worst thing was, she wasn't even right. How could she be? Her sons were a gift of God, an answer to prayer. Without God, she would have no sons. So if he wanted them to be raised by the great prophet Abraham rather than by a foolish woman like Rebekah, how dare she covet her own children and refuse to let them have the gift that God's servant was offering them?

In her heart she offered a silent prayer: O Lord, forgive me. If it is thy will to have my sons raised by others, I will submit to thee. I beg thee not to do it, but I will bear it if that is thy will. Amen.

But then, in her most secret heart, without her even thinking of it first, a deep true prayer leapt out through her lips: "Please don't take away my beloved sons."

At once a thought came clear into her mind: Why do you think God gave you two sons, if not to take one of them to himself?

She rested her hands on her belly and wept. One of them would belong to God, and only the other one would be her own to raise.

But there would be the one. God was kind and merciful. She would have one son to be her own, and the other to be turned into whatever it was that Abraham wished Isaac had been.

Abraham did not even stay the night, but got up on his camel and rode back to Kirjath-arba. And Isaac—whatever he was thinking, he kept it to himself.

So much of Isaac's behavior made sense to Rebekah now.

He had lived most of his life with the knowledge that, forced to choose between his child and his God, Isaac's father had chosen God. What could Isaac do, except agree with his father? Agree to die for him. Agree that his whole life was nothing but a taw in a game between God and his prophet. Agree that he had no worth in himself, no life, no dreams, no plans, no hopes that could not be swept away as if they were nothing.

And Abraham thought that God had been testing *him*.

Rebekah hardly emerged from her tent in the days and weeks to come, wondering in the shadows of her cloth-walled chamber what God was trying to do with their lives, where it all might lead.

Is it thy plan for every parent to be willing to give up their child?

And if that *is* thy plan, why didst thou create us to have so much love for them?

These quarrelsome, troublesome boys who wrestle with each other here just under my heart—why didst thou make me so my heart breaks with love for them before I've even seen them?

I am being asked to do no worse a thing than my mother was forced to do. No, a much easier thing, because I won't be cut off from my sons, I can be right there with them. Only my stubbornness and selfishness, my irritation with Keturah, my resentment of Abraham's treatment of my husband—only these low, petty human feelings kept me from peacefully accepting Uncle Abraham's invitation and moving to Kirjath-arba to have my babies.

So by the time the babies were born, by the time she felt them shove their way out between her thighs with the lusty selfishness of infants, she had already reconciled herself to the will of God. Or maybe just the will of Abraham, but either way, she knew what she had to do.

"The first is covered all over with red hair!" cried Deborah during the birthing.

"And look," said the midwife. "The second one's hand came out gripping the heel of the first. You little usurper, what do you think, you can pull your brother back into the womb and come out first yourself?"

"Supplanter," said Rebekah as she leaned back and gave the last push that sent her second child into the world. "I name him Jacob."

"And the first?" asked the midwife.

"Red hair," said Rebekah. "And the birthright is his. I name him Esau."

"Name him what you will, you know they'll end up calling him Edom," said the midwife. It's what redheads always ended up being called.

"What's that to me?" said Rebekah. "I told you the names. Now go tell their father he has two sons. And eight days from now we'll take them to Kirjath-arba."

"Why?" asked Deborah.

"For the circumcision, of course," said the midwife.

"No," said Rebekah. "We're going to live there now. So these boys can grow up in the household of Abraham."

PART V

BLESSINGS

CHAPTER 13

Keturah had arranged for two wetnurses to be sent to Lahai-roi so they could begin to suckle the babies as soon as they were born. But Rebekah refused to give them to someone else to be nursed. "I'll do it myself," she said.

"Two babies," said the midwife. "You won't have enough milk."

"God gave me just enough breasts for the babies," she said. "Or are you saying he can't count?"

"What about your responsibility to produce more children for the young master? If you're nursing, you won't conceive a child for years."

"He has two sons already," said Rebekah. "He can wait a few years to see his first daughter."

When the women finally allowed Isaac to come see her, he agreed with her. "Keep the children close. Since you've consented to move to Kirjath-arba, you won't have any duties with the women, so why shouldn't you suckle your own babies?"

Because the babies were both just a little smaller than normal, the birth had not been particularly bad—there had been no tearing, and Rebekah recovered quickly. In fact, the nursing caused her more pain. No one had warned her how much it could hurt, to have a baby fasten onto her tender nipples like a wolf onto a donkey's leg. Of the two, Jacob was the one she got used to most quickly, for once he was locked in place, he set to sucking away as placidly as could be, his cheeks pumping in and out, his breathing heavy, his eyes closed.

Esau, on the other hand, kept looking around, and would frequently stop sucking and let the breast fall away from his mouth. In moments, though, he would protest as if someone else had done this to him, and then reattach savagely, gnawing on the nipple to punish it, Rebekah supposed, for not having followed when he turned his head. It got so that she dreaded nursing Esau, and even though she understood that a baby that age had no idea of the pain it might cause someone else, she spent more time scolding him than singing to him.

So it was Jacob who heard all her songs every time she nursed him, and Esau who heard her complaints. "Don't do that, you silly selfish greedy little boy," she said. "I haven't committed any sins worthy of *that* punishment." She tried to be pleasant-sounding even as she scolded him, but in later years, when Esau drifted away from her while Jacob remained close, she wondered if the seeds of that had not been planted in those earliest days of their lives. Or was it the other way around? Esau's tendency to look away, to constantly search for something better to look at than his mother's breast, was it the first expression of his need to roam, his unwillingness to bend his will to someone else's?

Abraham came out to meet them when they arrived at Kirjath-arba, and when Isaac took Esau from her arms, he gave the child to Abraham to hold. Then he went to the kneeling camel on which Deborah sat, and took Jacob from her, and brought him also to Abraham, and the old man nodded. But he did not relinquish Esau or even touch Jacob. As Rebekah clambered down from the camel, she realized that this must be what the Lord intended. Abraham's heart would belong to the heir. The other son would be hers to raise. She grieved at the thought of Esau being drawn away from her as he got older; but at least God in his mercy had seen to it that she would not be left without a son to raise herself.

Abraham called to her. "Daughter!" he said. "You've made this old man's heart glad, to hold this child in my arms today."

"May he grow to be a man of God like his father and grandfather," said Rebekah.

Now that she was closer, Abraham spoke more softly. "I know how hard this was for you. It shows the greatness of your heart, that you could find compassion for me." There were tears in his eyes.

Rebekah was surprised and a little ashamed. He was not, in fact, the stubborn enemy that she had supposed him to be. He was an old man who wanted to be sure his life's work had not been in vain. Who wanted to be a part of his own family's life. She was almost glad, in that moment, that she had decided to bend to his will.

And then he spoiled it all by saying, "And *this* boy will grow up to be a *man*."

It made her want to scream with frustration. Didn't

Abraham see how utterly insulting his remark was? It implied that if they hadn't brought Esau to Abraham, the boy would *not* have grown up to be a real man. It also implied that some other boy had not grown up to be a man, and whom could he mean but Isaac?

He's an old man who says what's on his mind, Rebekah reminded herself.

He's an old man who should know better, she answered silently.

And I'm still the mother of both my sons. I'll cling to what I have, and leave God to watch out for the things that I can't control.

The circumcision was a simple ceremony. Isaac did it himself, and because Ishmael did not make the journey, though Keturah's sons were all on hand, there was no tension in the camp, only rejoicing.

And when the festivities ended and they settled in to their new life in Kirjath-arba, Rebekah was pleasantly surprised that she did not have the constant interference from Keturah that she had expected. Keturah came by at least once a day, but she offered no advice or criticism. Instead she brought figs or dates, or curdled milk or fresh cheese or some other particular treat, and cooed over Rebekah's sons without ever comparing them to her own.

When Rebekah commented on this to Isaac, he only smiled.

"You did something," Rebekah said.

"Father did," said Isaac.

"But you asked him to."

"I suggested to him that it was not so much him that you

310

wanted to avoid here in Kirjath-arba, but Keturah. He under-stood immediately."

For some reason, it really bothered her that Isaac would say such a thing to Abraham. "If that had been all, I would never have refused to come."

"You're here now, and Father doesn't feel as hurt and con-fused as he did, so what's the harm if I leaned a little more heavily on one side of the story than another?"

Now she realized why it bothered her so much. It was a lie between a son and his father. And she had no patience with people who told lies to the ones who trusted them most. "The way my father led me to believe my mother was dead, because it made things a little easier to explain?"

Isaac frowned. "I think your father's story made things easier for himself, while *my* story made things easier for my father."

She wasn't letting him off so easily. "And therefore easier for you, too."

Isaac thought for a moment, then got up as if to leave.

Suddenly all her words to him came back to her and she realized how awful she had been. "Wait, Isaac, please, I wasn't calling you a liar."

Isaac stood there, saying nothing.

"All right, I was, but I was wrong. It's not the same thing at all."

"Rebekah, I have work to do. Let's not make a quarrel out of this. Whether you like what I said or not, my purpose was to make things easier for *you*."

"Please don't go, Isaac. I won't quarrel. I really—what I want is to know what you meant by saying that your father felt—what did you say?—hurt and confused. I never saw that."

"I did," said Isaac. "I know him, so I know what it looks like."

"All I ever saw was him being stubborn. And disdainful of both of us."

"Rebekah, my father is a kind man. A loving, generous man. But this whole business with children—it frightens him. It's the most important thing in life, having children, raising them. And he thinks he didn't do a very good job."

"That's what makes me furious with him! He says it right in front of you, as if you were a terrible disappointment to him."

"I wish he wouldn't do that," said Isaac. "But it's not as if it's a secret. People have only to meet Ishmael, and then meet me, to know that any father would be disappointed that I was the heir, and Ishmael was not. Ishmael has the strength to hold on to what he's been given."

"To the cattle, yes. The sheep, the men with swords, the *things*, yes."

"It's how the world measures a man, Rebekah. It's as unfair as the way the world measures women according to the children they've produced. My mother was a great woman before she gave birth to me. You were the best woman alive even before these boys were born."

She waved his flattery aside. "But a prophet of God shouldn't measure his son the way the world does. No father should."

"How did this become about me?" asked Isaac. "And why are we discussing this?"

"Because I want to understand your father. I loved him all

my life, and now . . . now he seems to be my most relentless opponent."

"How can you say that? We live in the circle of his protection, his love and goodness are all around us in the loyalty and love of the men and women who serve him. He's my father!"

"What greater enemy could I have, than the man who hurts my husband most deeply and who wants to raise our firstborn without our influence?"

"That's not who my father is at all."

"It's all I've seen."

Isaac just stood there, shaking his head.

"Then explain it to me!" Rebekah pleaded.

"Maybe the best reason for us to come to Kirjath-arba is for you to see who my father really is."

"Maybe I'll see who he is about the same time he sees who *you* are."

"He sees me," said Isaac. "You don't. But I'm glad you don't. It feels good to have your love and respect, even though the fact that I don't deserve it turns it to ashes sometimes in my mouth."

She would have answered that, but he kissed her to silence her and then Esau started complaining and Rebekah had no choice but to let Isaac leave.

As the boys learned to walk and talk, toddling about the camp, the differences between them became clear to everyone. If there was something to climb, Esau climbed it; something to get stuck in, Esau was stuck in it. Rebekah assigned two of her handmaidens to take turns watching Esau even when he was sleeping—it took him only a few moments after waking up to be in a place where he might fall into a crevice or tumble onto a fire, or where a scorpion or a serpent or even a prowling lion might find him. It did no good to tell Esau what to do—he was deaf whenever he was being told what he may not do.

Jacob, on the other hand, while he was every bit as curious, was also obedient. When Rebekah told him not to follow his brother into danger, he heard her, and while he might protest, he stayed close by. And he was more predictable. Once he got interested in something, he would stay at it for hours. Not that what he did was always good. He once dug up an entire row of onions just to see if they all had those little bulbs growing among their roots under the soil, and he once endangered the whole camp by systematically dropping rocks down the well to hear them splash, running the risk of filling it higher than the water level. Jacob seemed oblivious to the rebukes of the servants until Rebekah explained to him why it was bad to fill the well with rocks. "That's something an enemy might do," said Rebekah. "We protect our own wells and keep the water clear so we and all the animals can have plenty to drink." When he understood that he might have deprived the flocks of their water, he began to cry, and he never threw anything down a well again.

Esau and Jacob were both fascinated by animals, but again, in different ways. The only time Esau showed patience was in stalking some hapless creature—an insect, a bird, a spider, a cat. He could move so slowly and imperceptibly until the moment that he pounced that he caught mice with his bare hands, and once Rebekah saw him come within a handsbreadth of catching a quail.

Jacob never stalked anything, but he seemed to have a natural affection for the herding animals and the beasts of burden. He was riding kids as if they were full-grown asses when he looked too small even to climb onto one, and when he adopted a runt puppy or a sick lamb, it always thrived under his care.

They were both remarkable boys, and there were stories to be told about both of them. But it bothered Rebekah more and more that Abraham and Isaac only told visitors the stories about Esau, especially reveling in the tales of how headstrong and daring he was—never disobedient or foolhardy, though in Rebekah's view those were the more appropriate terms. The boy's mouth was still full of childish mispronunciations, and he had already learned that when he disobeyed his mother or did something breathtakingly dangerous, Mother would be full of rebukes, but Father and Grandfather would laugh about it later as they told the tale again and again.

"You're encouraging him to be rebellious," said Rebekah to Isaac. "The more you laugh at his antics, the more he thinks that by disobeying me, he's pleasing you."

"He's a good boy," said Isaac. "He has to be brave. He has to think for himself, trust his own abilities."

"Don't you care that he could die doing some of the things he does?"

"The Lord will watch out for him," said Isaac.

"Why do you think that?" said Rebekah. "Because he's the heir? Because in case you didn't notice, the Lord sent us two boys. Did it never occur to you that he did that because we might well need a spare?"

"He is constantly watched over," said Isaac. "You see to that, and I don't interfere. He can hardly breathe without some woman's voice saying, 'Don't do that, Esau, don't go there, little Edom.'"

"Like your mother used to do with you."

"My mother never had to," said Isaac. "I would never

have dared to do the things Esau does. He's going to be a great man, like his grandfather."

"More like his uncle," said Rebekah.

"We'll make sure he grows up loving the Lord. After all, he doesn't have Hagar breathing poison into his ear every day the way Ishmael did."

"He'll become the man he thinks you want him to be," said Rebekah, "you and your father."

"Exactly," said Isaac. "What do you want to do, turn him into another Jacob? Puttering around after his mother as if he were attached to you at the ankle?"

"What are you talking about?"

"You're making the boy weak. Always hugging the animals and crying when they're hurt."

"As, for instance, the time Esau threw stones at a puppy until he blinded it."

"A dog that slow is no use to us anyway," said Isaac.

"I can't believe you said that."

"Oh, of course that was wrong, and didn't I punish Esau for it?"

"And then sat there while his grandfather told Keturah's boys about how it showed Esau was a born hunter. 'If he can do that to a puppy when he's five, what do you think he'll do to a lion when he's fifteen?'"

"Father's greatest joy is to watch the boys."

"To watch Esau."

"He loves Jacob, too."

"Your father said that the vision I had while they were in the womb was a true one. Well, part of that vision was that the elder boy would serve the younger."

"Yes, I remember that well," said Isaac.

"You treat Jacob as if he didn't exist."

"Oh, I'm quite aware that he exists. What you don't seem to understand is that those words in your vision weren't a commandment, they were a warning."

"A warning!"

"To beware of the younger boy, or else the elder will end up serving him."

"Look at the two boys!" cried Rebekah. "They're both clever and quick, but Jacob is obedient whenever he understands what we expect of him, trying to be a good boy always, while Esau seems to look for ways to flout the rules we lay down for him and make us angry."

"Esau is the elder son," said Isaac. "And the heir."

"Jacob is the son who might grow up to be as good a man as his father," said Rebekah.

"As weak a man, you mean," said Isaac. And, as usual, he cut off the argument at that point, refusing to hear for the hundredth time Rebekah's protests about how Isaac was not weak at all.

What made Rebekah most furious, though, was when Abraham tried to get five-year-old Esau interested in the holy writings. At age five! When Rebekah was still barred from so much as looking at them, Esau was taken into his grandfather's tent and shown them all and told that someday they'd be his. Predictably, of course, he became bored almost immediately, and this time, at least, Abraham did not appreciate his disobedience. It became a contest of wills between them, and on the third attempt, Esau ended the matter by tearing one of the fragile parchments on which one of the most ancient documents was written. Abraham's roar could be heard all over the camp, and Isaac spent the next three days making ink and copying the document onto a fresh parchment while it could still be pieced together and read.

Yet not once did anyone suggest that Jacob should be taught to read.

"When your father had no son," said Rebekah, "my father was trained to read so that he could preserve the birthright, if it happened to fall to him. Shouldn't we train Jacob, too, in case something happens to Esau?"

"The Lord will protect him."

"From himself? Yes, I trust the Lord to protect him from falling off a cliff, though sometimes I wonder if there *are* enough angels to watch out for him all the time. But can the Lord protect him from his own disobedient choices that make him unworthy of the birthright?"

"If Esau proves unworthy, there's plenty of time to teach Jacob. But we're *not* going to put it in his head to covet a birthright that will never be his."

So that was it, thought Rebekah. The Lord's prophecy made them suspicious of Jacob, made them want to keep even the knowledge of reading and writing away from him.

But Rebekah had no patience with such nonsense. She told Jacob that very afternoon that she had a new game to teach him, and soon he was learning his letters. She told him to keep it a secret between them until he was good enough to show his father and grandfather, and so every day they worked on the letters until Jacob could read anything she wrote, even when he had never heard the word before, and could write quite legibly, too.

She should have known, however, that such a secret could not be kept. Jacob didn't tell anyone, but he did scratch the letters into the dirt when the shepherds wouldn't let him get close to the flashing knives at shearing time. The next day Isaac saw the random letters and words written in the dirt—including the sentence "Yes I am old enough" in a very bold and angry hand—and he immediately came to Rebekah.

"I told you that boy was not to be taught!" he said. It was the first time he had ever been openly angry with her, and instead of being contrite, she was angry right back at him.

"You said that you and your father wouldn't teach him the writing in the holy books."

"That didn't mean for you to do it in our place."

"But Isaac, I didn't teach him the letters of the holy writings. I taught him the letters my father's household used to communicate with him."

"It's the same thing! Almost."

"How would I know that? I've never seen the holy writings, and you've never shown the slightest interest in seeing the writing I did know. So I'm passing along my family's writing to Jacob, just as you're passing your family's writing to Esau. Someday. When he sits still long enough and doesn't rip the ancient parchments."

"Now I understand," said Isaac, "why your father was so angry with your mother for her defiance!"

The words struck her so hard she lost her breath and couldn't answer. Isaac realized at once that he'd gone too far, but his effort at amelioration only made it worse. "Not that teaching Jacob to read is the same as worshiping Asherah."

"I'm glad you can see the difference," said Rebekah acidly.

"But the fact remains that you disobeyed my decision."

"The fact remains," said Rebekah, "that I did no such thing, because you never made it a commandment to *me*."

"Well I make it a commandment *now*."

"And what would you have me do? Go into Jacob's memory and strike out all his knowledge of writing?"

"Leave it alone and he'll forget it."

"You would deliberately make your second son, who loves learning, as ignorant as your firstborn, who hates it?"

"Esau is not ignorant."

"He's ignorant and disobedient by his own choice, and because you and Abraham encourage it."

"Maybe if he thought his mother loved him . . ."

Rebekah was furious at such a slander, but she kept her voice quiet to answer him. "I'm the only one who loves Esau enough to try to teach him to do right. And what does it say about you and Abraham, that you treat Jacob like nothing, precisely because he *is* obedient?"

"More obedient than his mother."

"Funny, isn't it?" said Rebekah. "My father never thought I was disobedient. Maybe I am, though, and maybe Esau got his disobedience from me. But when *he* disobeys, you say he's bold and needs to find his own way."

"You're not a five-year-old."

"And Esau won't always be, either. At what age do you plan to start teaching him to obey?"

"Let's see," said Isaac. "How old are *you?*"

Whereupon, as usual, he stalked away from her without allowing her any chance to reply.

This breach between them remained, though they smoothed it over with gentle words before the end of the day. It festered under the surface, and Rebekah knew that Isaac was as irritated with her as she was with him. Both of them, though, had a stubborn streak, and so Isaac became, if anything, even more indulgent of Esau, encouraging him in his hunting and teaching him his letters at a glacial pace, while Rebekah intensified her teaching of Jacob. She might not have the holy writings, but she knew the stories, and told them to Jacob, and encouraged him to write them down. She made one of the younger skinners teach her how to make parchment out of kidskin, and encouraged little Jacob to write down the stories she had told him. His versions, of course, were childish, with no real coherence, and with very odd emphases—he went on and on, for instance, with his list of the animals taken aboard Noah's ark, including some that he simply made up.

He wrote with such earnestness and enthusiasm that Rebekah was sure that Isaac would be charmed by it and soften his opposition to Jacob's learning. When she showed it to him, however, she saw at once that it had been a grave mistake. He grew more and more still as he read, and then turned his back on her and left with the parchment. Only a few moments later, a boy came to her tent and told her that Abraham wanted to see her and Jacob at once.

When she arrived, Jacob holding her hand, Abraham and Isaac were waiting, not inside Abraham's tent, but in front of it, the parchment lying in the dirt beside a small fire. She realized at once what they were going to do, and it became worse after a moment when Esau leaned out from behind his grandfather's back—they intended him to be a witness.

"I won't let you do this to him," Rebekah said, and started to take Jacob away, but Abraham snapped, "Stay!" and she stayed.

"It's not his fault, if there's something wrong," said Rebekah. "He did only what I asked him to do."

Abraham held up the parchment. "This is false scripture, like the counterfeit scriptures of the Pharaohs in Egypt."

"It's a child practicing his writing by setting down his memory of stories he loves."

"The writings have to be copied letter for letter, word for word, or the plain and precious truth will be replaced by foolish imaginings."

"We didn't think we were writing scripture," said Rebekah. "We're aware of the difference."

"Maybe you are," said Isaac. "But is he?"

"No more arguing with me in front of the boy, woman," said Abraham. "This is a lesson that has to be learned once and for all time." He held a corner of the parchment in the fire. Because it was new, it was still somewhat moist and burned only reluctantly. But Abraham burned it all, as Jacob watched, his face unreadably still. "That," said Abraham when the parchment had turned to ash, "is what will happen, in the end, to all false writings and imitation scriptures."

"May I take the boy away now?" said Rebekah. "Or do you have any further lessons to teach him?"

"To teach *him*? No," said Abraham. "But when you've taken him to one of the women to look after him, I'll expect you to come back here."

Rebekah looked at Isaac, but his face was unreadable.

Esau, however, was grinning at Jacob, who had tears streaking his cheeks.

She led Jacob away, her fury barely contained. Once she got him inside her tent, he began crying openly, and so did she. She dropped to her knees and hugged him to her, holding him tightly. "You did nothing wrong," she said to Jacob. "I thought they would be proud, that's why I showed it to them. If there was a sin, it was *my* sin."

"I'll never remember all the animals again," said Jacob.

322

So he did not understand the magnitude of his humiliation. That was good.

"I'll tell you what," said Rebekah. "We'll remember them, together, before you sleep tonight, and then we'll keep remembering them forever. We just won't write them down on parchment anymore. How's that?"

"I'll forget some. I already forgot some."

"We'll do our best," said Rebekah. "That's all we can do."

"Why didn't papa stop him from burning my writing?" asked Jacob.

"Because . . ." She paused a moment, trying to find a way to say it that wouldn't diminish Jacob's father in his eyes. "Because Grandfather is *his* papa, and so he has to be obedient."

"I thought when you got big you didn't have to do everything your papa says."

"When you get big," said Rebekah, "you'll obey all the commandments because you believe they're right. But when you're little, you don't understand everything yet, so you obey the commandments because your papa and mama say so."

"Isn't Papa big?"

"Papa's definitely big."

"Then he must think it's right to burn my letters."

"I don't know," said Rebekah. "But you stay here with Deborah. I have to go back."

"Did I get you in trouble too?" asked Jacob.

"No, silly."

"Grandfather sounded like he was mad at you."

"Well, if he is, it's not for anything *you* did. And he won't be very mad at me, I promise. You be good for Aunt Deborah, won't you?"

Deborah laughed. "He's always an angel, Rebekah, you silly." To Jacob she said, "You tell me all the animals you can think of."

The list was well under way when Rebekah reluctantly left the tent and returned to Abraham's. They were no longer in front of the tent, and the fire had been put out. She was relieved, upon entering, to see that Esau was no longer a witness. Presumably he also had been given over to someone to watch. Apparently they did not think it important to tell her.

She should not have spoken first, but she could not contain herself. "You didn't need to humiliate Jacob in front of his brother."

"Watch your rebellious tone, girl," said Abraham. "The lesson needed to be learned by both boys."

"But it was Jacob's writing that was burned, and Esau reveled in it."

"It's hardly my fault that Esau did not commit the offense," said Abraham.

"No," said Rebekah. "Besides, Esau couldn't write his own name. Didn't either of you even notice how *well* Jacob is writing? Why wasn't that part of the lesson? Look, Esau—learn how to write, and you too can have your writings burned by the men you love most in all the world. I'll be surprised if he ever learns another letter. Then what will become of your birthright?"

Abraham rose to his feet, trembling with anger; Isaac had to help him, he was so feeble and so furious.

Rebekah at once repented of her sharp words. What she had said had truth enough in it, but it did not help Jacob or Esau or anybody that she spoke so disrespectfully. "I'm sorry," she said, sinking to her knees. "I spoke in anger, and I was wrong to do it."

"Are you trying to curse the last days of my life?" said Abraham. "Are you trying to show me a family riven in half because my son's wife plays favorites with her children?"

"Plays favorites!" The charge was so ludicrous that she could hardly believe it. "I teach them both the same rules of behavior, I watch over them both—and if you two weren't always encouraging Esau's defiance, maybe he would have learned some obedience by now!"

"So much for your sorrow about speaking in anger," said Abraham.

"How can I hold my tongue when you're so unjust?" said Rebekah.

"What injustice have I committed, girl?" said Abraham. "What lesson is it that you have to teach me?"

"You're right," said Rebekah. "You stopped learning years ago."

She felt Isaac's hand on her shoulder, and the grip was not kind.

"You have been at war with me since you came here," said Abraham. "I don't know why God chose you, and believe me, I've asked him many times. But when I think of what will happen to my family after I die, my heart breaks."

"Then why don't you tell Isaac to send me away? He'd do it, if you told him to."

"If you believe that, you foolish girl, then you don't know your husband."

"So you've suggested it? And he said no?"

"What God gave me, I do not refuse," said Abraham.

"No, I guess we've learned *that*, haven't we. So which is

worse? Having me as a daughter-in-law, or being commanded to sacrifice your son?"

Abraham recoiled from her words—staggered backward, and if Isaac had not been holding him up, he might have fallen.

"Go back to your tent, Rebekah," Isaac said.

"Oh, is your father finished with me?"

"My father hasn't been able to get a word in between your accusations," said Isaac.

"My accusations! You're the ones who called Jacob's sweet little writings 'false scriptures'! You're the ones who said I was a curse on the family!"

"While we were waiting for you to return," said Isaac, "I explained to Father that I thought he was wrong to burn the parchment in front of the boys. That it would have been better to leave it among the adults."

"Don't pretend you didn't know he was going to burn it from the start. Why else would he have that fire burning in front of the tent where we never have a fire?"

"Now she accuses her husband of lying," murmured Abraham.

"So you agree that you were wrong to burn the parchment?" Rebekah asked Abraham.

"No I do not," said Abraham.

"I didn't think so," said Rebekah.

"And Isaac didn't say that I agreed. He only said that *he* told me I was wrong."

"Why do I find it so hard to imagine the scene? Isaac actually suggesting to his father that something he said was less than perfect."

"Isaac isn't as rash as I am," said Abraham. "He speaks in private, when his words won't shame me openly."

"If only someone had been as thoughtful of poor Jacob. Not to mention Esau, who has now been shown as plainly as possible that it's all right for him to despise his brother, because after all, his father and grandfather do."

"That's what Isaac said," Abraham replied. "And maybe there *is* some truth to it. I was thinking only of the lesson about the scriptures. I didn't think of what it might do to the way the boys regard each other."

"So what prompted this sudden change? A moment ago you said you *weren't* wrong."

"Unlike you," said Abraham, "I actually listen to what other people are saying, and occasionally allow their words to change my mind."

This was so unfair that she couldn't find words to answer him.

"Instead of listening only to think of arguments to destroy them with," said Abraham.

"Like me."

"Isn't that what you were doing just now? Struggling to find some retort that would devastate me for daring to say that I was able to change my mind, and you were not?"

"Because you're wrong," she said, "and you can't see it."

"Sometimes I'm wrong, and like every other human being, I don't see it until I do. And sometimes that takes longer than it should, in my ignorance. Which is made worse by the fact that I'm old and have the foolish idea that I might actually have learned something from my experiences. But you don't have that problem, because you already know what's right and wrong and what matters most and what doesn't matter at all."

"I've never made any such claim."

"Of course you haven't," said Abraham. "To *claim* the supremacy of your judgment would show that you knew it was possible to doubt it."

Her mind raced with sharp answers, but underneath it she could feel another thought that she couldn't put in words, and it was that inarticulate thought that she knew most needed to be said.

So in the silence, there was a moment for Isaac's voice to emerge again. "We are all good people," he said, "trying to do good things for those we love. Because we disagree about what is the best thing to do doesn't make any of us evil."

Gentle as his voice was, it was a sharp yet fair rebuke to all of them, and from Abraham's face, Rebekah could see that he felt it as keenly as she did. "I know," she said. "But you treated me as if you thought I was horrible to have taught my son to read."

"And you treated me as if you thought I was a monster for having taught my grandsons that the sacred writings are not to be trifled with."

She started to renew the argument with a sharp retort, but again the unframed thought floating just under the level of consciousness distracted her from saying the harsh words that came to mind.

"Who is to say," said Isaac, "which lesson was most important to learn today?"

And then the unspoken thought took shape. "Isaac, Father Abraham, do you see what's happening in our family? This struggle between us is going to turn into a struggle between the boys. Esau and Jacob are as different as two brothers can be, but you are teaching Esau that he is the worthy, manly son and Jacob is weak and womanly."

"While you're teaching Jacob that he ought to covet the birthright."

"I'm teaching him to love the words and stories of God," said Rebekah.

And it was Abraham's turn to visibly stifle the retort he so plainly wanted to say.

And when he spoke, it was not a retort at all. "They both need to learn it all," he said. "They need to learn together. We've been wrong to try to keep Jacob away from the writings." Abraham looked at Rebekah. "It's the words the Lord gave you. Warning us that the younger would usurp the place of the older."

"Those weren't the words," said Rebekah, "and it wasn't a warning. It was just . . . a prophecy."

"The Lord gives us prophecies so we can figure out what to do before the moment of decision arrives."

"Yes," said Rebekah. "And if the younger will someday rule, shouldn't he be prepared to do it righteously?"

"It's not his right to do it at all," said Abraham.

"What if he has to rule because the older brother refuses to do it?" asked Rebekah. "Then it *would* be his right, even if he never sought it."

"But you *do* seek it for him," said Isaac softly.

"I don't!" cried Rebekah. "I want Esau to be worthy, I want him to—"

"How could he ever have any kind of faith or confidence, when you disapprove of everything he does?"

"And you *approve* of everything!"

"So he doesn't grow up surrounded by rebukes at every turn."

"And how does Jacob feel, with you two always praising Esau and completely ignoring him?"

"When do we have a chance even to see who Jacob is, when he's always with you and never with me?" said Isaac.

"He wants to be with you, but you never even see him. All you see is Esau."

"Because Jacob just . . . just tags along, just *clings* instead of *doing* things."

"He does things," said Rebekah. "But when he tends the animals, you mock him for hugging them instead of throwing rocks at them and . . . and *blinding* them." She couldn't help weeping at the unfairness of Isaac's treatment of Jacob.

"How can we love each other so much," said Isaac, "and yet see nothing but bad in the way we treat our sons?"

"All Jacob wants is your love."

"He has my love. You know he does, and *he* knows he does."

And that was true. Rebekah realized it now, that Isaac was affectionate with Jacob, that he listened to him—which was sometimes a challenge, since Jacob was a determined talker, more like Rebekah than like Isaac in that way. "Yes, you're right, it's not your love that he's missing, it's . . . your respect."

"Respect is earned," said Abraham.

"And how has Esau earned it? What great deeds of righteousness?"

"They're five. They can't tell right from wrong yet," said Abraham. "Esau's willfulness is not wicked."

"But it's not a great achievement, either," said Rebekah.

"You and Isaac revel in it as if it were something to be proud of."

"When I was Esau's age," said Abraham, "I already had a mind of my own."

"So does Jacob," said Rebekah. "But it's not wrong that he's able to listen and *change* his mind when he learns what is expected of him."

"No, it's not wrong," said Abraham.

Isaac sighed. "At long last," he said, "the two of you are actually trying to understand each other."

"So when will the two of *you* try it?" asked Abraham. He sounded as if he meant them to take the remark as a joke.

"It takes a lifetime," said Isaac. "Or so Mother told me."

What Rebekah did not say was, When will *you* two begin to understand each other? They were on the verge of making peace. She was not going to spoil it by provoking a new argument in which she would definitely be the outsider with no right to speak.

They ended the conversation with a new resolve to treat the boys even-handedly, and from that day forward, Abraham included Jacob with Esau in his lessons, and Isaac included Jacob with Esau when he taught them how to care for animals, and how to hunt, and how to fight in battle. Teaching them side by side was not always pleasant, because the two competed relentlessly, and each took it hard when he came out second best. But that competition made it so Esau worked hard at his reading in order to catch up with Jacob, who was so far ahead, and it made Jacob work hard at the games of hunting and war at which Esau excelled and in which Jacob had shown so little interest before.

And now that they were all trying to work together to

raise the boys well, Rebekah found that Abraham was not at all autocratic and arbitrary. He had reasons for everything he decided, and when she spoke to him respectfully instead of picking a quarrel, he listened to her and explained things to her so that most of the time they ended up in agreement. Isaac seemed much happier, too, to have peace between his father and his wife, and as she eventually became pregnant with each of the three girls, he could not have been more attentive.

But the tensions were all still there. Working in harmony did not mean that they were truly of one mind, only that they were determined to find a way to keep the peace and willing to compromise with or tolerate each other in order to do it.

When the twins were old enough that they began to reach the stature of men, and beards first began to grow on their faces—heavily on Esau's face, lightly on Jacob's—Abraham began to grow not just frail, but unwell, with pains that kept him from rising from his bed more and more hours of each day, until it was clear to everyone that he was dying. One by one he called his sons and grandsons to him and blessed them—beginning with Ishmael and his sons, and then Keturah's sons and the grandsons who were old enough to sit still under Abraham's hands. Each of Keturah's sons was given a substantial gift of breeding stock that would bring them prosperity if they cared for them properly, along with a few good servants to help them with the labor and protection of their household. Keturah herself was given a household, and her sons were charged with helping maintain her all the rest of her life with the flocks and herds that Abraham settled upon her.

So blessed was Abraham with flocks and herds, lands and servants, that when he had given gifts to all his sons and to his last wife, and they had all moved away to their own places of settlement, it hardly seemed that the wealth that would be inherited by Isaac was diminished at all.

Abraham blessed Esau and Jacob, charging them especially with a solemn obligation not to take wives from among the daughters of the Canaanites, "or your children will grow up to hate God and love the idols of Canaan." Both boys vowed to obey him in this, and to serve God all their lives.

Then, to Rebekah's surprise, he called her in. He did not lay hands on her head, but he talked to her for a while, and his words were gentle. "I think I looked for you to be Sarah," said Abraham, "and in some ways you have been—in your strength and boldness and . . . your desire to serve God. Maybe in that you're even fiercer than Sarah was."

Rebekah blushed at the thought that in Abraham's eyes she might have surpassed Sarah in anything at all. And she found that she liked the word "fierce" when applied to her faith.

"But there are ways that you aren't like Sarah, and ways that I didn't want you to be like her because I thought she and I had made mistakes together with our sons," said Abraham.

That again, thought Rebekah. But on his deathbed she would not argue.

"Especially . . ."

Oh, please, don't show disrespect to my husband now!

" . . . Ishmael."

Rebekah was glad she had held her tongue.

"Sometimes the things we do out of fear help to bring about the very things we dreaded. But what's done is done, and like every man and woman, Ishmael has to do the best he can with the errors of his parents. As your children will become the men and women they choose to be, either because of or in spite of what you and Isaac do well or badly in raising them."

These words filled her with confidence, even though she also heard them as a warning and was sure Abraham meant them partly that way as well. It was good to remember that the children were themselves first and eternally, and sons and daughters only second.

"Be good to your husband, Rebekah," said Abraham. "You are the fire in his hearth. He wasn't complete until you came to him." He laughed, a papery dry laugh that made her think of locusts on a dry desert wind. "What man *is* complete, without a woman who completes him and needs him as much in her turn?"

"I'll try to make you proud of me," said Rebekah. "All my life, I only wanted to serve the God of Abraham."

"The God of Abraham and Isaac," said Abraham. "And Esau, if God is willing."

Or if Esau is, Rebekah said silently.

"I never even hoped that I might be blessed to spend so many years in your household, learning from you. God has been kind to me."

He smiled then, and did not remind her of how much she had resisted living in his household and learning from him. He didn't need to.

"Send my boy to me now," he said. "Send me Isaac. I need to hold him to my heart again before I die." He sighed, and his breath caught with emotion. "God sent us such a good and pure spirit to be our son. We couldn't bear to think of the world soiling him or hurting him, and we protected him too much. We should have known that his goodness was strong enough to stand anything."

Those were the words she had longed to hear. The words she hoped he would also say to Isaac, for if there was any shadow in Isaac's life, it was his hunger to know his father loved and honored him. Why couldn't he have said them before, to Isaac's face, or to others in Isaac's presence?

She leaned over and kissed Abraham's brow, and thanked him, and bade him farewell, and then went out to fetch her husband.

Isaac went in to his father and remained alone with him until he died.

CHAPTER 14

Rebekah had expected that Abraham's death, when it came, would change their lives completely, and things were in fact different. They moved back to Lahai-roi, because Rebekah and Isaac both preferred it there—and because it was farther from the cities of the Philistines, where Esau now was being inexorably drawn. With Keturah gone, Rebekah was the undisputed ruler of the women, and because they already knew her, and because Rebekah was a fairer and more patient mistress than Keturah had been, she found no lack of loyalty and help among the women.

But those were all relatively small changes, really. Rebekah had hoped for a more profound change—that without his father's overwhelming presence, Isaac would become less diffident with the servants, more willing to issue firm commands. But he remained as he always had been, kind and compassionate but prone not to make decisions unless they were of particular urgency. His patience was as inexhaustible as ever—even in cases where firm action could have solved a problem before it got started. It was frustrating that one of Isaac's finest virtues as a man should be a weakness, at least sometimes, as a ruler.

On the other hand, Rebekah was relieved that contrary to Sarah's old fears, Ishmael did not make any kind of move against Isaac at all. Ishmael came to Abraham's burial as he had come for his blessing, with only a small retinue of men. Cousin Moab actually brought more men from his town east of the Jordan. And when Isaac gave Ishmael a gift of a vast number of cattle—which Eliezer had counseled against, lest it be interpreted as tribute—Ishmael responded by giving Isaac a gift of even more sheep, so that neither could be said to have enriched—or intimidated—the other.

As the brothers laid their father's wrapped body in the cave of Machpelah beside the dried, mummified body of Sarah, Rebekah felt nothing but relief in her heart, for instead of quarreling they embraced each other and wept for their father. Perhaps they wept for different things—Ishmael for the loss of his company when he was a youth and needed him; Isaac for the way Abraham never seemed satisfied with him despite all his effort to be worthy—or perhaps they wept for the same thing, because he was a good man that they loved deeply and whose absence would be keenly felt. Either way, they were at peace with each other there at the tomb Abraham had bought to hold the body of his beloved wife.

And the house of Isaac remained at peace with all his kin, and as for possible enemies outside the family, any who had power enough to be a threat simply had no motive. Abraham had been a man of peace with the strength and will to preserve it. Isaac was no less peaceful, and at first, no one tried to test his will or strength.

Only Rebekah could see that Abraham's death, rather than liberating Isaac from the burdens that his father had placed upon him, only guaranteed that there would be no relief as long as Isaac lived. That memory of his father choosing to obey God and offer up his life, however he might understand it and even agree with it in his mind, still preyed on him in his heart and showed itself in Isaac's contempt for his own abilities. Whatever Abraham might have said to him on his deathbed, whatever blessing he might have given, it was not enough to counter all the years of self-doubt, the hopeless self-evaluation that had become a part of Isaac's character.

The one gift I long most to give him, thought Rebekah, the one that a wife *should* be able to give, is simply beyond my power. Whatever preys on Isaac's soul, only God can take from him; whatever happiness he hungers for, only God can give it.

With time, however, changes did come. As the Philistine cities grew, so did their need for farmland to support their growing populations, and soon Philistine farmers were deliberately filling the wells near their cities that Abraham's herds depended on. It was an act of war, but when Isaac sent complaints to the king of this or that Philistine city, the king always protested that he had never given permission for such a thing, that he deplored it, and that he would surely find and punish the perpetrators.

Isaac, Eliezer, and Rebekah conferred about it, and decided that there was no point in dying or killing over it. "If we had fewer herds," said Isaac, "we'd have no need of those wells."

Eliezer's response was, "If you had no herds at all, we'd need no water except for ourselves."

He meant it to be a joke, but Isaac didn't laugh. "I couldn't feed the men and women who have served my father all these years if I did that. But I've found a middle way. I have a loyal servant whose grandsons are now grown men, and it's wrong to keep him in service to the end of his days. He has earned an inheritance to give to his sons and grandsons, and so I'll give him all the flocks and herds that are watered at the wells of the Philistines, along with the servants who now tend them. If he's wise, he'll move them immediately to other pastures, and avoid quarreling with the Philistines. But since they'll belong to him, that decision is his as well."

"That's nearly half your wealth," said Eliezer.

"That's how this servant deserves to be rewarded," said Isaac. "Though in another sense he will still be lifting half my burden, so even this gift gives back as much to me."

"And who is the servant who will receive this burdensome gift?"

Rebekah sighed. "Why can't we just say these things plainly?"

Isaac laughed. "All right, then. Eliezer, you're the man, of course—who else could it be?"

"You are discharging me from your service?"

"Of course not. I'm finally paying for it."

"But I bound myself to Abraham forever."

"Stay bound to Abraham. I'm Isaac, and I declare that you and all your children are free. What I give you now will be your inheritance to pass on to your children. Even if you think you shouldn't receive so much, remember how little it will be divided among your grandsons."

"But if I'm not the steward of Isaac, I'm only Eliezer. Who is Eliezer?"

"All your cattle and sheep and goats will low and bleat your name. Soon everyone will know it."

Eliezer bowed himself to the earth then, and wept, and accepted the gift that Isaac gave him.

After Eliezer left Isaac's tent, Isaac sat heavily on the rug and said, "It wasn't about the wells or the Philistines, you know."

"I should hope not," said Rebekah. "The right to water is precious and shouldn't be so easily abandoned."

"I thought my father should have done this before he died. I even suggested it, but Father said that I'd need all my strength and all my wealth to maintain my position. Which I suppose is true. Father never needed wealth—he could walk into a king's palace without a single servant, without being armed himself, and still be treated with the respect due to a great lord. While I need to have a few hundred thousand sheep and cows and goats under my control before anyone will take me seriously."

"You underestimate yourself."

"You overestimate me," said Isaac. "But I'm getting older and my vision is beginning to fail. It's better if I rule over a smaller household. It's more in line with my abilities."

"Well, I could rule over a household twice this size," said Rebekah.

When Isaac looked at her with dismay, she laughed and nudged him. "Isaac, you and I are both very good at ruling a household peacefully. If you were king of the whole earth, there's not a city that wouldn't be better governed. But I'm content with half of what your father had, or half of that, or half of that, though you should keep in mind that a vast household will be left alone by enemies the way a snake never bothers to try to swallow a sheep. But if you shrink your holdings small enough, then some ambitious desert snake or city viper will begin to think he can swallow you up and add what you have to his domain."

"I'll heed the warning," said Isaac. "I have no one else to give another half of my wealth to."

"Until you decide to divide what you have between your sons."

"The inheritance is whole. It will go to one son, not the other."

"The birthright is whole," said Rebekah, "but you know you'll give half of the flocks and herds and servants to one son as a gift, and the other half to your heir as his inheritance. Call it what you will, it amounts to the same thing. They'll each get half of the half of your holdings that you now have left."

"So I leave each of them with a quarter of the strength that my father left to me." Isaac said it with a note of despair in his voice.

"That's absurd," said Rebekah. "The strength of your father was always faith in God, and when he and Sarah were alone in Egypt during the drought, God made them mightier than Pharaoh."

"Yes, well, that was Father. And Mother."

"And this is you. All the flocks and herds could be swept away in a moment, and you would still be Isaac."

"And you would still be Rebekah. But we'd be very very poor."

They laughed together.

"The wealth is what we give our children who haven't the faith to rely on God," said Rebekah.

"The girls will all be like their mother—like stone in their faith," said Isaac.

"I only worry about Esau," said Rebekah.

"You don't need to worry about him," said Isaac. "His faith is strong."

Rebekah wondered how he could say that with such confidence. "What sign of faith have you seen in him?"

"He and I speak of the things of God often," said Isaac.

"Even if Esau really does think of God when he's talking to you," said Rebekah, "that still doesn't account for when he's out on the hunt with his wild friends or with one of Ishmael's sons, which is even worse. Do you think he's thinking of God when he's out stalking some animal to kill it, or in some town or other, playing at whatever games he plays?"

"Games?" asked Isaac. "What kind of games do you think a young man Esau's age plays?"

"I don't know. I've never been a boy. Not that Esau is a boy anymore. He says he's going hunting, and he comes back with a smirk on his face and says the deer were elusive today, and I keep thinking it's no hart he hunts, but hinds."

Isaac got a distant look on his face. "He knows the law of chastity," he said. "He assures me that there is no girl whose virtue is in danger from him."

"Which leaves a vast number of girls whose virtue was ruined long ago," said Rebekah. "My concern is whether Esau's virtue is in danger from *them*."

"How did we get from our children's inheritance to Esau's *endless* faults?"

"His faults aren't endless, and I see his virtues as well as you do," said Rebekah. "I'm proud of him. But what kind of keeper of the birthright will he be, when he takes no thought of the teachings of the prophets except when he needs to do it to impress you?"

"Do you think I'm so easily deceived as that?" asked Isaac.

"Yes, you are," said Rebekah.

Isaac got the cold look that told Rebekah she was one sentence away from having him leave in silence.

"Isaac, it's one of your virtues. You're so absolutely honest yourself that it never crosses your mind that the person you're talking to might be telling you only what you want to hear."

"Esau loves the Lord."

"And I tell you that he doesn't," said Rebekah.

"And Jacob does?"

"With all his heart."

"And you know this because *he* tells *you*. How is that any different?"

"Because I *don't* know it just from that. I see it in everything he does. Jacob keeps his word, even when it isn't convenient. Can you say that about Esau?"

"Are you calling him an oath-breaker?"

"I'm saying he doesn't do what he tells me he's going to do, and when I remind him he either gets angry with me—'Mother, I'm going to do it!'—or he laughs and says, 'Didn't I already do that?'"

"He's just irresponsible."

"All right, that's as good a word as any."

"But all boys are. They grow out of it."

"Jacob isn't. When he tells me a job will be done, he does it. Carefully and well, and takes pride in having done it for me. When will Esau *start* to grow out of this . . . irresponsibility?"

Isaac's eyes flashed. Time for the silence now?

No. Though he didn't look at her, his voice was hard and set—as angry-sounding as Rebekah could remember his ever being with her. "When will you understand that God's decision in making Esau the firstborn is an irrevocable one? I'm not going to throw my firstborn out of his place and put his younger brother there, even if Jacob *is* your favorite child."

"I love both my sons, and I want what's best for them."

"And somehow you decided it's best for Esau to be rejected as firstborn? How much will he love God then?"

"Can you hear your own words, Isaac? Even *you* realize that if Esau were deprived of the birthright, his love of God would evaporate at once."

"If he's hurt that badly by his parents, in anger he might rebel against God in order to hurt us back."

"But *you* were hurt by your father, and you didn't rebel against God."

"Rebekah. The birthright is Esau's. And it's the great sorrow of my life, that my wife despises her own firstborn."

The words outraged her with their unfairness, and Rebekah answered quickly, in the first heat of her anger. "The great sorrow of *my* life is that my husband is blind to the son who loves God and obeys his parents."

Isaac left her then. As usual, the argument quickly receded and they conversed normally again, but the words stayed in Rebekah's memory and poisoned everything that happened afterward. There were times when she would have rebuked Esau and charged him to do better, but she held her peace because her husband would think she hated her firstborn.

And there were times when she would have delighted in Esau and shown her deep love for him, but in her stubbornness she refused to let her husband see her delight in the young hunter, when Isaac still showed no favor to the son who deserved it more.

As for Jacob, what could she do except try to help him move beyond the deep void in his life that only his father's love and respect could truly fill?

The wall in the family was fully built, and named, and she and Jacob stayed on one side of it, and Isaac and Esau on the other, even as they went through the motions of being one family, unchanged.

The girls felt it, too. Little Deborah, the eldest of the three, doted on Jacob, who always had time for her even when he was hard at work with the sheep or in the fields. Little Sarah, the second, was devoted to Esau, who always brought her snatches of bright cloth from the city, or a soft rabbit skin from his hunting, or a strange butterfly, or a rare fruit. Only the baby, Qira, did not choose sides—but when Rebekah was upset, Qira would fuss at her breast, as if the milk had soured and Qira could not abide the taste of anger.

With Rebekah fussing at him less, and Isaac favoring him all the more no matter what he did, Esau slipped ever further out of control. Jacob came to her once and told her, "I think Esau has taken a wife in the city of Gerar."

"It's not a wife you take when your parents haven't been told," said Rebekah, but despite her ironic tone, her heart was sinking at the thought of what it would mean for the birthright, to be in a household headed by an idolatrous woman.

"I heard his friends tease him about having a baby coming."

"In front of you?"

"Esau was quick to deny it, and his friends saw how angry and worried he was and immediately they denied it. But Mother, even if she's a Canaanite and not a Philistine, how much better is it to have the holy writings in a house where Asherah is worshiped than in a house that serves Molech?"

"Oh, it's better," said Rebekah. "Better in the sense that a quick death in battle is better than a death by torture."

"I know the birthright isn't mine," said Jacob. "But can't I do anything to protect the holy writings?"

"Have you told your father?"

"What's the point? He'll accuse me of being envious and then call Esau in to confront me, and Esau will deny everything and afterward he'll threaten to kill me if I ever tell lies about him again."

"Kill you? He threatens your life?"

"He doesn't mean it," said Jacob. "I mean, he *means* it, but he won't do it."

"You mean he hasn't done it, because you haven't cost him anything. But if you told and your father believed you and took away the birthright, then we'd see what Esau might do."

"He's not a killer, Mother."

"How many times has he come home with blood on his hands?"

"The blood of the beasts he kills and brings home to Father."

"Like a cat showing off the mice it kills."

"Father loves the taste of wild game. I understand—I'm tired of the taste of mutton and lentils myself. But someone has to stay home and manage the flocks and herds. Esau has no more interest in the work of the camp than he has in . . ."

"In the birthright."

"Oh, he's interested in the birthright, Mother!"

"He's interested in having it, not in studying the holy writings and living by them."

"I know Father's eyes are weak, Mother, but why can't he see how Esau mocks everything that matters to our family?"

"Because Esau is smart enough not to show that side of himself in front of his father."

"But what if I had proof?"

"What could possibly prove it to your father? He won't believe what he's told, and he can't see it for himself."

"I'm the most helpless person in all this, Mother," said Jacob. "Because if I do anything to show Father who Esau really is, Father thinks I'm envious and want the birthright. Sometimes I think the only way I can help to save the birthright is to renounce it myself."

"And then whom would it go to?"

"One of Keturah's boys, maybe. Midian's a good man, Mother. He'd make a worthy guardian."

"And then your father's line would be cut off from the birthright, if it went to his half-brother."

"If the birthright goes to Esau, the way he is right now, then it will be lost to the whole world, because he'll never care for it."

"All we can do," said Rebekah, "is pray to the Lord to help your brother grow up and grow out of his rebelliousness and repent of his sins and become . . ."

"A good servant to the Lord."

"Like you."

"I'm not a good servant to the Lord, Mother, because I'm not the one chosen to *be* his servant. If I take it upon myself, I'll be a usurper."

"You don't have to have the birthright to be a servant of God," said Rebekah. "There was never a chance for *me* to have the birthright, but still I spent my childhood trying to serve God. And finally my day came. As yours will, my son."

"My day? My day for what—to be at war with my brother?"

"To have your father show you that he sees the man you are."

"Fathers never see their sons for what they are," said Jacob.

"That's not so."

"You've told me yourself how Grandfather never valued Father, either."

"He never really *showed* Isaac how he valued him."

"It's the same thing."

"No it's not," said Rebekah. "And I didn't mean your father Isaac, anyway. I meant your Father in heaven."

"He knows me. He knows us all."

"Sometimes I wonder why he doesn't just tell your father the way things should be."

"Because the problem isn't that Father *can't* see, it's that he *won't* see, and the Lord doesn't make us do things, he only teaches us and hopes we'll use the things he taught."

"So what has God taught you? And how are you going to use it?"

"What are you asking me to do, Mother?"

"Just keep being the man you are, and pray that your

---

brother will realize what road he's headed down and come back."

"Or that Father will finally get the proof he needs to see what Esau is becoming. Proof that is witnessed by someone other than me."

Later, Rebekah would realize that Jacob must have started planning then the incident that finally brought things to a head.

But at the time, the only thing Rebekah worried about was that she shouldn't have spoken so openly to Jacob about her worries concerning Esau. Yet within the family, Jacob was the only one besides Rebekah who understood the danger from Esau's behavior. And should she let him feel completely isolated in the family? Wasn't it good for the obedient son to know that his mother understood the man he had become, even if his father didn't see it and his brother despised him for it?

I didn't make Esau's choices for him. Nor is it my fault Isaac refuses to see. Though it's unbearable that he doesn't. Jacob *is* Isaac as he must have been as a child. He even looks more like Isaac—Esau looks like my father, except for the red hair.

Maybe that's the problem. Isaac can't love or value any man who even *looks* like himself.

For a while Rebekah believed that if Esau felt himself truly needed by the family, he might stop the things he was doing and settle down to life as Isaac's heir and the future head of the family. So when such a time came, she watched for his response.

It was the climate that changed their lives, as it had been in Abraham's day. Another drought, so severe that many wells went dry, and others simply didn't have the water to sustain the flocks. They got word that Eliezer and his sons had sold off much of their stock and then traded the rest to Ezbaal's cousin in exchange for orchards and wheatfields in the plain near the Great Sea, and they moved into one of the growing towns that was trying to compete with the growing Philistine cities. But Isaac knew that wasn't the right choice for his household. "If we settle on one piece of land, then we're bound to one city, to one people, generation after generation. Only when we have the ability to leave and carry what we have with us are we truly free, and only if we're free can we serve God."

Esau heard this with an outward show of respect—"That's very wise, Father"—but Jacob told Rebekah later that Esau and his Canaanite friends later mocked what Father had said.

For days, Isaac tried to decide what to do. If he moved from Lahai-roi and started wandering, he'd find himself struggling to find water that wasn't already defended. Eventually, a wandering life was bound to mean war. Finally he sat down with Rebekah and told her that as he searched the holy writings, he kept coming back to his father's account of his journey to Egypt during the depths of the last drought. "There's always grain in Egypt," he said.

"But Egypt isn't the same place where your father went. These days the country is dominated by a strong Pharaoh, and he hasn't forgotten what happened the last time he allowed wanderers like us into the country."

"How do you know so much about Egypt?" asked Isaac.

"From you! From the stories you've told me out of the holy writings. And from the traders who come through here, of course."

"Then why is it that I've talked to the same traders and I read the same scriptures and they seem to be guiding me to Egypt?"

"It's not enough to read the holy writings and then try to do what they did. Noah built an ark, after all, but I don't think that would help *us*."

"Noah was commanded to build an ark. We aren't being commanded to do anything."

"Are we asking?"

"Of course."

"No, I mean it, Isaac. Egypt is dangerous, and staying here is impossible, and it's at times like this that the keeper of the birthright has a right, has the *duty* to consult the Lord and find out what to do."

"If the Lord wanted to speak to me, Rebekah, he could have done it a thousand times before now. Including this morning when I prayed to him about exactly this matter."

"In every crisis before now, your father was head of the household and the Lord spoke to *him*. Now you're the patriarch. Expect to be answered, *clearly*. It's your *right* to be led by the Lord."

"As I recall, you've had more actual visions than I have," said Isaac. "Maybe *you* should pray."

"I *once* received a vision about the babies in my womb," said Rebekah. "And it was in answer to *your* prayers. You have responsibility for all these people. The Lord answers you all the time when you pray for them."

"And if he doesn't?"

"Then it only means that the choice is up to you, and whatever you choose will please the Lord."

Isaac grinned at her. "Now you're sounding like the kind

of believer you said your mother was—you've set a test for the Lord that the Lord can't fail."

"But we're not testing the Lord," said Rebekah. "We already know that the Lord is God. We're seeking to know his will. And he *will* answer."

"How do you know?"

"Because we need him, and he won't fail us."

"No. But *I* might fail us."

"The only way you could fail us, Isaac, is if you heard the Lord's answer and disobeyed it. Or if you refused to ask him, because you didn't believe he loved us enough to answer."

So Isaac, full of self-doubt and clinging to his faith in God, went to pray. In the morning he awoke Rebekah by coming into her tent and whispering in her ear. "I dreamed a dream," he said.

She came out of the fog of sleep to hear him telling of how he saw himself among dying cattle, and dipping down into a well only to come up with jars full of sand. In his dream he said what he had been saying in his prayers—I see nothing for us to do but to go down into Egypt. "And then there was a voice in my dream telling me not to go to Egypt, but to stay in Canaan. The wells our family used to control near the cities of the coast are no longer used, with Eliezer gone. If I go to Abimelech, the king of Gerar, he'll let us use the wells as long as we need them."

"*Let* us use them? They're ours by right. Your father dug them!"

"Let him think he rules, let him think the wells are his to share with us," said Isaac. "I have the Lord's promise—the same one he gave to Father, only now he has sworn to fulfill the oath with me. My children will multiply as the stars of heaven, he said, and they'll be given all these countries, and through my seed all nations of the earth will be blessed."

Then Isaac wept in her embrace, in gratitude that the Lord at last had spoken to him, as he spoke to Abraham, and accepted him as the heir to Abraham's covenant. "You believed when I did not."

"You always believed in God," said Rebekah. "It's yourself you doubted, and I knew better, because I can *see* you."

"And I can't see anything," said Isaac ruefully, for his eyes were getting old and he couldn't see far-off things clearly. Worse, there were white patches in his eyes growing out over the pupils, cutting off part of his field of vision. But for now, he could see what he needed to—that the Lord had not abandoned him, but would lead him to safety.

Only Esau resisted the move. "I can't hunt there in the plains," he said. "It's all farmland, orchards, *tame.*"

"You can hunt where you've always hunted," said Isaac. "You'll just have to go farther and work harder to get there."

"You might try staying with the camp and helping us redig the wells near Gerar," said Jacob.

"I'm not a well-digger," said Esau contemptuously.

"We'll all be well-diggers," said Isaac, "until our flocks have the water they need."

"Of course, Father. I was only teasing Jacob. As if *he* needed to teach me my duty!"

They went to the wells near Gerar and it all happened as the Lord had promised. It wasn't exactly a miracle—the Lord didn't force Abimelech to be generous where his father had been haughty back when Isaac first gave up the wells. What Rebekah gathered from the ladies of Gerar whom she visited with while Isaac negotiated with the king was that the crown rested very loosely on the head of this current Abimelech, whose mother had been only a concubine and whose people had actually preferred a different brother who had happened to be away from Gerar when the old king suddenly died. Having Isaac's large camp and hundreds of servants in the hills overlooking the city changed the balance of power in the city, for Abimelech made a great show of his friendship with Isaac, implying that if anyone attempted to revolt against him, he'd be able to flee to the camp of his friend Isaac and bring down an army of Hebrews to subdue Gerar and restore Abimelech to power.

But the Lord had known the weakness of Abimelech's position, and that's why he sent Isaac there. The miracle was not that Abimelech exploited their presence and in exchange Isaac got water for his flocks during a drought. The miracle was that Isaac asked the Lord with faith that he would be answered—or at least with hope—and the Lord answered him, and for the first time in his life Isaac was happy in the confidence of the Lord.

Esau, true to form, lasted only one day at well-digging, and then he was off with Nebajoth, one of Ishmael's sons, on a hunting expedition into the rocky country south of Gerar. "We have meat," said Rebekah. "We have enough meat to feed ten thousand. What we need is water. Will you find us water in the desert and bring it home to us on the backs of asses?"

"Father likes the venison I bring him," said Esau. "He's an old man. Don't you think an old man should have things he likes?"

"He needs your help more than he needs venison."

"He has servants," said Esau. "But he has no deer in all his flocks and herds." Then Esau laughed and went on his way.

Jacob saw it all, of course, and when Esau was gone said to his mother, "He thinks it'll be like hunting in the hills near Kirjath-arba."

"And it won't be?" asked Rebekah.

"There are streams and pools in the mountains of Canaan. But south in the Negev there are no streams."

"Why do you know this and he doesn't?" asked Rebekah.

"Because I know everything the shepherds know, and the shepherds know that they can't take a flock into the Negev and hope to bring back even half of them. The lions know where there are tiny shaded pools they can lap from, and so do the small deer and mountain goats they prey on. So there are always lions to take the sheep that don't die of thirst."

"Is your brother in danger?"

"In danger of coming home exhausted and empty-handed."

"Of dying? Is it that bad?"

"Mother, Esau's a good hunter. He'll have the water he needs with him, and when he sees that he's running low, he'll come home. As for the lions—Esau will no doubt bring home a lion skin to show off. Even if he finds no deer, he'll not come home without blood on his hands."

"What about you?" asked Rebekah, suddenly curious.

"What about me?"

"Could *you* kill a lion?"

"I *have* killed lions, Mother. I'm a shepherd, and it's a season of drought. The lions come down out of the mountains, following the game, and they're following the water."

"But you never bring home the skin. I never hear of your doing such things."

"It would shame me in front of the other shepherds, to be

355

caught bragging to my father and mother about doing what every shepherd does."

"The other shepherds brag all the time."

"They're not the son of the patriarch," said Jacob.

As long as she was asking, she might as well learn the rest. "What about in battle?"

"Against what foe?"

"The enemies we sometimes face. Raiders. Soldiers."

"I don't know. I've never fought against a man."

"Oh."

"Why are you asking such questions, Mother? Is there something you know about, that you haven't told me? Is there a war coming?"

"No, I don't—I hope not. I just wondered—because you've killed lions and I didn't know it . . ."

"I'm no match for Esau when it comes to fighting, Mother. He loves it and he's been practicing all his life. I hate it and I've learned only what I need to in order to fend off raiders and thieves. They aren't usually the best fighters anyway so they're easily frightened away. That's the total of my experience of battle—frightening away marauders by showing them that we won't run away ourselves at the sight of them."

Something sank inside Rebekah's heart. Because she could not forget that Esau had once threatened to kill Jacob, and even though he almost certainly didn't mean it, it would have been nice to think that Jacob could protect himself.

Though in truth, no one was safe if someone wanted to murder him and didn't care about the consequences. Unless the Lord was protecting you, and then no enemy could touch you. Jacob's protection would never be sword or spear in his hand, but rather faith and goodness in his heart.

And in faith and goodness, he was as skilled and practiced as Esau was with bow and javelin.

Esau came home empty-handed, as Jacob had foretold, and he and Nebajoth and the men they had taken with them were all exhausted and famished. Jacob had seen to it that plenty of lentil pottage was kept ready for them, so that whenever they returned they could eat without waiting. They were so hungry they ate it all—though apparently it never occurred to Esau to thank Jacob for having provided for him. Rather he took it as his right to be served by his younger brother.

During their time in Gerar, true disaster struck. The blotches in Isaac's eyes finally grew to block his pupils entirely. He was utterly blind.

Rebekah came to find him on one of his last days with vision, and found him in his tent, bowed over a parchment, weeping.

"What is it?" she asked.

"I can't remember what it says."

"What do you mean?"

"I could always make out enough of the writing to remember the words and say them aloud, but I can't even tell which prophet's story this is."

Rebekah glanced down at the parchment. It was the first time she had been allowed to read one of the holy writings for herself—and she hadn't actually been allowed this time, either. Yet she felt no excitement about it, because everything was swallowed up in Isaac's grief at his blindness. "At the head of the parchment," Rebekah said, "it says that it's the book of Enoch, written in his own hand as a testament to and condemnation of the people who for their love of bloodshed have rejected the Lord their God."

Isaac sat in silence.

Was he angry that she had read from the scripture? "Do you need me to read more?"

He shook his head.

She reached out and took his hand, meaning to comfort him. Instead, he wept again.

She saw how old he had become. His hair was white, his beard speckled like new-broken granite. And with the white splotches on his eyes, he seemed to have lost much of the fire that she had always seen burning in him.

He was going to die.

Not tomorrow or the next day, but his body was aging faster than his father's had. And with his vision gone, as it nearly was, he would lose much of his hope, much of his reason to live.

She thought of her father then, and how he had raged when he lost his hearing. But his deafness had been caused by an accident and a sickness that followed it. It came on him suddenly, in the robustness of his middle age—and even he had lost much of his vigor because of it, until Laban and Rebekah had restored it to him with their efforts to write to him, to be his ears.

"Isaac, you won't have to go without reading the holy writings. Let me and Jacob and Esau read them to you."

"It's too late," said Isaac. "I always thought I had more time."

"More time for what?"

"For copying," he said. "Father didn't let me have them during his old age—I think he was more and more afraid that I might lose one or damage it. And after I got them, I copied a few but I knew I'd have plenty of time after my sons took over the work of the camp."

"So let your sons do the work of copying. It's their work eventually." Well, it was Esau's work, but she knew which son actually had the patience to do it. As for that, why not make the most audacious offer? "I can help. My hand is as clear and clean as this."

If he even heard her, he gave no sign.

"I'll never see the words again."

"Neither will your father. The advantage you have is that you're not dead, so at least you'll hear the words as we read them to you."

"Yes," said Isaac. "Yes, I see the wisdom of that." He stilled his weeping. "I'm sorry you saw me being so weak. Grieving for my eyes like a child who lost a toy."

"I saw my father's grief when he lost his hearing. Losing your vision is harder. Of course you grieve."

"It wasn't for my eyes, Rebekah, truly it wasn't. I give thanks that I ever had them. I grieved because . . . just when the Lord gave me vision in the spirit for the first time, he's taken away the vision of my eyes. What have I done to be so unworthy?"

"This isn't a punishment," said Rebekah. "It's . . . part of life. These things happen to people. You're not the first blind man, or we wouldn't already have a word for it, would we?"

"I know," he said. "And yes, Rebekah, the work of copying must be done. If the Lord makes me blind, then my sons have to be my eyes and hands. And if the Lord has given me a wife who can read and write, I would be ungrateful not to let you be my helpmeet in this as in all other things."

He had heard her offer, had thought about it, and without

Abraham here to be adamant, he could see that the old rule was not helpful now, and change it.

He reached out and touched her face. "There's one gift in my blindness, though. You'll always be as beautiful in my eyes as you are today."

"You're so silly, Isaac. My beauty fled years ago, such as it was. I'm an old woman. Though of course I'm still but a child compared to *you*."

He laughed. "Ah, but you've stayed beautiful. In fact, you've grown more beautiful with every day and year that's passed. Even when we argue, you know, I still marvel that the Lord loved me enough to give you to me as my wife."

"Oh, come now. You just didn't know it, but I was the first of the plagues the Lord sent to you, blindness being by far the lesser one."

He kissed her, and then let his lips explore her cheeks, her eyes, her brow. "I can depend on you," he said.

"For everything."

"You'll be my eyes. Whatever you see, you'll tell me."

"I will."

"I'll always see truly, with you as my eyes."

"As truly as I see. I can't be any wiser for you than I am for myself."

"That's vision enough for me," said Isaac.

"And you have the Lord to speak truth into your heart."

"Yes. I do."

Thus began the precious months in which Jacob and Rebekah copied the scriptures, reading aloud to Isaac as they did. He would interrupt them and explain what Abraham had told them this or that passage meant, and when they copied it out, they would add Isaac's explanations and read them back to him. They would sometimes interrupt with questions, and Jacob often discussed doctrine with his father while Rebekah kept on writing.

It was wonderful to see Jacob and Isaac sharing the holy writings this way. To hear how Jacob's voice was the same as Isaac's, how his tone echoed his father's inflections. And gradually Jacob began adding his own insights and speculations about the implications of the scriptures, as Isaac nodded encouragement or offered countersuggestions.

Through all of this, Esau came once or twice, early on, but he quickly lost patience and left, and then stopped coming in the first place. Rebekah never bothered to point out Esau's absence to Isaac. Why provoke a quarrel, when the point was so obvious that even a blind man could see it? Especially a blind man.

But if Isaac saw, he gave no sign.

Meanwhile, Isaac's people had prospered so much in the land near Gerar that he needed more servants to tend his flocks and fields and orchards, until he had as many servants as he had had before he sent half of them with Eliezer. The people of Gerar began to be envious, and then frightened. "How do we know they won't decide they want to possess our city?" they said, and there began to be quarrels between men of Gerar and Isaac's men over the use of the wells. Of course Abimelech denied any knowledge of what his citizens were doing, and of course Isaac and Rebekah pretended to believe his protestations. But they understood that Abimelech did not dare to stop his people from what they were doing, or he would be accused of already being under Isaac's control, and one of his many rivals would rally support against him.

Since Abimelech was helpless to stop the fighting, Isaac's

answer was to send his men to dig another well farther from the city, and even as they were digging it, men of Gerar came to harass them, claiming that any water that came out of it should belong to them because it was on land within sight of the walls of Gerar. Isaac named the well Esek, meaning "strife," and they used it for a few months, till a new well even farther away could be dug, at Sitnah.

But even that one became a point of contention, until Isaac had his men dig yet another well in poorer land that was so far from Gerar that it would take half a day for the men of Gerar to reach them to cause trouble. And at this well, Rehoboth, there was no more contention.

But of course it did not have as much water in it as the previous wells had had, and they needed yet another. Isaac rode a camel that was led in front of the others, following a winding path among hills pocked with outcroppings of rock and covered with sun-browned grass. Finally Isaac told the boy leading him to stop. The spot seemed to Rebekah to be no more inviting than any other, but Isaac said, "Tomorrow we'll begin to dig here."

Such was their respect for him that none of the servants said, This is just the sort of place a blind man would choose. But they had to be thinking it.

That night, sleeping in the same traveling tent with Isaac, Rebekah awoke to hear him mumbling in his sleep. It seemed not to be a nightmare, and so she did not waken him, but lay there and listened. The words surfaced in isolation and meant nothing to her. Finally he grew still, and she realized from the way he was breathing that he was no longer asleep.

"What was your dream?" she asked him.

"The Lord came to me," said Isaac.

She became more alert, and leaned over him. In the darkness she saw nothing, yet his voice told her that he was filled with emotion. She glided her hand along his chest to his neck, then up to his cheeks. Sure enough, tears had flowed from his eyes across his temples and into his beard.

"What did he say?" asked Rebekah.

"He said he was the God of my father, and told me not to be afraid, because he's with me. He said he would bless me and multiply my seed for Abraham's sake, because he was such a good servant."

Rebekah knew that even in the midst of this vision, Isaac would hear only that it was Abraham's worthiness, not his own, that the Lord was honoring.

"Tomorrow we'll write the Lord's words," said Rebekah. "I'll be your hand, and we'll write an account of your vision in the book of Isaac."

"There *is* no book of Isaac," he said.

"Didn't you write about the Lord telling you to go to Gerar instead of Egypt?"

"It didn't seem important. Not like the visions my father had."

"If the Lord thinks it's important enough to speak to you, how can you say that it isn't important enough to write it down?"

"I can't write anything. In case you haven't noticed, I'm blind."

"But you have my hands, or Jacob's hands, if you think it has to be a man. You've had the vision you wanted all your life, and you have to write it down so your children and their children will know of it."

"If the Lord wanted me to write, he wouldn't have made me blind."

"If the Lord wanted you not to write, he would have taken you home. He hasn't, so you're still here, and as long as you're here, you're the only one who *can* write, or cause your words to be written down by another. *Your* words, Isaac. That's what matters, not whose hand makes the actual letters on the parchment."

He was silent for a moment. "You'll write faithfully the words I say."

"Of course."

"But I don't know how to say it."

"Just tell what happened. Tell what the Lord said. You don't have to write eloquently. You're not giving a speech to an army, urging them to battle. You're telling what the Lord did. Tonight in your sleep he came and spoke to you. That's all you have to say."

"To you it's easy, because the responsibility isn't yours. There won't be copyists year after year, writing down the same ill-sorted words and thinking, 'Isaac—his writing is nothing like his father's.'"

"They won't think such a foolish thing, and even if they did, would you let pride or shame stop you from writing? What do you care what they think of *you*, as long as they know of what the Lord has said and done?"

"I don't care. I mean, I'd never let that stop me. But it's all right for me to hate the fact that I'm no good at this."

"The Lord will make you as good a speaker as you need to be, as long as you have the faith to speak in his name."

"As good as I need to be," said Isaac. "But never as good as I want to be. I'm ashamed that the Lord always has to make do with me. I'm an ordinary man who keeps the records between the great prophets, a place holder."

"Place holders aren't visited in the night by the Lord."

"He visited me for my father's sake."

"But he didn't visit Ishmael or any of the sons of Keturah, and they have the same father."

"Enough," said Isaac. "You've comforted me, now go back to sleep."

What Rebekah didn't understand was why a man who had just received a vision from God should even need comforting. But to Isaac, the vision only left him feeling more keenly aware of his unworthiness.

Perhaps that was why the Lord did not come to him more. Out of mercy, because it made him so miserable.

It was on the third day of working on the new well that Abimelech himself came out to them with a party of soldiers, bringing gifts to show that he wanted nothing but friendship to prevail between the people of Isaac and the citizens of Gerar.

Rebekah wanted to say something brutally honest about what friendship with Abimelech was worth, but of course she said nothing, merely listening as Isaac spoke to Abimelech as if they were good friends. Isaac had Jacob give Abimelech gifts of twice the value, and sent him on his way with firm assurances of what mattered most to Abimelech—that Isaac wasn't angry and wouldn't seek vengeance against him or his city, even though the orchards and fields Isaac had planted were now in the possession of the people of Gerar.

"Poor Abimelech," said Rebekah after he was gone. "He doesn't understand that fields that produced a hundredfold for the servant of God will be ordinary soil for the servants of Molech."

By the time Abimelech was gone, it was nearly time to stop work on well-digging for the day, and Jacob had gone to tell the men that, when he suddenly returned at a run. "Water!" he cried. "They've struck water!"

"Impossible," said Isaac. "They haven't dug deep enough yet."

"It's close to the surface here," said Jacob. "There'll be plenty of water."

"Then this is where we'll stay," said Isaac. "Call the place the Well of Shebah. Beersheba. This is our camping place now."

"Who can doubt that the Lord loves the house of Isaac?" said Rebekah.

"No one doubts it," said Isaac. "And may they never doubt that the house of Isaac loves the Lord."

Then he had her lead him to where the workmen were celebrating, so he could commend them and then give a prayer of thanks and a burnt offering to the Lord for having blessed them yet one more time.

CHAPTER 15

From Beersheba, wild mountain country was never far away, and Esau had found he had a taste for testing himself against the rocks and the sun and the animals that dwelt among the crags and canyons. Rebekah worried about him every time he went, but since there was no stopping him, she learned to stop begging him not to go, and instead prayed for his safety and kept her mind on the work that surrounded her in Beersheba.

Much of the burden of the camp now fell on their shoulders, since Isaac could no longer inspect the animals or oversee any tasks. He still made the decisions and heard everyone's reports, and except for a tendency to be a little impatient with people whose storytelling style meandered too much, he showed remarkable patience with his affliction. Still, what he lived for were the hours he spent listening to Jacob or Rebekah read aloud from the scriptures as they copied them. As a result, they not only made one new copy of everything, but by the end of the third year of Isaac's blindness they had made a second complete set.

It was Isaac's idea to have someone outside his household keep the duplicate copies. "You were right all along, Rebekah," he said. "There's more safety in having several people read these writings than in keeping it with just one. Father kept them hidden to keep enemies from stealing them. But there could be a fire, or they could become waterlogged, or mice could get at them, and then where would we be, if all the copies are in the same place?"

After some thought, they decided to invite Keturah's fourth son, Midian, to stay with them for a year in order to learn how to read and write. At the end of the year he would become the keeper of the second set of writings. "It's not the birthright," Isaac was careful to explain to both Midian and Keturah. "There's more to it than that. But you should keep the parchments and copy them every generation, and pass them along father to son. It's a priestly responsibility, so I'll ordain you, when the time comes."

Midian took the responsibility seriously. More than once during the year he was with them, Rebekah found herself wishing that Esau had chosen Midian to be his companion on his adventures. Midian took the commandments seriously and studied the scriptures zealously, so he'd be sure to understand them well enough not to make foolish errors in copying. He and Jacob became good friends, able to laugh and be outrageously silly when they had no pressing duties, and then drop the frivolity and become intensely serious when the time came.

As far as Rebekah knew, Esau barely noticed that Midian

was in the camp. He was so disconnected from the holy writings now that Rebekah sometimes wondered if he still remembered how to read.

At the end of his year, Midian wasn't inclined to leave, even though Isaac pointed out that the purpose of training him had been to have a copy of the writings maintained in a widely separated place. "Don't be in a hurry to send me away," said Midian. "Jacob has a head start of a dozen years in his study of the writings, and I still have a lot of catching up to do."

And when Rebekah pointed out that it was good for Jacob to have a friend in the camp, Isaac relented and Midian was not sent away—though Keturah began sending servants to relay petulant messages about someone having abducted her son or he would surely have come back, at least for a visit.

Perhaps it began as a joke that Jacob and Midian meant to play on Esau—certainly that's how Midian explained it, later. But Rebekah suspected that Jacob, at least, had a serious purpose all along. He might have daydreamed his plot for years, but because he now had a friend to confide in, what had been a dream now became reality.

It was Esau's custom to return from a hunting trip exhausted and hungry. If he arrived before supper was ready, he became angry if he wasn't allowed to eat until everyone came in for the meal; if he came home after supper was finished, he was furious if food hadn't been saved for him. So Jacob had taken to keeping a pot of soup or stew simmering by the fire from midafternoon on, whenever Esau was out on an expedition. Rebekah saw this and approved. It not only kept peace in the camp, it was also, or so she saw it, a chance for the brothers to become close.

Well into Midian's second year with them, he came to Rebekah as she read to Isaac in the doorway of his tent. "Jacob asked me if the two of you would be willing to come to the tent near the cookfire."

"What for?"

"He has something for you to hear."

"Well, let him come and tell us himself," said Rebekah. Isaac didn't like to walk around the camp too much—it reminded everyone of his infirmity, to see how he had to be led wherever he went.

"It's not something to tell, it's something to *hear*. And it won't work unless you're quiet. Nobody should know you're there."

"No," said Isaac. "It sounds like some kind of game and I've got better things to do."

"It *is* a game, I guess," said Midian. "Or a joke. A surprise, anyway."

"A joke on whom?" asked Rebekah.

"That's the surprise. But it's not on either of you, if that's what you're worried about."

Rebekah sighed. "It's not as if Jacob asks us to do this all the time."

"He's a grown man, he shouldn't be playing games."

"You know that when he and Midian get in one of their moods, they become twelve-year-olds again."

"Jacob was never twelve," said Midian. "He was born thirty."

"Believe me," said Rebekah, "if *that* were true, I'd've remembered it."

They ended up coming down the gentle slope to the storage shed near the cookfire. It was hotter there, and even

though Jacob and Midian had cleared enough space in the
shed for them to sit comfortably, the fact remained that it was
poorly ventilated and soon both Isaac and Rebekah were
sweating profusely.

"This is foolish," said Isaac. "We've waited here long
enough."

"I agree," said Rebekah. "There are limits to how much we
should have to put up with for children who have beards."

"If you can call them beards."

Before they could leave, however, they heard a loud conversation going on behind the shed, near the cookfire. Voices
were raised. And one voice was loudest of all.

"Esau's home," said Isaac.

Rebekah was suddenly filled with foreboding. Esau was
home. Esau always went straight to the cookfire. And Jacob
had arranged for his father and mother to be sitting inside the
shed where they could hear but could not be seen. What could
it be, except that Jacob had finally figured out a way to force
his father to see just how unworthy of the birthright Esau
was?

Esau was angry, and when Rebekah and Isaac were seated
again, listening, it became clear that Jacob was demanding
something from him.

"You don't ever bring *me* any meat from these hunting
trips, but you come here and expect to eat pottage I made,
from lentils I grew."

"I haven't eaten in two days," Esau said. "And you have
food there that nobody's going to eat at this hour of the day!"

"And it's yours, if you pay."

"All right, then, what is it you want? You're the one who
knows all the sheep—"

"By name," said Nebajoth, and he laughed nastily.

"I don't want sheep from you," said Jacob. "In fact, what I want is something you don't even care about."

"What's that?"

"The birthright."

Inside the shed, Isaac immediately became angry. "I'm going to put a stop to this at once."

But he was whispering. Which meant he didn't want to be heard.

"Let's stay," said Rebekah. "Don't you think it will be interesting to hear what Esau says?"

Esau was laughing. "Sell you the birthright? Why not! It's yours! Now dish up the soup!"

Isaac whispered to Rebekah. "Of course he'll agree. He knows the birthright is mine to give, and I'd never transfer it to Jacob because he bought it with pottage."

"First put your seal on this parchment," said Jacob.

"What's that?" Esau asked.

"Read it."

"Just tell me."

Once again, Rebekah wondered if Esau remembered how to read, or even what all the marks of the alphabet were.

Jacob was answering Esau. "It says what you just agreed to. That in exchange for as much of my pottage as you want to eat, you relinquish all claim to the birthright and give it to me."

"This is a joke," said Esau. "You know Father will never stand for it."

"Even if he did allow it, what difference does it make to you?" said Jacob. "You don't care about the holy writings."

"I care about them."

"Not about reading them. Not about copying them."

"I'll always have women like you who can do that for me, Jacob. In fact, after Father's dead I think I'll make you my steward, and you can spend all day copying the holy writings over and over till you go as blind as Father."

Isaac was not happy with the direction the conversation was going. "He's leading Esau to say things that he doesn't mean, because he doesn't know I can hear."

"I don't know, Isaac. Aren't we more likely to hear things Esau *does* mean, *because* he thinks we won't hear of it?"

Outside by the cookfire, Jacob was dishing up pottage. Esau must have signed the parchment, then.

"Well, thank you, Esau," said Jacob. "I'll take good care of the parchments and make sure there are good copies to pass on to the next generation."

Esau's mouth was full, but he still laughed.

"Come on, Esau, you're spitting all over me," said Nebajoth.

"I spit on your parchment," said Esau, apparently to Jacob. "Do you think it means anything?"

"It will when Father finds out you signed away the birthright for a mess of pottage."

"He won't care. He doesn't care what I do. I'm the first-born, in case you didn't notice it, you little heel-grasping bloodsucker."

"The birthright goes to the oldest *worthy* son," said Jacob. "Grandfather Abraham was not Terah's firstborn son."

"Oh, I don't care if Father bestows it on you," said Esau. "You won't be able to keep it."

"What do you mean?"

"I mean I can have anything you own, whenever I want it."

"Oh, that's a good idea. *Steal* the birthright."

"Why not? *You* tried to get it by withholding food from a starving man."

"Rough trip, I guess. Didn't catch anything, I take it."

"We don't *catch* them, you halfwit, we *kill* them."

"Looks like you didn't do either."

Nobody but Jacob laughed.

"As I said, Jacob, my dear brother, you can't possibly keep those records away from me, if I decide I want them."

"What are you threatening?"

"I'm not threatening anything, Jacob. I'm just giving you fair warning. Once Father is dead, I'll have anything of yours I want. Have some flocks and herds? They're mine if I want them. Marry a pretty girl? She's mine if I want her. Because you don't have the strength or the courage to stand up to me for five minutes."

"So when Father dies, you'll take away whatever gifts he might have given me."

"If I feel like it, yes, they're all mine. Including the birthright."

Rebekah felt a chill shudder through her. "Are you hearing this, Isaac?"

"To my disgust, yes," said Isaac.

Outside, Esau was laughing uproariously, joined by Nebajoth. The sound faded. He was moving away to eat his pottage, apparently.

Midian appeared in the doorway of the shed. "That was it," he said.

"Get away from me," said Isaac, his voice full of loathing. "You're going home to your mother."

"What?" Midian was confused. "What did I do?"

"We'll talk later," said Rebekah.

Isaac was getting up from his rug. "Take me back to my tent," he said.

Midian thought he was being addressed and took Isaac by the arm, but Isaac recoiled as if he were a leper. "Don't touch me. I want you out of here come morning. Clearly you stayed too long."

"I didn't do anything," said Midian.

"You didn't stop Jacob from this vile plot of his."

"Jacob!" said Rebekah. "All he did was show you what—"

"He showed me that he thought the birthright could be purchased."

"He thought nothing of the kind," said Rebekah.

"Oh, so you plotted this with him?"

"I found out about it when you did," said Rebekah.

"Let's not have this discussion in front of Midian."

"He's gone. Back to Jacob, I imagine, to tell him that his father is deaf as well as blind."

Isaac said nothing, but pulled his arm away from Rebekah.

"Isaac, what are you doing?"

He stumbled on ahead of her, the uneven ground causing him to lurch this way and that as he quickly became headed in the wrong direction.

"You're heading for the orchard," said Rebekah.

Isaac adjusted his course but also hurried his pace. He fell. Obviously in pain, he got back up and began to walk again. Rebekah was able to catch up with him and took him firmly by the arm. "No matter what you think of me, you need me to guide your steps."

"How lucky your father was," said Isaac. "I would rather be deaf than hear what I heard today."

"I have no idea what you heard," said Rebekah, "because if you had heard what I did, you wouldn't be sending Midian away."

"Are you really proud of Jacob, setting a trap for his brother like that?"

"It was a test that Esau could easily have passed. All he had to do was say he'd rather go hungry a few minutes longer than to sign away the birthright."

"Esau is young and foolish, and I'm not surprised at his attitude. It takes time to understand the value of the holy writings."

"Did it take *you* so much time? He's a grown man. When do you think he's going to understand? And it wasn't just the selling of the birthright. It was his threats against Jacob."

"I have a few threats against Jacob myself," said Isaac.

"Well, Esau was certainly right when he said 'Father doesn't care what I do, I'm the firstborn.'"

"I care about everything my children do. Including lying."

"Jacob didn't lie."

"He didn't tell Esau he had his parents hidden in the kitchen shed, listening."

"He didn't tell him that we *weren't* there, and Esau wasn't speaking quietly anyway. We might have heard him simply by chance."

"But it wasn't by chance. Jacob laid a trap."

"A trap which Esau could not have fallen into if he had had even the tiniest shred of respect for the birthright."

"So you defend your precious Jacob even now."

"He did nothing that needs defending. But Esau's attitude—if you give the birthright to someone who thinks and talks like that, how long do you think it will last? If he'd sell it for pottage, he'd sell it for gold, or even more readily for the favor of a king."

"He didn't *sell* it at all. He signed a meaningless piece of parchment in order to get his brother to give him some food when he was hungry. Esau doesn't *own* the birthright, so it isn't his to sell."

"Who does own it?" asked Rebekah.

"I do," said Isaac.

"How odd," said Rebekah. "I always thought it belonged to God."

"Oh, I see. Now you're digging pits for *me* to fall into. Of course it belongs to God, but I'm the steward of it here."

"What kind of steward are you, even to *think* of passing it along to the man Esau has become?"

"He hasn't *become* anything. He isn't finished growing up yet. He has plenty of time to mature before it matters. I'm not dying yet."

"How do you know?" said Rebekah. "Death can come to anyone at any time."

"It's simple," said Isaac. "God won't take me *until* Esau is ready to receive the birthright."

"No, it's not simple," said Rebekah. "Maybe you're being tested the way your father was tested."

"What do you mean?"

"When he was commanded to sacrifice you. Maybe the Lord is expecting you to sacrifice Esau's privileges as firstborn for the sake of preserving the holy writings in good hands."

"Good hands? You mean the hands of that lying snake of a boy?"

"He's a man—the man who stays here day after day and manages your household like a steward. The man who sits at your feet and studies the scriptures. Haven't you been listening to him? Jacob's questions are important and deep, and he's a righteous, prayerful man."

"It's all part of his ambition. Pleasing me in hopes of getting what belongs to someone else."

"He's not ambitious," said Rebekah. "He cares about the birthright and doesn't want it in the hands of a worldly man who despises it. Why don't you test him? Give the birthright to Midian, and see what Jacob does."

"Midian! The birthright is more than just copying the scriptures."

"I know. It's adding to them," said Rebekah. "Writing down the acts of God that you witness during your life. Now, what do you think Esau will write? What do you think the book of Esau will contain? Accounts of the virgins he's deflowered in Gerar and Mamre?"

"Get away from me," said Isaac, his voice low and the words bitten off.

They were at the door of his tent, and Isaac's hand was on the post that held the flap, so she could step away. "So you hate me now for telling you the truth."

"I don't need you to tell me the truth," said Isaac. "I need a wife who loves *both* her sons and doesn't play favorites."

Rebekah wanted to scream back at him in rage. It was so unfair of him to accuse her of the very thing he had done for the boys' entire lives. No one had ever made her so angry. But she controlled herself and spoke in measured tones. "I did my best with both boys. Esau chose to reject every good teaching, and Jacob embraced them. You've been blind to Esau's faults all along, and to Jacob's virtues. The worse Esau behaved the better you liked him. No, let me state it plainly. The more he behaved like Ishmael, the better you liked him. And the more like *you* Jacob became, the more you despised him. But the man who is like *you* is the man who should have the birthright. And you fail in your duty to God when you refuse to see that."

"So you've judged *me* unworthy of the birthright," said Isaac. "Very well, be a judge. But what I need is a wife. Go away. I'm done with you."

She understood at once that she had gone too far—but she had never thought he would respond like this. "Isaac, I beg you, don't send me away from my children, I'll speak no more about this, but don't do to me what was done to my mother!"

"What are you talking about?"

She sank to the ground. "Please, Isaac, I beg you on my knees. I was trying to help you see, but I'll keep my silence, only don't send me away."

"I was telling you to get away from my tent, I wasn't divorcing you! I'm not like your father. My marriage doesn't end just because my wife hates me."

"I don't hate you!"

"Oh, is it love that tells me I'm unworthy to be my father's son?"

"I never said that!"

"I've failed in my duty to God, I heard you say it. I'm not deaf, just blind."

"I said you're about to fail. Or that's what I meant, anyway. I'm trying to give you good and honest counsel!"

"You've given it. I disagree with you. The decision is mine. I'll hear no more about it."

"Yes, I agree," said Rebekah. "I've said what I've said. I don't unsay any of it. You heard me. I don't need to say it again."

"Good. Now leave me in peace."

"I can leave. But you'll have no peace if you throw the birthright into a pit."

Still shaking, she walked back to her tent, went inside, and threw herself onto her sleeping rugs and wept until she could weep no more.

Deborah came to her after a while and, saying nothing, lay down beside her and held her until she fell asleep.

This was a quarrel that did not dissipate with time. It remained between Rebekah and Isaac for days, weeks, months afterward. Ironically, Jacob and Esau were soon back to normal—which included sniping at each other, but they also had many times when they laughed together over one thing or another. In fact, Rebekah suspected that Esau knew that his parents had heard about the business of selling the birthright for pottage, though neither Isaac nor Rebekah had spoken to either of them about it. Why else would Esau suddenly take a new interest in the scriptures? He came several times to their copying sessions, and though he didn't actually write anything—she still suspected that he wasn't quite sure how to make all the letters, though it might be he was simply ashamed of his unpracticed hand—he took part in the discussion and vied with Jacob to ask the most searching or challenging questions.

However, Jacob caught on at once to what was happening, and just as Rebekah would have expected, he immediately backed away and asked questions only when he wasn't sure what an obscure passage meant, and he wanted to make sure he was putting the letters together to form the right words. Jacob had no interest in competing with Esau for the birthright. If only Isaac could see that. Not that she'd point it out to him, or discuss it with him in any way. He had put a ban on that topic, and she intended to keep it. Still, she could guess what he'd say in response: Jacob held his silence when Esau was there because he was a coward who could only be bold when his manly brother wasn't there. Or perhaps he would say: Jacob is ambitious enough to know how to make a good impression, but Isaac wasn't fooled.

Who can fool a man who insists on fooling himself?

Something had to be done. Rebekah prayed morning and night and many times in between, begging the Lord to intervene somehow, to make Isaac see what had to be done—or, better yet, to help Esau to repent of his rebellious nature, his love of worldliness.

But the only answer she got came the day Esau came to his father to inform him that he was going to marry and needed a bride gift. No, two bride gifts—for he had fallen in love, he said, with two Hittite girls, Judith the daughter of Beeri, and Bashemath the daughter of Elon.

Rebekah chanced upon the conversation when it was already well under way, arriving in time to hear Esau half-mockingly say, "Well, Father, you always warned me not to marry a Canaanite girl. So I'm marrying two Hittite women!"

Two women at the same time. What was he thinking? And both of them full wives, able to bear children who could inherit.

Didn't the boy—no, the man, he couldn't be called a boy

anymore—didn't the man see that taking wives and having sons was something that couldn't easily be undone? How could Isaac give the birthright to a man whose sons had been raised by idolatrous women?

Rebekah didn't say anything, however—for she suspected that if she criticized Esau in any way, it would provoke Isaac into taking Esau's side, and the last thing she needed was for Isaac to start finding justifications or excuses for this.

"I'll give you no bride gift for Hittite women," said Isaac.

"As you wish, Father. It will be said that Isaac is too poor to provide for his son's wives, but what's that to me?"

"You're the one who's too poor, Esau. What do you plan to do, hunt for their meat? You have no flocks and herds."

"Am I your firstborn or not? Are the flocks and herds here someday to be mine, or not? Have I no claim upon them now to support my wives? Or will you shame me in front of everyone, leaving me as poor as if I had no father?"

Rebekah wished Isaac could see the smirk on Esau's face as he said these things. From the tone of his voice, Isaac might think Esau was making reasonable arguments. But Rebekah could see that he was mocking his father even as he demanded the right to bring these wives into the camp and set up his own household here.

"No idols," said Isaac.

"What are you talking about?" said Esau.

"I'll have no idols in my camp."

"Neither of them is particularly religious, Father."

"I didn't suppose they were," said Isaac. "But I tell you now, so you won't be surprised later. In my camp, idolatry is forbidden."

"I'll tell you what, Father. Do for me what your father did

for you. Set me up in my own household, with my own servants and my own flocks and herds. Lahai-roi was good enough for you, wasn't it?"

"There isn't water enough there."

"Have you checked lately? There were good rains this past year."

"The best you can say is that there were rains at all. It wasn't disastrous. Lahai-roi will still be dry."

"Well, Father, I happen to have checked already. There's water in the well there."

"There's always water in the well. The question is how much water there'll be after you've drawn from it enough to satisfy a few hundred sheep. The well at Lahai-roi doesn't recover quickly in dry years."

"I can't believe you'd try to use a well as an excuse to keep me from setting up my own household."

"It won't be your household. It will be my flocks, my servants, and you will be my steward. I still forbid idolatry."

"I forbid it too. I've already told them. No idols. I'm not completely ignorant, Father. I know we worship a God who doesn't appreciate rivals."

"He has no rivals," said Isaac. "The other gods don't exist. Only God is real."

"That's what I meant, Father. Don't try to catch me in some trap because I used the wrong words."

Rebekah could see, in Isaac's silence, how infuriated it made him to be accused of trapping Esau when he intended no such thing. Well, let him chew on that for a while, thought Rebekah. It's only just, since that's the very thing he did to me in our last argument.

Despite Isaac's opposition, Esau went ahead with both

weddings. Isaac did not go, but Rebekah and Jacob did. Isaac claimed that the journey was too dangerous for a blind man, but Rebekah knew better. And she was secretly pleased at how furious Isaac was over the marriages, not because she wished him to be unhappy, but because maybe now he would awaken to what kind of man Esau was.

The girls were beautiful, as Rebekah expected; what she did not expect was that they gave no sign of being the kind of wild woman that Esau had a reputation for consorting with when he visited a town. Judith was nearly twenty, but it wasn't for lack of beauty and grace that she had not taken a husband before now. From what other guests at the wedding said, she gathered that Esau had been courting her for three years, and it took this long for her father to give consent for her to marry a man who didn't worship the gods of Heth! The other girl, Bashemath, was small of stature and quite a bit younger—was she even fifteen yet? Still, she too was quiet and respectful, and her father and mother seemed to dote on Esau as if he were a fine jewel someone had given to them.

And he was, wasn't he? Sometimes it was hard for Rebekah to remember, in all her worrying about Esau, that he was still a fine-looking man who had learned the gracious manners of a desert prince. For all that he could be snide and overbearing with his younger brother and his parents, he was still a man of intelligence and considerable knowledge. He had the look of a warrior about him. He was generous with his friends—and with his family, too. And he did love them. Ever since he first started hunting, it wasn't enough for him to bring home the game—he cooked the meat and proudly served it to the household, and prepared the skins and gave them as gifts. Rebekah herself had received his first rabbit skin. It had been raggedly removed and unevenly tanned, but she had treasured it then.

After the wedding, she went home to Beersheba and searched until she found it, that first rabbit skin. It was badly worn—the girls had used it pretty roughly in their games when they were little, and since it hadn't been all that well prepared, it wouldn't have held up well in any case. But it was good to have it, all the same. Her proof that there had been a time when Esau loved her.

Or did he love her still? Was the man with the smirk who enjoyed showing his independence from his parents still the boy who had wanted to please her?

Why did he stop wanting to please her? She didn't like to think of it, but it was possible that he simply gave up when it seemed she could not be pleased by anything he did. Maybe it seemed to him as he was growing up that anything he did well, Mother didn't much care about, and anything she cared about, he did badly and had to be corrected.

Having thought of it, the idea preyed upon her. Did I cause this? If I had been less critical of him, would he have kept that generous, giving spirit in his relationship with me?

After several days in which Rebekah had lived with—and prayed about—an overwhelming sense of guilt about this, Esau came home with his brides for a visit. She saw how disdainful he was with his father—enough so that Judith, at least, looked a bit shocked—and Rebekah realized that while she might have been too critical of him, his father and Abraham had certainly not been, and Isaac now got even worse treatment than she did. Of course, that might be simply because he was blind so Esau could get away with more right in front of him. For all she knew, he mocked her viciously behind her back. But the important thing was that the parent who indulged him and approved of him all the time got treated as badly as, or worse than, the overly stern parent. It wasn't the way they treated him. It was Esau. It was his own choice.

The girls were nice enough, though it made Rebekah feel old to have her son married to such children—even Judith seemed like a child to her. And she was glad that his wives were kind, and treated her and Isaac's daughters well. Young Deborah, especially, hovered around Bashemath like a bee around a flower, wanting to take possession of her, which was not surprising, since Deborah was only a couple of years younger than the bride.

Which meant that soon they would need to arrange a marriage for her. It made Rebekah tired and sad, to think of her daughters getting married and leaving her. All this work to raise children, and just when they become interesting, everything changes. The girls get married and leave and you never see them again, and the boys—well, Esau, at least, had become a stranger in many ways.

Marriage did change him. It subdued him, a little. He still went hunting with Nebajoth, but they didn't go into town anymore. Esau's wives wanted him to stay home with them, and he was happy to oblige. In fact, Nebajoth got so bored that he actually got married, too.

And Esau turned out to be a reasonably competent herdsman. Apparently during all the years that he had avoided the work of the camp as much as possible, he still managed to pick up enough skill and knowledge not to embarrass himself with the men. And where the servants loved Jacob and trusted him, they were dazzled by Esau and vied for his attention in a way that made Rebekah a little sad for Jacob. He had to see the difference in the way they were treated, and she knew him well enough to know that though he would never speak of it, it must bother him. It must make him feel . . . unvalued.

Like Isaac.

What Jacob is going through, watching how Esau, after having ignored the herdsmen's work for so many years, becomes the hero of the herders from the moment he finally pays attention to them—that's what Isaac had to go through as well. It must have been just like this for him, whenever Ishmael came to visit, watching how everyone—Abraham included—hung on every word, laughed at every jest, jostled each other for pride of place, for the chance to be noticed by Ishmael. While Isaac was just . . . Isaac.

Abraham never disdained Isaac—quite the contrary, he loved his only son by his beloved Sarah. But Isaac never got to see his father look at him with those shining, dazzled eyes that Ishmael always got to see. That was the root of it all, the reason why Isaac had never been able to believe in his own value.

But that meant that poor Jacob's experience was much worse, for unlike Isaac, he had only disdain from his father, which had recently turned to hostility. If Isaac's life has been stained with a sense of worthlessness because of the contrast between him and Ishmael, how much more damage is Jacob going to suffer?

Of course, there was another difference—Jacob had never seen his father with a knife raised to kill him. But which was worse? At least Abraham had been commanded by God. Isaac's dislike of Jacob was entirely his own choice.

And I don't treat Esau the way Sarah treated Ishmael, for that matter. I did not play favorites. I expected them to follow the same rules. If Esau ended up in conflict with me and Jacob didn't, it wasn't by my choice.

It's really Isaac's fault. Why should Esau ever learn to obey me, when he knew Isaac would always indulge him?

And yet Isaac indulged Esau because Esau was everything Isaac wished he could have been. He couldn't help how he loved this wild son. The seeds planted by Abraham and Sarah grew in Isaac and bore fruit in the way he treated his own sons. And it would happen again in the next generation. However hurt Jacob was, or however spoiled Esau was, it would show up in the way each treated his children. And so on, and so on, in a never-ending cycle that began with nothing worse than good people trying to do what was right and getting it wrong without meaning to.

Like my father, divorcing my mother for the sake of the children. Like my mother, defying my father because she truly believed that it would harm me if I weren't offered to Asherah. Everyone trying to do the right thing.

Which of the right things I'm trying to do are really wrong?

Round and round in circles these thoughts went, day after day. Esau's visit ended and camp life settled back to normal—but Rebekah noticed that the buoyancy had left Jacob, and he began to find excuses not to come and work on copying the holy writings with her and Isaac. She couldn't blame him—Isaac's answers were perfunctory now, as if answering Jacob were an onerous duty that he'd just as soon avoid.

Still, unpleasant as things were, they might have gone on in relative peace if Rebekah hadn't come upon her younger two daughters, Sarah and Qira, playing in an odd way with their dolls. They were in the tent they shared with their older sister Deborah—much to Deborah's disgust, of course, since she considered herself to be a woman and vastly above these mere children. Rebekah was seeking them out because she wanted them to help her make a robe, so they could learn some of the finer points of sewing and get some practice. To her shock, she found three poppets perched on top of a chest with lamps lighted in front of them, and both of the younger girls stark naked.

"What in the world are you doing?" Rebekah demanded.

Immediately the girls shrieked and dived for their clothing. Since they were so frantic to dress, they got everything inside out and backward and knotted and stuck, and by the time Rebekah had got them dressed again, she had had time to think about what they had been doing. She remembered seeing her mother kneel before an image of Asherah.

"What game were you playing?" asked Rebekah, keeping her voice calm so they'd not be afraid to tell her the truth.

"Just a game," said Sarah.

Which meant that she knew she had been doing something wrong, and so didn't want to name it.

"You were pretending that your dolls were gods, weren't you?" said Rebekah.

Sarah clammed up—she had inherited her father's taciturnity—but Qira burst into tears.

"Where did you see someone do this?" asked Rebekah.

Through her tears, Qira said, "Judith and Bashemath showed us."

"They said for us not to tell," said Sarah.

"If someone tells you *not* to tell your mother something, then that means they know it's wrong and want to hide it. So that's exactly the thing that you *must* tell me."

"I promised not to," said Sarah.

"If you promise to commit a terrible sin, will God punish you for breaking the promise?"

Sarah thought about that for a moment. "I suppose not," she said.

"Why were you taking off your clothes, Sarah?"

"Because that's how Judith and Bashemath did it."

"In our house," said Rebekah, "we worship only the Lord God. We make no images of him. We worship no images of any of the false gods, either."

"We weren't worshiping, we were just playing," said Qira.

"Pretending," said Sarah.

"No, children. I'm afraid that isn't true. When you lit these lamps before your dolls and bowed down, you turned these dolls into images of false gods, and what you did was worship, whether you were sincere about it or not. So I'm going to have to take these dolls to your father and have him destroy them."

They wailed and pleaded, but Rebekah was adamant. "You have turned these toys into images of gods," she said. "No one did that but you, and I taught you all your life that images of gods are forbidden here."

"But Judith's and Bashemath's gods weren't destroyed!" said Qira.

"Darling girl, that's because your father and I didn't know they were worshiping them. But you may be sure that they *will* be destroyed."

"No, you can't!" cried Sarah. "Then they'll know we told!"

"But I knew before you told me. How else could you have learned such a thing? I'll make sure they know you didn't tell."

Rebekah took the dolls and left her daughters weeping. There would be time to comfort them later. Isaac had to know.

She found him in his tent, of course. He heard her story, which she told as simply as possible, without comment, and when she was done he turned his face away from her. "My son's wives have brought evil into my household," he said. "Burn the dolls, and send me a man I can use as a messenger."

Isaac sent the man with a command that Esau bring him the gods his wives had dared to worship in his own camp, so he could destroy them.

The message came back that his wives had not worshiped any gods, because they knew it was forbidden.

Isaac's return message was short: Send me the gods, or send me the wives. One or the other will be destroyed. And he did not send it with a single messenger. He sent it with ten men, armed as if for war.

They came back with three statues of wood, two of stone, and one carved from the antler of a hart. Isaac had the wood burnt, the stone crushed, the antler ground to dust.

That evening, Esau himself arrived about dusk, his wives weeping behind him. They had walked the whole way, and the women's feet were bloody. There was dried blood in their scalps, and bruises on their faces as well. Esau dragged them to his father's tent and threw them to the ground.

"Here they are, Father!" shouted Esau. "The liars who told me they had no gods! The blasphemers who broke the oath they made to me, that they would forsake their old gods and never worship them again!"

Secretly Rebekah rejoiced to hear this. She had not known that Esau cared enough to exact such an oath from them.

Isaac came out of his tent and stood there in judgment, as

Esau named their sins. "For idolatry they are worthy of death," said Esau. "For breaking their oath to me, I should put them to death, or if I let them live, I should divorce them and send them out to be harlots. For lying to me and saying they had no gods, I have already beaten them. For teaching my sisters to imitate their evil idolatry, I have made them walk barefoot from Lahai-roi. Now, Father, you are the judge. Their sins against me I have punished. But their sins against God are for God's prophet to punish."

Esau's talk of putting people to death or divorcing them filled Rebekah with dismay. If Rebekah was any judge of character, these women had never realized how serious Esau was about the religion of his father. They could hardly be blamed for that—Rebekah herself had not been sure until now that Esau even cared. But Judith and Bashemath could not repent of their sin and learn to serve the Lord with honest hearts if they were dead. And if Esau divorced them, they would hate God and never learn to love him.

"Husband," said Rebekah. "May I speak on behalf of these women?"

Isaac looked surprised, and Esau turned to her with consternation on his face. "You would plead *for* them?" he asked.

"I think God will be better served if they are given a chance to repent of their sins and learn to obey their husband and keep their covenants."

"I don't want them near me," said Esau. "I can't believe anything they say to me."

"You're angry now, but that anger will pass, and you'll see that from now on they'll be honest with you. They don't have lying hearts."

The abject women, weeping, sobbed their agreement with Rebekah's words.

"My father divorced my mother for a similar offense," said Rebekah. "The result was that my brother and I grew up without a mother, and my mother never learned to love God, but worships Asherah to this day. Show them mercy, Isaac, and perhaps they will become worthy wives for your son Esau."

There was silence for a while as Isaac thought. Finally he said, "Esau, you heard your mother plead for your wives. What do you think now?"

"If you judge that they should live, and that they should remain my wives, then I'll take them back. But only because you command it."

"Judith, Bashemath, you heard your husband's mother plead for you. Will you learn to worship the Lord God, and serve only him and no other?"

Not surprisingly, they agreed.

"This is a solemn oath," said Isaac, "but an oath made under threat of death is no oath at all. So I tell you now that no matter what you say, you will not be put to death. Is your answer the same? Will you forsake your false gods and worship only the Lord God?"

Again they agreed.

"Then I will give you a year in which to show perfect obedience. If you keep this oath for a year, then this sin will be blotted out. I'll remove all mention of it from the record I write, and it will be as if it never happened. But if you break this oath, then you'll stand worthy of punishment as if you had never repented. Now thank your mother-in-law. You owe it to her that you were not sent out of this camp and back to your fathers this very night."

They crawled to Rebekah and wept into the hem of her robe, until she bent over and raised them up and embraced them. "They can't go home like this," said Rebekah. "They'll have to stay until their feet are healed."

"I can lend them camels to ride," said Isaac. "I don't want them here."

"You can't see them, Isaac, but they're not fit to ride. They can sleep in my tent."

Isaac relented and they ended up staying for several weeks. For the first few days, Rebekah taught them about God for hours each day, and they listened contritely. But then, with their wounds healing nicely, they began to be restless during the lessons, and finally one day Bashemath said, "Haven't we been punished enough?"

"This isn't punishment," said Rebekah. "You promised to serve the Lord God. I'm teaching you who he is and what he's done for us and our ancestors."

"All right, I'll listen," she said. But her tone was full of weariness, and Rebekah realized that all Esau had accomplished by beating them was to make them resentful. They would go through the motions of serving God because they had learned how harshly they would be dealt with if they didn't. They probably wouldn't have any more idols, or if they did, they'd make very sure not to be observed doing it. What they would never do was repent and become true daughters of God.

It made Rebekah heartsick and weary. She longed to be able to tell Isaac of her frustration and disappointment with Esau's wives, but she didn't dare. He might decide that their repentance was insincere and the penalty had to be paid after all. It was better for everyone if Rebekah held her tongue, even though it meant keeping in the camp two women who worshiped false gods in their hearts. They could keep it a secret from their husband, but as their children grew, their true beliefs could not be hidden from the little ones. Children always knew what their parents really believed, absorbing the attitudes of their parents without even realizing it. Esau's children by these women would not grow up to serve God with an open heart.

She put them out of her tent, claiming that she needed her sleep and that the girls had learned everything she could teach them. Both statements were true, as far as they went.

In the long run, of course, the fault was with Esau, not his wives. Hadn't Isaac and Rebekah always taught him that he must marry a woman—or women—who served the Lord? That if he married a woman of Canaan, whether she called herself a Canaanite or a daughter of Heth, in the long run it would mean that his children would not worship God?

Besides, was his anger at them really because they worshiped false gods, or because they had deceived him and embarrassed him in front of his parents? There was no sign that Esau had learned anything important or true from this.

The girls kept their covenant, outwardly at least, and at the end of a year, Isaac made a show of having Esau blot out the story of their transgression and judgment where it was written on parchment. "Your sins were recorded as black marks," he told them. "But now where they were, not one word can be read."

Judith and Bashemath took their revenge in subtle ways. Esau almost never came to visit. When he came, they almost never came with him. His children were rarely brought to their grandparents' camp. Isaac and Esau should not have responded so harshly. Beatings don't bring repentance, they lead to concealment and lies. No one's mind was ever changed with a stick, only their mouths.

Isaac never seemed to recover from the pain of having his firstborn marry idolatrous women. It only got worse as first Bashemath, then Judith gave birth to sons. After the circumcisions, Isaac's life seemed to fade within him. He came out of his tent less and less, and then only to sit in the sunlight to get warm. And before long he took to his bed and did not get up.

Rebekah came to him then, and tried to encourage him. "You aren't sick, you silly old man, you're just too lazy to get out of bed."

But he didn't respond to her cheerfulness, perhaps because it sounded forced to him. "Don't try to deceive me, Rebekah," he said. "I know every sound of your voice and what it means. You're worried about me. I'm old and blind and you're afraid I'm going to die."

"Isaac," she said. She knew she couldn't refute his words, so she didn't try. She could only take his hand. He clasped her hand, and his grip had lost much of its strength.

"The fact is, I *am* going to die, sooner or later. I think you were the one who pointed that out to me some time ago."

"Please, Isaac."

"There are things I need to take care of, in case I die soon."

She waited for him to tell her what he needed her to do.

"I need to ordain Esau," said Isaac, "and turn the records over to him."

"No!" cried Rebekah. The word slipped out before she could stop herself.

He withdrew his hand.

"Isaac, please," she said. "I obeyed you and haven't

spoken of the matter since, but his wives haven't become servants of God. They pretend, that's all."

"Are you saying they still worship their false gods?" asked Isaac.

"I don't know how they feel about their old false gods. But I do know that they hate the Lord God, and they'll never raise their children to worship him."

"Then Esau will have to raise them to love and serve God."

"Do you really believe that? If it were so easy, why did your father send Eliezer to fetch me back to be your wife? Why did you and he forbid your sons to marry Canaanite women? You know why. If you give the holy writings to Esau, they'll be in the hands of idolaters within a generation."

"Did God tell you this?" said Isaac.

"No, *you* told me this. And Abraham. I'm doing nothing more than returning to you the truths you taught me long ago."

"If God didn't tell you," said Isaac, "then maybe you ought to keep your prophecies to yourself."

"Isaac, as surely as you love God, you can't give the birthright to Esau."

"I'm through with hearing your meaningless oaths," said Isaac coldly. He turned his face toward the wall of the tent. "Bring me my firstborn son, so I can give him what he was born to receive from me."

Weeping silently, Rebekah left the tent. When she had calmed down a little, she sent a messenger to Lahai-roi to summon Esau.

Esau came by the next morning, and when Isaac

summoned him to his tent, Rebekah not only came herself but brought Jacob with her.

"What are you here for?" asked Isaac.

"You'll give the birthright to Esau," Rebekah said, "but surely you also have a blessing for your other son."

"Another day, another time," said Isaac impatiently. "Besides, I'm not ordaining Esau today. I don't want Jacob here. This has nothing to do with him."

Jacob, wordless, left the tent. Rebekah's heart broke for the unloved son.

Isaac reached out a hand. "Esau?"

"Here I am, Father," said Esau.

"Let me feel your hands."

Esau held out his hands, but instead of taking hold of them, Isaac first slid his fingers up Esau's wrist, to feel the thick matted hair that grew on his arms.

"You're as hairy as a beast yourself," said Isaac, chuckling.

"I'm always afraid some lion is going to tan *my* skin and use it to keep himself warm on cold nights."

Isaac chuckled. Then he clasped Esau's hand in his and said, "Son, I'm old, and I might die any day. I'm weak. Before I ordain you, my son, take your quiver of arrows and your bow and go into the field and take the life of a deer. Cook me the choice meat, spiced the way you know I like it. I think then I'll have the strength to sacrifice the rest of the animal and then give you the blessing of the birthright before I die."

"I will, Father," said Esau.

"Go at once."

Esau left the tent.

Isaac lay there in silence.

"You're going to do this," said Rebekah quietly. "You'll be

the last prophet to write in the holy books. Their long history ends with you."

"I've had enough," said Isaac. "Once you were a joy to me, Rebekah, but now your hatred of my firstborn son makes me weary of life."

"I love our firstborn son," said Rebekah. "I'm weary of *my* life because of the daughters of Heth. Esau made choices and now he must bear the consequences."

"He's the one God chose by letting him come first from the womb."

"God gave him no more than the *chance* to have the birthright, if he proved worthy. His own actions have made it impossible for the holy writings to be passed to him and his children."

"When he comes back with my venison, Rebekah, you'll see just what is possible and what isn't."

"All you can do is pass it to him," said Rebekah. "You can do nothing about his children."

"That's right. I learned the lesson you taught to Abraham—the next generation is not my responsibility. Those children are Esau's to raise. He'll have to make sure his first-born son is ready to receive the writings and the priesthood. I know that Esau cares about the Lord and is determined to serve him. And now if you're through condemning me, I'd like to sleep." He turned his face to the wall and she left the tent.

She immediately looked for Jacob. He wasn't in his tent, and it took more than an hour before she saw him walking up from the thicket on the far side of the well. He waved—sadly, it seemed to her, but maybe that was because of her own sadness for him.

She told him of all that Isaac had said.

"Then it's done," said Jacob. "Esau will surely rise to the responsibility."

"It's too late for him to do anything about it," said Rebekah. "His firstborn is already being raised by a mother who's an idolater in her heart."

"It's in God's hands now," said Jacob. "I'm content with it, Mother. Truly I am."

"It's not God's will," said Rebekah. "It's Isaac's blindness and stubbornness."

"Remember that Midian has copies of everything."

"Copies, but no authority. Words on parchment, but no prophetic gift to write any more of the words and works of God."

Jacob put his arm around her. "Nothing will be lost, Mother. The Lord is watching out for these books."

"The Lord allows his children to make their mistakes. He won't stop Isaac from making this one. But I will. You are the son who's worthy of having the birthright, and I'll see to it you have it."

"How?" asked Jacob. "I don't know about you, but I've never seen Father change his mind. Especially when it has anything to do with me. He decided who I was before I can remember, and nothing I do can change his mind."

So he saw it, and bore it.

"Jacob," said Rebekah, "I have a plan. Bring me two strong young kids out of the herd of goats. I know how to cook them so they'll taste like venison, including all the spices Esau uses. Where do you think he learned to cook the meat the way his father likes it, if not from me?"

"Mother, I know what you're thinking," said Jacob, "but it

won't work. I know our voices sound alike, but Father's hearing is sharp and he can tell the difference between our voices even when other people can't. And look at my arms and my chest, Mother. I'm smooth as a baby's bottom, and Esau's as hairy as a goat. You saw how Father checked his wrists to make sure it was him. He'll know it's me and then he'll be confirmed in his belief that I'm an ambitious sneak, and I'll get a curse instead of a blessing."

"Do you have a better plan?"

"Yes," said Jacob. "I'll leave it in the hands of God."

"No, Jacob. By doing nothing, you leave the birthright in the hands of Esau's Hittite wives. My plan is the way to put it back in the hands of God. Your father is blind to the man you are, Jacob, but God is not. If it's God's will for you to have the birthright, Isaac will give you the blessing when you go to him."

"If he gives it to me, thinking I'm Esau, what will it be worth?"

"As someone once said to me, leave it in the hands of God."

"Mother, Father isn't a fool."

"No, he's not. We have to help him avoid the consequences of this foolish, foolish decision. Now go, get me the two kids. Even if you decide not to do it, it won't hurt for me to cook them."

Jacob left, and returned not long after with two kids, already gutted and drained. She had him disjoint the animals and carve off the flank meat and the loin and chop it into large pieces, which she put into the cooking pot where she already had a broth of spices boiling. Two of the shoulders she saved for the burnt offering; the rest of the unused meat she set aside to go into a different stew for the camp's supper.

Hours later, she had Jacob, despite his objections, wearing the robe Esau always wore for sacrifices, and bound to his arms within the sleeves of the robe he wore the hairy skin of the kids he had slaughtered that day. She had already sent the servants away from camp, some on errands, and some with the explanation that today's rituals needed no witnesses. Only Deborah complained about it—her place was with Rebekah, she said, and Rebekah understood her feeling. But they all had to be gone, Deborah most of all—she wanted no chance of someone calling out Jacob's name at the wrong moment, or, worse, shouting a greeting to Esau if he came home earlier than she expected. Deborah was the one most likely to forget and let something slip. So Rebekah was firm about needing Deborah to watch over the younger handmaidens, and she was gone with the others.

"How can I get the birthright with a lie?" asked Jacob.

"It's not a lie," said Rebekah.

"Oh, I really *am* Esau?"

"You really are the son to whom the birthright has to go," said Rebekah. "It happens that your father mistakenly uses the name 'Esau' for that son. So by calling yourself 'Esau,' you are truthfully declaring yourself to be the son worthy of the birthright."

"All that means is that you've found an even grander lie to tell yourself in order to justify the lie you're having me tell."

"Do you care about the holy writings, Jacob?"

"You know I do, Mother."

"Then what's *your* plan to keep them safe, since you don't like mine?"

"I don't have a plan, Mother. I'm counting on the Lord to stop Father the way he stopped Grandfather just before he sacrificed his son."

"This is my doing, Jacob," said Rebekah. "You're only obeying your mother."

Jacob shook his head. "Come up with all the justifications you want, Mother, but I know what I'm doing. And yes, I *am* going to do it. Because I really do believe, Mother, that when you want something to happen, your will is so strong that the whole world bends to accommodate you."

"If only *that* were true, my life would be so much easier."

"Not really, Mother. The truth is that if you *weren't* that strong, your life would be that much worse."

"It's all on my head, my good son, my obedient son."

"Esau's a good man, too, Mother."

"Esau's a man of violence by his own choice, Jacob. When this is done and discovered, I won't be surprised if he tries to kill you. So I'm going to have you guarded."

"If this is the will of the Lord, Mother, he'll protect me."

"Jacob, haven't you been paying attention? The Lord uses us frail humans to do his work. Miracles are rare. Blessings most commonly come to those who have worked hard and done all that was within their power to bring them to pass."

Jacob nodded his agreement. "I'll do this, Mother, because I feel something within me that whispers that I must do it. I hope that feeling comes from God, assuring me that what you're having me do is right."

"It does," said Rebekah.

"Mother, when you're *that* sure I know you're just encouraging me. You really don't know, do you?"

"I know that I think God is guiding us both right now."

"You know that you think—"

"Sometimes that's the best we can do."

"Then why does it feel as though we're doing the very worst thing we could do?"

"Because that's also true."

"The best and the worst are the same thing?"

"We offer the best lamb of the flock for a sacrifice. We give the best; but to the lamb, we do our worst."

"So who's the sacrificial lamb? Me? Or Father?"

"The sacrifice is the shoulder of a kid."

"Shoulders," said Jacob. "And make sure you don't have two left shoulders instead of a left and a right. Father might check that, too."

She slapped him lightly. "Enough joking. I'm going to pray that this goes well, the whole time you're doing it."

"So will I. And also that when Esau kills me, my death will be mercifully swift."

"Enough of that," she said.

Then she sent him in to Isaac's tent, carrying the wide bowl of savory meat that smelled like Esau's venison.

She stood outside the wall of the tent, listening.

"Father," said Jacob.

"Here I am," said Isaac, as if Jacob were the blind one. Though in the darkness of the tent, perhaps he was.

A pause, perhaps as Jacob set down the bowl before his father.

"Who are you, my son?" asked Isaac.

"I'm Esau, your firstborn. I've done what you asked. Now sit up, Father, and eat the venison I've prepared for you, so you'll have the strength to bless me."

"How did you find a deer so quickly?"

"Because the Lord brought it to me."

To Rebekah, Jacob sounded exactly like Esau. Right down to the way he let the words glide out of his mouth lazily. Jacob was mimicking him perfectly.

Yet not perfectly enough. Isaac said, "Come closer to me, my son."

Rebekah knew what was happening—the hands probing under the sleeve. She felt bad about deceiving her husband like this. And yet she also felt good when she heard him through the tent wall, saying, "There's something of Jacob in your voice today, but those are the arms of my son Esau. Did you save the shoulders of the deer for sacrifice?"

"Yes, Father."

"When we're done here, you'll have the authority to give all the burnt offerings to the Lord, and the same power to bless that I have. All that I have from God will be yours then, my son."

"I pray that God will have as much from me as he's had from you."

It was then that Isaac fell silent as he ate and drank. She hadn't come from Haran yet when Abraham did all this with Isaac, but he had told her about it, and he knew that Isaac would be giving Jacob morsels of meat from the bowl. It was a good thing that Jacob's beard had finally come in thickly. If Isaac should brush against it with his hand, he wouldn't be able to tell the difference from that.

Isaac wasn't well, and he ate only a little before he called again for his son to come near him. "Kiss me, Esau," he said.

After a moment, Rebekah heard him say, "Ah, the smell of my son is the smell of the open field which the Lord has blessed. Therefore God will give you the dew of heaven, the fatness of the earth, and plenty of grain and wine. People will serve you willingly, and the nations of the earth will bow down to you. Be a good ruler over your brother, and your mother's son will bow down to you." Then he said the words that conferred the full authority that he had received from Abraham, ending with the formula, "God will bless those who bless you, and curse those who curse you. Whatever you do upon the earth in God's name will stand in heaven, and whatever you record on earth will be recorded in heaven."

And it was done.

Jacob emerged weeping from the tent, carrying the bowl, his tears falling into the nearly-untouched meat. Rebekah led him to his tent, where she waited while he stripped off Esau's robe so she could return it to his tent.

Which she did just in time, for as she emerged from his tent to return to Jacob's, she saw Esau down by the cookfire, cutting fresh-killed venison into a stewpot.

"Jacob," she called softly as she stood outside his tent.

"Come in, Mother," he said.

She found him looking dejected, sitting on the rug, the kidskins he had worn on his arms lying where he had dropped them.

"Esau's back," she said.

"I know," he answered.

"I think you should leave, just for a few days. He's going to be very angry."

"I'm not leaving," said Jacob. "Not unless Father sends me away."

"I'm afraid for you," said Rebekah.

"But you weren't afraid when you cooked the meat and

put it in my hands, when you wrapped my wrists with kidskin, when you told me to call myself Esau."

"I was afraid then, too."

"So am I afraid now," said Jacob. "What I have is a lie. I haven't saved the birthright. I've destroyed it."

"Pray with me," said Rebekah. "Pray *for* me. For if there was any sin today, it was mine."

"You don't have the power to take my sin and bear it yourself," said Jacob. "Father was right. I was ambitious. I did resent Esau for having what he didn't value and I did. But I shouldn't have taken what Father meant for him." He wept then. "I didn't want the blessing," he said. "I wanted Father to want me to have it."

"I know," said Rebekah, kneeling beside him, holding him. "Just as your father wanted *his* father to love him too much to sacrifice him. But what matters is that God's purposes are served."

"No, that isn't all that matters," said Jacob. "It also matters how we treat each other."

They heard Esau walking up the path heading for Father's tent. Jacob stopped weeping and got up. Rebekah followed him out of the tent.

Esau saw him, saw how his eyes were red from weeping. "Poor Jacob," he said. "Don't grieve, little brother. At least you have that paper I signed." Esau grinned.

Rebekah felt only a slight stirring of anger at his taunting of Jacob. It was immediately swallowed up in her grief for what she knew Esau was about to go through.

Esau passed through the door of his father's tent. Rebekah was not standing close enough to hear what was said this time, but she could have been on the far side of the orchard and she would have heard Esau's wail of anguish.

After that, their voices were loud enough for Rebekah to hear them even by Jacob's tent.

"It was a lie! How can the blessing count for him when you thought you were giving it to me? It's mine, Father!"

"The blessing will stand. It belongs to Jacob now."

"That supplanter! That sneak!"

"He has been blessed." The tone of Isaac's voice made it clear—the decision was final.

"Bless me, Father! Bless me too! Isn't there something left for me?"

"I've made him your lord," said Isaac. "I've made all men his servants. The keys to the priesthood of God are his. What is there besides that?"

"Is there only one blessing in the world?" cried Esau. "You have another, Father. Bless me also."

And he wept.

Outside the tent, so did Jacob, sinking to the ground and weeping for his brother. Or perhaps, at least partly, weeping because when his father could have renounced the blessing he had given Jacob, he chose not to. He let it stand.

"Yes, Esau, I can bless you with the fatness of the earth, and I do. I bless you with the dew from heaven. By the sword you will live, and though you serve your brother, in the day when you become a true servant of God, you will come into your dominion. You'll break the yoke of subservience and be a free man, because only the servants of God are truly free."

Rebekah wondered if Esau would understand what Isaac had blessed him with. If he would only obey the Lord, then he would have his own place in the kingdom of God. He might never have the authority that Isaac had confirmed upon Jacob, but he would have a place in God's favor, if he changed his life and earned it. Please, Esau, hear what your father said, and live by it. Please, God, help my son Esau to fulfill his father's blessing.

When Esau emerged from the tent, he saw Jacob curled up on the ground, weeping. He said nothing, but he stood there gazing at Jacob for a long moment. And as he did, Rebekah heard his voice, the words of his heart, not from his lips, but inside her mind. "Father will die soon," he was saying, "and when he does, you'll also die, and I'll have everything you stole from me." Then he burst into bitter tears himself, and fled, not to the tent he slept in when he visited Beersheba, but down the hill to the corral, where he prepared his camel for the journey back to his wives.

His wives, who were the reason that he had lost the birthright.

The tent door opened again, and Isaac emerged into the light, though his eyes showed no sign of responding to it. He had a sturdy chest in his arms. Rebekah recognized it. All the holy writings were kept within it.

"Jacob!" Isaac called. His voice was also ragged with weeping.

"Father," said Jacob. "I'm sorry, I'm sorry."

"I forbid you to be sorry," said Isaac. "What you did today came from God."

Jacob wept.

"Listen to me, my son," said Isaac. "I knew it was your voice. I was about to curse you and send you out of the tent, perhaps banish you from my household. But then I felt the spirit of God within me, and it whispered, This is the right son. Bless him. At that moment I thought the Lord meant that it really was Esau, and so when I felt your arms and smelled your clothing I was reassured and I gave you the blessing knowing that I was giving it to the son that God intended to have it. Then when Esau came in, and I realized that it *was* you the first time, as I had thought, then the Lord's meaning became clear to me. It wasn't Esau, but it *was* the son who should receive the birthright."

"Father, I know you love Esau. I know you wanted him to have it."

"No, Jacob. No, I wanted it to be given to the one the Lord chose. I thought it was Esau. I thought the Lord chose him by making him come first out of the womb. All these years, watching him turn away from everything that mattered to me, ignoring so many of God's commandments, despising what was precious, and finally marrying idolatrous women— through all of it, I kept thinking, The Lord must have chosen him for a reason, it has to turn out right. And when I saw you, how good you were, how obedient, I kept thinking, There must be some reason God did *not* choose this one. It must be that all his goodness is false, and God knows that in his heart he's unworthy, a hypocrite, a deceiver. I thought all your goodness had to be a trick to try to steal your brother's birthright. But I was wrong. All these years, I had to work so hard not to love you." Isaac wept. "Jacob, come to me, take these holy writings from me! They belong to you. You're the one with eyes. You're the one whose vision is clear. I'm the one who was blind even when I could see."

Jacob rose to his feet and ran to his father, took the chest from his arms and set it down in the grass. Then he embraced his father and they wept into each other's shoulders.

Rebekah went to the chest and picked it up. The sacred writings were safe. They would be preserved. They would be added to. Jacob would write of God's doings all the days of his life. He would write as a prophet, and in due time would pass the birthright on to the right son. Maybe the firstborn. Maybe not. It wasn't a matter of law. It was a matter of worthiness.

And I, what of my worthiness? What of my vow never to lie to anyone I loved? What of my promises to my husband that I would be his eyes and tell him truthfully all that I saw? Those vows never even came to my mind during all the hours that I worked to prepare Jacob to deceive his father. Only now, when the Lord has made it come out right, only now do I remember my promises.

I have no business holding these holy writings. Jacob was chosen, and in the end, the birthright went to the right son. But not because of my deception of my husband. No, the Lord spoke to Isaac and told him which son to give the blessing to. I should have known that he would do that. I should have trusted God, as Jacob begged me to do.

Where is Deborah? How could I have sent her away? She's the one who loves me even when I've broken my promises. Even when I don't deserve to be loved, she loves me.

Rebekah set down the chest and walked toward her tent through the blear of her tears. She was nearly there when she heard Isaac call out for her. "Rebekah, where are you! Rebekah! Can you hear me!"

"Mother!" called Jacob.

I don't want to talk to you, she thought. I don't want to face either of you, after what I did.

And then she remembered—she had to see them. She had

an urgent piece of information to tell them. She had heard Esau's threat, and she had to warn Jacob that he needed to leave Beersheba until Esau's rage cooled.

Haran, she thought. He must go to Haran. It's past time for him to marry. In Haran, he can go to my brother's house and Laban will help him find a wife among our kindred there. Laban will take him in, for my sake. He'll be safe there, out of Esau's reach until a time comes when they can come together peacefully.

The whole thing was so clear in her mind. And she realized: Of course it's clear. It comes from God. Just as it was a gift of God when I heard the words of Esau's heart. His lips said nothing, but God let me hear the warning.

Was this how it was for Sarah, when she knew she had to send Ishmael away to save baby Isaac's life? God's hand was in it. Thank God Sarah had faith enough to hear, and to obey.

And I also heard, as she heard. The Lord has not rejected me. My sin is not so great that God would cut me off. He can still find a place to dwell in my heart.

She turned and headed back to her husband, to her obedient son, and now her eyes were filled with tears for a different reason. For joy.

"Isaac," she said. And would have said more, but he reached out a blind hand and touched her face and stilled her lips.

"You grew up in a deaf man's house," said Isaac, "but you found a way to make your father hear you. I was blind and deaf by my own stubbornness, but you found a way to make me see and hear. Forgive me for making it so hard for you. I thank God for you, Rebekah."

She wrapped her arms around him and pressed her cheek

into his chest and held on to him, the sound of his heartbeat in her ear, the warmth of his body against the skin of her face. I belong here, she thought. This is the place I was born to have. All our work is done, our sons raised to be the men they chose to be, and the holy writings and the priesthood of God have been passed on. Jacob will leave for another land and find a wife there and build his life without me now. My daughters will also marry and be gone. But I belong here. With my arms around this man, with the sound and smell and heat of his body surrounding me, with his voice in my ear, with his face and his hands and all his works and all the people who love him in my gaze forever. And when we both are dead, and our bodies are in the ground, I will still be at home with him forever.